Becoming a Judge:
An Inside Story

Michael S. Jordan

Bethesda Communications Group

Copyright @ Michael S. Jordan 2022

Published by the Bethesda Communications Group
49 Wellesley Circle
Glen Echo, MD 20812
www.bcgpub.com

ISBN-13: 978-1-7367773-1-2
ISBN-10: 1-7367773-1-9

No right or privilege is waived or licensed to others by sharing the contents to get ideas, criticism, or help in getting the writing published.

This autobiography is a narrative of my personal and professional life based solely and entirely upon my personal opinions, memories, beliefs, thoughts, feelings and ideas; as such, all information herein represents a potentially imperfect retelling as documented to the best of my knowledge and therefore must not be misconstrued as uncontested, absolute fact. Any potential or actual inaccuracies or deviations from fact are completely unintentional and, if present, were mistakenly generated without any animus or malice aforethought to any referenced individuals, living or dead. Any and all assertions, implications, conclusions, representations, attributions, associations, conceptualizations and recollections in this body of work completely and without exception represent my own, good faith thoughts, opinions and beliefs.

— Michael S. Jordan

Cover photo: The *Chicago Tribune* captioned this photo "Babysitter on the Bench" when it snapped Michael S. Jordan holding his daughter Elizabeth while getting the news he would be installed as a judge.

I dedicate this book to my loving wife, Maureen, who is the best mother my children could ever have. Maureen always reminds me it is best to have faith and show humility, patience, kindness, hospitality, love, caring, and endurance. Maureen raised our two independent children, so much alike in character traits of honesty, caring, reliability, and faithfulness, but with different views of the world. While they act and respond so differently to situations, they understand each other and have an enduring love that will outlive all of us.

Michael S. Jordan and Maureen Lynn Jordan

Acknowledgements

The motivation for this book comes from my son Jeff. He asked me to expand on the transcripts of my oral interviews by researchers at Loyola University. I had been selected by my friends Ted Swain and Jim Henry, who assisted the researchers in finding a cross section of judges from various backgrounds to examine the commonalities in their path to the judiciary. Jeff believed that if I expanded the narrative, he and others would more easily appreciate my life and my accomplishments. It was my daughter Elizabeth who encouraged me to paint a vivid picture and "show my life" rather than just "telling about my life." My wife said if I could find the time or make the time to do the work, do it.

I am grateful to those in my family who gave me the motivation and help to pursue an education, have faith in myself, and to be open to public service to protect the guardrails of our democratic society and help to respect those less fortunate than we are. I offer this book as a beacon of hope that the freedoms we have enjoyed in this nation will expand and long endure and that rights most recently abated may be restored so that all in our country can prosper in a safe environment and our nation will remain a beacon of light for other nations.

In writing this book, I acknowledge the many women and men who choose to guide and mentor me. Many are acknowledged in this book but some are not mentioned. I also reflect upon the men and women whose lives I affected in some small way by my actions and words. Some, like Justice John Paul Stevens, affected millions of people and their words and deeds are well known, while others hopefully became better co-workers, supervisors, mothers, fathers, brothers, or sisters with little or no fanfare or notice by the greater population.

There are some people I think of such as Nick, whose custody I determined. What gifts has he given the world? He is symbolic of many persons whose lives intersected with mine where

I touched them for only a moment and do not know the lasting consequence of that interaction.

I had to decide where to start. I reread the oral history transcripts and began to fill in the details. The more I wrote, the more memories flowed into my consciousness. When I had a need to fill a gap in my memory, I would call upon those involved and ask them their recollections, which refreshed my recollections. I thank the scores of people in my life I was able to reach. I enjoyed the opportunity to catch up and reminisce. I had the opportunity to thank them for their companionship, help, and support, whether it was in grade school, high school, college, law school, or after.

To further my efforts to write a credible book, I decided to take a course on book writing to learn what mistakes to avoid and learn what I would need to do. I took a self-directed course from the local community college, Oakton Community College. I was lucky, however, to take the course by video. It was a nationwide course given at colleges around the county. I benefitted from the class. I also called members of my high school class who had written nonfiction pieces themselves to get some inspiration and guidance. I thank Professor Kenneth Manaster and Rabbi Sheldon Lewis for their time and support.

After I had reached a point where I felt I could show my work to others, I shared an early draft with members of my high school class to get feedback and learn if my project was one for a small audience of my immediate family or possibly a slightly larger audience. I heard that beyond my family, those involved in the events would be interested, but that I also had some national and international themes, since I made reference to the history of guardrails for democracy. I show how anyone can affect larger events in history and the body politic. One classmate said he could see this book being of interest to Chicagoland historians, those questioning or supporting faith-based systems, those interested in Watergate, Greylord, civil rights, and just a man's place in the world. Can we each achieve our own impossible dream?

I have profound gratitude and admiration for Debbie Davison Lange, my editor and publisher, and offer my thanks to her for her patience, teaching me again the rules of English grammar that I must have forgotten. Her success in guiding me through rewrites was amazing. I could see how fantastic she must have been as an English teacher at South Shore, working as a peer with our most admired teacher, Dr. Margaret Annan. Debbie was deserving of her membership in the National Honor Society. She suggested that after we made our final changes, we have several other persons read the work. She suggested Jeanne Alexander Pass, another former classmate from high school. I said Jeanne would be perfect. We were still in contact. She was bright and sharp and had been in the National Honor Society. Importantly, I also liked her. She was my senior prom date. I also asked my long-time mentor in writing, Dennis Dohm, to review my book. He too is sharp and bright as always. Both Jeanne and Dennis quickly agreed; and my book is better for their efforts.

I am of course grateful to you, the reader. I hope you enjoy the book and learn something in the process. If I inspired anyone in any positive way, I am delighted.

Contents

Acknowledgements 5
Preface 11
Introduction 13
1 BECOMING A JUDGE 15
   April 1, 1974 15
   The Process 21
   The Effort 24
2 CALM BEFORE THE STORM 28
   A New Supervisor—Man of details 28
   Career Development 31
   The New Boss Enters 35
   The Lay of the Land 39
   My First Office Mate 41
   Making Connections 43
   Starting from Scratch 46
   Sage Advice 50
   Successful Classmates 51
3 ENTERING THE FRAY 54
   Judges Get Dirty Assignments 54
   Experience Acquired 61
4 PERSONAL LIFE 67
   A Story of Attraction at First Sight 67
5 WORKING FOR WHAT YOU WANT 69
   Get the Votes 69
   Despres vs Holman 71
   Another Lesson Learned 74
   Protections Provided 78
6 STEPPING UP FOR GREATNESS 85
   My Opportunity to Change History 85
7 RECOGNIZING THE SUPREME POWER 95
   Gratitude 95
   Mentors and Guides 100

8 THE FORMATIVE YEARS	103
College Begins	103
Immaturity at College	108
Career Plan Change	112
First Year Law School	115
Religious Education	117
9 SURPRISE! SURPRISE!	124
Front Page News—Babysitter Becomes Judge	124
10 WHERE DO VALUES COME FROM?	126
My Father Helped Me Help Others	126
11 MINDGAMES	135
Thoughts Before Being Sworn into Office and Dangers to Face	135
Other Interesting Divorce and Family-Related Case Histories	146
12 GROWTH	150
My Experience Widens and Deepens	150
Perspectives	152
Using My Experience to Help Others	155
13 11:00 AM	160
My Installation as a Judge	160
Who am I?	163
My First Companions	168
Moving from Hyde Park to South Shore	173
Another Bully	178
14 TRIAL BY ORDEAL	189
Operation Greylord	189
Overcoming Corruption	193
15 TRANSFER	202
Skokie, Illinois	202
16 LOOKING BACK	207
Reflections	207
On the Positive Side	210
Fear of Depression	216

17 LOOKING AHEAD 224
I Had Plans for a New Career 224
Mediation & Arbitration Services 230
Some Plans Actualize and Other Plans Dissolve 235
Writing Can be Fun 237
An Arbitration Experiment 242
Planning Ahead 245
18 GIVING BACK MEANS LIFE RENEWED 246
Peer Review 246
Back Story on Process 247
Giveback Time is Due 250
Surprise Consequences 251
Some Conclusions from Working on Judicial Evaluations . 257
Betrayal and Let Down 260
Deja Vu, All Over Again 264
A Little Here and a Little There, But Not Everywhere 267
19 THE WIDE VIEW 269
A Perspective of History 269
My Mentor Goes Home, But Creates My Path Forward ... 271
The Perk That Lasts Until Death 274
Extended Perks and the Value of a Good Name 282
Brotherly Love and Concern 288
20 WHO CARES ABOUT ONE PERSON'S LIFE? 296
Why Tell My Story? 296

Preface

Many of us have seen television reruns of the 1946 movie, "It's a Wonderful Life", where actor James Stewart, as George Bailey, has a chance to see what the world might have been if he were not born and never existed. George is saved from himself by his guardian angel, Clarence, when he contemplates suicide by jumping off a bridge. George acts instead to "save" Clarence who actually jumps into the cold swirling waters. The guardian angel then shows George how the world would be changed without him being in it to convince him how important George's life has been.

George's younger brother would not have been saved by him as a child and then lived years later to serve in the military and win the Congressional Medal of Honor saving the lives of many other American servicemen in World War II. Jimmy Stewart's character would not have married his childhood sweetheart. She would have become an old maid rather than the mother of his four children. His uncle would have been committed to an insane asylum rather than living out his life working in the family business helping humanity. Mr. Gower, the pharmacist he worked for as a child, would have served a lengthy jail term for negligently placing poison in medicine killing a patient, had a younger Bailey not intervened and not delivered the medicine on the day the pharmacist learned his son had died and was distracted from his duties compounding medicine in a safe manner. The town would become a city of sin under the thumb of the corrupt and ruthless financier, Potter, for whom the city would be renamed and have no affordable housing built with George's efforts, but only have slums for most people. The story shows many lives were changed in some way but most for the worse without George.

Yes, one man can change the lives of many by his deeds, for the good, or for the bad. My story is one where I try to show that each of us in some way can help improve and save the lives of people around us. Sometimes we see the results; but sometimes we do not see the results. Yet, every one of our acts do have consequences! Let us begin a trip back into my life and see how many people affect the lives of others from the very poor to even a modern age president.

Introduction

 You may wonder why I have written this story. I wondered as I have been writing. My dear son Jeff thought it would be healthy to gather my memories to reread later and for others to understand how I got to my place in life. He read the transcript of my oral biography given to the Loyola University sociology researchers, led by Professor Christopher Manning, after I had been contacted by my friends Ted Swain and Jim Henry, who thought I had an interesting background.

 Jeff had questions regarding many of the events and thought it would be good for me and for him and he believed for others in a wider audience for me to expand on the information I had given. When I again read my oral history, I realized how much more there was to add while I was still able. My daughter Elizabeth learned of this project and said that she did not even know of some of the stories I was referring to but she bet that others might find my life story interesting and inspirational. She felt that my life showed how one person can affect the lives of many for good or for bad, and she argued my life has been for the good. If we see the good in people, most people will show their goodness. There has always been evil and we need not allow ourselves to be naïve to that fact and we must be watchful. Both of my children observed that my actions had surely affected their lives but also affected more of society, especially in

Chicagoland, but also the country and perhaps the world. Elizabeth cautioned me to stress the positive or I would be viewed as negative. Yet, I could not ignore the people who entered my space who were evil.

Just a few days ago I was driving to a food store for groceries and had the soundtrack of the Broadway musical Hamilton playing. I heard Alexander Hamilton's final words after the duel when Vice President Burr fired the fatal shot mortally wounding Hamilton. As his life passes before him, he asks who will tell his story. Every man and woman has a story. The question is really who will tell that story. Victors following the war tell everything favorable to their cause and impugn every act of the losers. When Hamilton died, he feared the worst side of his life would be exposed rather than his good deeds. Everyone has done good and bad, but who will tell that important story. I thought who better than I to tell my story. My loving son with his great talent for word craft will be able to help edit, but only I know my story. I must begin before I forget the story. My wife Maureen encouraged me to initiate the project to better understand how so many kind and loving people helped us get to the place we reached.

1 BECOMING A JUDGE

April 1, 1974

Michael S. Jordan receiving his first judicial assignment from the Acting Chief Judge Eugene Wachowski on April 1, 1974 in the ceremonial courtroom of the Civic Center

It was April 1, 1974 in Room 2005, the ceremonial courtroom of the Chicago Civic Center, where a standing room crowd was gathering for the swearing-in ceremony of 12 new associate judges. The Civic Center has been known as the Richard J. Daley

Center since December 27, 1976, (seven days after the death of Chicago Mayor Richard Joseph Daley).

Everyone entering the ceremonial courtroom had their own reason for being there. Most of those entering looked around for people they expected to see. Some who had attended other such ceremonies went quickly to seats, knowing there were never enough seats and many people would be standing for over an hour during the ceremony, holding onto their jackets and hats as well as briefcases and other items. April 1 was usually cold in Chicago. Today was no different. With many coming from outside, the chill lingered with the winds coming from nearby Lake Michigan, only a half mile to the East. Many handshakes and smiles were exchanged in this festive atmosphere. Some hugs and kisses were exchanged as well. There were some who appeared to be alone, sitting quietly, just watching and waiting. The professional dress was suits and ties for men and conservative dresses for the women. Cameras were brought by some. As the crowd increased, the buzz in the room became a louder noisy backdrop where each person had to speak still louder to be heard, with all contributing to the rising din.

There were to be 13 new inductees that day, but one, Bernard Wolfe, then a Democratic state representative from Chicago's 40th Ward, had to be in the state capital. An important bill he sponsored dealing with education issues was being debated that day in Springfield. He was sworn in about two weeks later after resigning from his legislative seat and getting the bill he sponsored enacted into law. Instead of 13 inductees, therefore, there were 12. I was one of the 12. And yes, the installation took place on April Fools' Day. It was on April Fools' Day that I was to begin my judicial career. Was that an omen or just a new anniversary to remember?

I entered the room with a smile on my face. My wife Maureen was with me at my side and my parents were behind us. I looked around for my in-laws and saw they had just arrived as well. We got them all seats together, fairly close up to the two rows of seats reserved for the 12 new judges. I could see the pride, happiness, and excitement on the faces of our parents. I excused myself and began to say my hellos and express my thanks to people I recognized. My wife saw a few friends and greeted them as well. I saw how she brought a few to meet our parents. She was at ease and made the joy of our parents even greater by knowing who some of the people were who were in attendance.

Normally, the Chief Judge of the Circuit Court of Cook County, Illinois, John S. Boyle, would be the one to preside and administer the oath for new and retained judges in the circuit, but he was ill, and his designee, the Presiding Judge of the First Municipal District, Eugene Wachowski, oversaw the proceedings and administered the oath to the 12 of us.

Boyle was the first Chief Judge elected by the judges of the Circuit Court of Cook County when the unified court system was created in 1964, a few years before I was licensed as a lawyer. He had been recruited by the Mayor of Chicago, Richard J. Daley, who was also the Chairman of the Cook County Democratic Central Committee. Daley and Boyle were a generation older and came from an entirely different background, culture, and life style than what I knew. Daley rose to power in the Democrat party using the athletic social club, the Hamburgs, in the Bridgeport neighborhood, as his base of strength. I thought of his loyalty to the group when I learned that an elderly man who served as a messenger working in the Law Department of the City of Chicago had been in the Hamburgs with Daley. He had always supported Daley and his loyalty was rewarded. I knew then that loyalty to Daley would earn loyalty in return.

When I learned that Judge Wachowski would be in charge officiating at the installation, I felt relieved and happy. I had met Eugene Wachowski personally on several occasions. He was a short, podgy, full-fleshed older kindly man with an almost constant smile on his face. During the three weeks preceding the installation and during the hectic two-week period when I, then a candidate for associate judge of the Circuit Court, had to be interviewed by all of the 134 sitting Circuit Judges so I could solicit their votes, Judge Boyle was absent due to his illness. Boyle, the former Cook County States' Attorney who became a judge and then chief judge was merely a name to me. I did know from newspaper pictures that he was a large and imposing man. He had been the candidate of Mayor Daley, known by many as the "boss." Daley was the mayor and the chairman of the Cook County Democratic Party. At this time, Daley was like a king and he was definitely a king maker. He was bright and charismatic and he knew how to run the wheels of power in government. He was the king maker sought out by any and all politicians who sought office or sought a higher office at the local, county, state, and national levels. In his view, there was no separation of the branches of government and that vision prevailed wherever he had friends and allies, whether at the local, county, state, or national levels.

Daley was at the top of a strong and firmly entrenched patronage system started in the 1930s by Mayor Anton Cermak, who was elected Mayor as a Democrat in 1931, defeating Republican "Big Bill" Thompson. Mayor Edward Joseph Kelly, the 46th Mayor of Chicago, succeeded Cermak, who died after taking an assassin's bullet aimed at President Franklin Delano Roosevelt. Under the system started by Cermak, jobs in government were the rewards for work in the political machine as precinct captains or assistants under the elected ward and township committeemen of the Cook County Democrat Party. There were 50 wards with committeemen in Chicago and 30 township committeemen in the suburban Cook County area. The 80 committeemen constituted the Cook County Democratic Party and they selected a chairman who ran the party apparatus to ensure Democrats were elected to public office. Each committeeman was allocated the number of votes cast in the last Democratic primary election for committeeman whenever a vote was taken by the county central committee. Certain committeemen therefore had a much bigger voice in matters than others in weaker areas. The office holders elected to their office with the help of the committeemen hired employees who were recommended by the committeemen in letters brought to the officeholder by the prospective employee from his committeeman.

Chicago Mayor Richard J. Daley was the County Democratic chair from 1953 until his death on December 20, 1976. Daley was the committeeman from the 11th Ward, the base of several mayors before and after him. Some people believed that just about every resident of the 11th Ward had a job in some government agency and most quickly became supervisors, if not superintendents, commissioners, or board members. They were not all smarter or more capable than other workers from other wards or townships, but they were connected to the man in the room where it happened on the 5th floor of City Hall. Daley made sure his base in the 11th Ward was content with all the perks he could provide. One of the mayor's administrative assistants was in charge of overseeing the patronage dispensed by the city. The mayor had installed others in each government agency in a well-coordinated effort and process. The committeemen all knew for each agency the person to address their "recommendations."

All of these committeemen had power; but I came to realize that even people without any apparent power had the ability to change the world. Each of us has the ability to set in motion a chain of events and make things happen that we could not even imagine when we take the action and engage in a situation. In Judaism, I had learned that if a person saves one person, it is as though he saved the world; and if one's actions bring harm to another, it's as though the person is causing harm to the world.

The Republicans had the same process under the law, but they usually held few political offices in Chicago and Cook Country government except until recently in the Republican suburban townships. There were a few breakthrough Republicans who were elected to countywide offices, such as Richard Ogilvie who was Sheriff and then President of the County Board of Commissioners before he became the state's governor. Another breakthrough Republican was Joe Woods, who became sheriff. His sister was President Richard Nixon's personal secretary who erased recorded conversations in the White House during the Watergate Scandal. Of course, judges running in suburban Cook County were elected as Republicans and sometimes, though rarely, elected when running countywide when candidates like Woods and Ogilvie would drag them in on their coattails.

Daley's position as mayor, was ultimately filled after he died, following a political struggle between the Black and White forces in the city council, with the county committeemen as well as other county political officeholders weighing in and exerting pressure or influence. The White power elite prevailed with the election as mayor of the 11th Ward Alderman, Michael Bilandic. He, in turn, however, was defeated in the next Democratic primary election by the first female mayor of Chicago, Jayne Byrne, who had been the Director of Chicago's Department of Consumer Weights and Measures under Daley. Not only was she not a man, but she was not a resident of the 11th Ward. She was a member of the Democratic party organization.

As I will relate later, she had assisted me when I was a judge in creating a useful program for the economically challenged in the years after Daley's death and before she became mayor. Daley had made Byrne the vice chair of the Democratic Party, to the chagrin of many committeemen feeling it unseemly to have a woman in the newly created position. While there was a committeewoman designated in each ward and township, the elected committeeman made appointments of a committeewoman, but the committeewoman position was only ceremonial. In the 50s, 60s, and 70s, women did not enjoy the power or positions they later discovered. A few were put into office, usually as successors to their deceased husbands to serve as place holders.

Jayne Byrne was a hard driving dynamic competent lady. She ran her department well and had a hands-on approach. My colleagues and I prosecuted several cases she and her department brought for license revocations when I served in the General Counsel Division of the City Law Department. She defeated Bilandic as mayor after he was perceived by most Black voters as acting in a racist manner following a major snow storm in Chicago in January 1969 when CTA officials under his control decided to have CTA rapid transit trains run express through densely Black neighborhoods, getting White suburban residents to the city for jobs, but leaving the Blacks stranded. Bilandic was a reserved, quiet man, a bachelor until he was in his fifties. He never spoke much and therefore made few close friends to defend him when he needed allies. He was bright and polite but soft-spoken. While Daley was alive, he was a reliable vote in the city council. When trouble emerged, most potential allies deserted him.

Ultimately, Bilandic went on to become a justice of the Illinois Supreme Court. His intelligence and loyalty were rewarded. The State of Illinois Building at 160 North LaSalle Street in Chicago was named in his memory. While on the Supreme Court, Bilandic was responsible for my close friend Dan Pascale's appointment as a Cook County Circuit Court Judge and later, when Bilandic was chief justice, for Dan's appointment as Director of the Administrative Office of the Illinois Courts. To his credit, Bilandic always recognized Dan's brilliance and honesty.

I met then Alderman Bilandic when he would visit the law department of the city, sometimes to see Dan and others for legal advice. I would like to think Bilandic may have helped me become a judge as well, but I will never know. He was very closed-mouthed and humble. But I am getting ahead of myself. I will get to Dan again in a while.

The Process

I was one of 26 lawyers certified by the nominating committee of the Circuit Court in late February 1974. The nominating committee members had all been appointed by Boyle who, in turn, had been supported for his position by Daley. The top 13 vote getters would be declared the designees to be sworn in as associate judges. The balloting to select those 13 was administered by the Administrative Office of the Illinois Courts under a procedure established by the Illinois Supreme Court in its Rule 39, dealing with the selection and retention of associate judges.

The Administrative Office of the Illinois Courts was at that time led by Roy O. Gulley, a former judge from downstate Illinois. He had become a judge in his county at the age of 26 and a circuit judge at about age 31. While I was young to become a judge, especially in Cook County, he and others had been younger still. Some believe for Cook County, I may have been the youngest judge in a long, long time. I would learn that youth could be a negative factor in getting along with others or others not wanting to get along with me.

Gulley was an institutionalist and he ran a very efficient office. His deputy in Chicago was William Madden. He and his Chicago staff had counted the ballots certifying me and the others in my group. One member of the Chicago-based staff of the Administrative Office of the Illinois Courts was a very bright and conscientious public servant, Dennis Dohm, who became a close and lasting friend after Judge Wachowski and Justice Glenn T. Johnson had me put on the Judicial Administration Section Council of the Illinois State Bar Association where Dennis was already the newsletter editor for the section. I became his assistant. Dennis was always the major and usually only contributor of the copy for the monthly newsletter. He put out more newsletters for our section than editors issued for any other section and sometimes had an extra thirteenth newsletter in a year. Dennis was a constant professional, looking for efficiency, economy, consistency, and adherence to the rule of law, taking the cues from Gulley as an institutionalist. The courts, as an independent co-equal branch of government, were more important than any individual.

I served as an editor by finding an occasional error in spelling, which was quite rare, or urged that we not include something that might appear to place someone in a negative light. I also had an aversion to one of the words Dennis used regularly to describe precedents—nice—as a "nice" case. Dennis was a dedicated researcher and good word crafter, reporting honest news, highlights, case analyses, and perspectives. Our newsletter was distributed to all section members, but importantly, also to all judges in the state. Dennis later was appointed a circuit judge in Cook County twice to fill vacancies.

The Judicial Administration Section later became known as the Bench Bar Section; I served on its Council as assistant editor, co-editor, secretary, vice chairman, and chairman, and ex-officio member for over 40 years with only a few years off. Dennis begged off as editor as I moved up into the leadership; I recruited a former journalist and great writer and a new team to replace us. The new editor, Al Swanson, had been an active member of the section council and I realized his great abilities and talents. He did a fantastic job and served for many years thereafter. He later was appointed a circuit judge. We too became good friends. I will reflect later on the activities and on other members of that important section council.

Pursuant to Supreme Court Rule 39, in Cook County, a nominating committee was required to propose double the number of candidates for the number of associate judge vacancies. The committee was composed of circuit judges from different divisions and departments of the court who had been elected under Democrat and Republican labels and were appointed to the committee by the Chief Judge.

The Democrats dominated the Court and the committee. The Circuit Court of Cook County was divided into various parts. There was the Municipal Department composed of the First Municipal District—Chicago, the Second Municipal District—the Northern Suburbs of Chicago in Cook County, the Third Municipal District—the Northwest Suburbs of Chicago in Cook County, the Fourth Municipal District—the Western Suburbs of Chicago in Cook County, the Fifth Municipal District—the Southwest Suburbs of Chicago in Cook County, and the Sixth Municipal District—the South Suburbs of Chicago in Cook County.

There was also the County Department composed of several Divisions including Criminal, Domestic Relations, Chancery, Law, Juvenile, and County. For a while, there was another division for support enforcement folded into the Domestic Relations Division. Additionally, there was the surety section attached to the

Chief Judge's Office for approval of bonding companies used in the other divisions where bonds were required to be posted.

The Effort

My first effort was to have my friends contact the members of the nominating committee by letter or telephone to provide good reasons why my training, experience, temperament, and maturity made me an ideal person to be selected for a judgeship. I found that the work I did for the city had put me in touch with many influential people of both political parties. Fortunately for me, many of my enlisted allies knew the committee members well on a first named basis. I always wondered what the conversation was on that committee. I could hear each member saying they heard from many good friends that Mike Jordan was a mature young man who had a lot of experience for his years and could be counted upon to do a great job and work hard. I also heard others saying what is he? Is he Black from the 4th Ward? No, he is Jewish from the 4th Ward. He must get along with everyone. He has Black, Hispanic, Irish, Polish, Italian, and Jewish support, additionally, many Republicans like him. Maybe, he is a winner!

I had worked with diligence, integrity, and competence at the many assignments given me as a lawyer, especially after leaving my entry position in the Law Department's Traffic Division and transferring to the General Counsel Division of the Corporation Counsel's office. I was transferred by the young Corporation Counsel, Raymond F. Simon. He was very bright and had been appointed to this position by Mayor Richard J. Daley only a few years before I started at the Law Department. I started when I was 24 years old, after I passed the bar examination but before being admitted to practice as a lawyer; and Simon was only 33 years old then. As I entered his large office, the first thing I noticed was that my sense of smell was awakened. I later came to recognize the scent of Simon's masculine cologne whenever I was in his office or near him. On that first visit, Simon told me that he heard good things about me from the head of the Traffic

Division and from my 4th Ward Alderman, Claude W. B. Holman, Chairman of the City Council Health Committee. Holman was a strong ally of the mayors and well known to Simon.

Before I was transferred to the Law Department's main City Hall offices on the 5th floor, down the hall from the mayor's office, while I was at traffic court, I had some memorable experiences. The first experience, was after passing the bar exam but before being sworn in as a lawyer. I was employed by the Law Department as a clerk. I was expected to learn the procedures and the way things were done.

I appeared in the various courtrooms at traffic court hearing cases where Chicago municipal ordinances were invoked to charge the offender. I was assigned to observe the lawyers there to learn the procedures, but since I was only a clerk and not a lawyer yet, I could not speak or participate in any manner or address the judge.

Years later, the Supreme Court did promulgate a rule to allow law school graduates who were called clerks and served in a government position to appear and speak in a courtroom setting under the supervision of an attorney. Those clerks would be referred to as 711s in recognition of the Rule. When I worked at traffic court before being sworn in as a lawyer, I had to remain silent. Years later, I would supervise 711 clerks who were designated in government offices such as a municipal law department.

One day I arrived in a courtroom that I was assigned to observe as the judge took the bench for a court call and saw the lawyer from my office was not yet present. The judge was very austere in his manner and appearance. He spoke quietly but sharply to me saying he did not want to wait any longer. He wanted to proceed. He told me to step up. His direction sounded to me like a sharp jab to my stomach that could be a mortal wound to my career. I tried to express myself with respect and clarity. I told the judge that I was not yet licensed. He said no one would know the difference. I felt like I was falling into a deep pit. I said I was going before the Character and Fitness Committee of the Supreme Court in a few days and I did not want to get myself in trouble. He insisted that I proceed. I felt cornered with nowhere to go. I was about to decline again, but fortunately the lawyer walked in to take his position as prosecutor. I did not have to defy the judge who had recently been the Republican County Chairman before being appointed to the bench. That was one of my first ethical challenges. Although I may have appeared calm on the outside, my stomach was churning. I saw it could be very difficult to speak truth to power.

A few days later, with much trepidation, I answered my summons to appear before the Character and Fitness Committee by presenting myself at a lawyer's law office. I found that Mr. Mulroy, the lawyer, was the only one present to interview me. He seemed very formal and had a file in front of him that apparently contained my application for admission to the Bar. He said he noticed I was from the south side and went to South Shore High School. As I said yes, I realized we might have a connection. I told him that the principal there was a very lovely and dynamic woman. After making that statement, I asked him if he was in any way related to her. He told me she was his older sister. I felt relieved that I suspected some connection since they both had the same last name and I knew she had never married. I had given only glowing reviews before he identified the relationship. It seemed to me that after that exchange he was less formal and more friendly and he became reassuring to me. He said his report to the full committee would be positive and I would be able to be sworn in shortly. I was greatly relieved and felt I had lucked out to have had a lawyer I had a connection to, even if tenuous. I had been more than lucky to have been assigned to a lawyer whose sister was my high school principal. If he mentioned me to his sister, she probably would not remember the time she summoned me to her office after I participated in a senior year prank.

Back then, many of my classmates decided to take out at least five books from the school library. When hundreds of books were taken, the librarian must have felt something was amiss and called the principal, who began calling into her office all of those students who had taken out books that morning. My history teacher told me that she received a note from the principal that I was wanted in her office. I felt perspiration under my arms and my stomach tightened as I stood up and walked out of the classroom and proceeded to the office. I had just a few minutes while walking to decide what I would say.

The principal asked me why I had taken out books and I told her I needed books on a certain subject and only had a few minutes between classes, so I merely found the books in the subject area and quickly grabbed five so I could more closely examine them in study hall later in the day. I was excused and went back to my class. My teacher said she was curious why I was called to the principal's office since I was a good student and a good boy. I said it was just a question that the principal had that needed clarification, but that everything was fine. I thanked her for her compliments and her concern. I learned that actions can have consequences. Just because others do something, that does not give me license to do it without good cause. Here, I was lucky again that my guilt could not be proven. I enjoyed the presumption of innocence. Maybe the experience taught me that some compassion might be necessary when a young or immature person acts without thinking. All of life's events can be used as a learning opportunity for the future.

2 CALM BEFORE THE STORM

A New Supervisor—Man of details

City of Chicago Corporation Counsel Ray Simon told me to report to my new supervisor, Allen Hartman, head of the General Counsel Division. I walked only about 100 feet wondering who this man would be. I hoped he was nice, but I would have to accept him as my new boss and go with the flow. I was told by his secretary, Harriet Peterson, a prim grey-haired serious woman, to wait in a nearby office, since he was out of the office. I sat alone in the nearby office for a few minutes and then shortly thereafter, I met two young men who were assigned to that adjoining office. I introduced myself to each as they came into their office. I said I was told by the secretary to sit and wait for Mr. Hartman. Each introduced himself to me. We discussed where I came from—traffic court—and what law schools we had gone to. I learned that one had an Irish name and lived on the southwest side while the other had an Italian name and lived on the north side. The Irishman, Mike Madigan, was fair skinned and blue eyed and had a charming twinkle in his eye and a warm reassuring smile. The Italian, Dan Pascale, was darker in complexion and seemed very warm and reassuring. Both seemed very bright and both were quite friendly and open to receiving me as an equal. Dan had gone to Harvard and the University of Chicago Law

School. Mike had gone to Notre Dame and Loyola Law School. The two men I met became close personal friends of mine.

The two would joke about each other in a way that showed their admiration and kindness for the other. Dan told me how strange it looked when they both attended the Bar Mitzvah service the previous Saturday for the son of a court reporter. Sonny Katz, the friendly court reporter, had invited both of them although neither was Jewish. Dan felt with his dark coloring he could pass as Jewish, but Mike stood out as a "sheygets"—a non-Jew, and looked funny wearing a kippah and prayer shawl during the service. A greeter welcomed both of these young men as they entered the synagogue and handed them each a kippah and prayer shawl (tallit) that they wore. Clearly, no one knew they did not know the prayer for adorning themselves with the tallit. I was amused hearing this story by one non-Jew seeing the humor in another non-Jew but not seeing himself as funny. I learned then and many times thereafter that neither had any aversion to Jews and their rituals.

A short time after my transfer to General Counsel, Dan was assigned to the Appeals Division, which was about 50 feet away on the side of the office where one would enter after passing through the main door to the 5th floor law offices. Dan later became its head after the current lawyer in charge, Sydney Drebin, retired and his successor, Marvin Aspen, became a state circuit judge before becoming a federal district judge and later the chief federal judge for the Northern District of Illinois in Chicago.

After Dan served as head of the Appeals Division, he was named deputy corporation counsel. All of these promotions came before Dan was appointed a circuit judge in Cook County and then the head of the Administrative Office of the Illinois Courts, a later successor to Roy Gulley. Dan's many promotions came under different administrations and bosses and were based on merit. Ray Simon had told Dan once that if Dan was ever asked who his political sponsor was, to say it was Simon. Ray Simon did not want to lose Dan, whose talents were endless. After public service with the city, he also served as counsel for a major corporation and was hired by a major law firm. Dan told me years ago that his most scary assignment for the city involved a helicopter ride to make an inspection. He said he tried not to look down while inspecting a parcel of land being reviewed for development, but did see the Earth moving about as he felt the vibrations. He felt relieved once he returned to the landing site and he could walk again.

Michael was then a clerk assigned to brief liquor and license police reports to be used by lawyers like me, who would prosecute licensees for violations of the law. They could lose their city licenses or receive suspensions of varying durations. Mike had been a secretary of his 13th Ward Alderman David W. Healy while he was a law student at Loyola University Law School. Not too long after we met and after Mike graduated and passed the bar, he took a job at the Illinois Commerce Commission, where he served under a very erudite gentlemen from my 4th Ward, Cyrus Culter, who also wrote many books of poetry. Mike reviewed briefs and helped draft opinions for the Commerce Commission.

Within a short time, Mike moved into several other important positions in government and politics, but our friendship continued. He became the Democrat ward committeeman for the 13th Ward, making him a member of the Democratic Cook County Central Committee. He served in the constitutional convention of 1970 as a delegate, with two delegates from each district. He showed his skills at Con Con. He was elected for service in the Illinois legislature and moved up through the ranks into leadership, ultimately becoming the Democratic leader and the Speaker of the House, serving longer than any other house speaker in the nation. He was the last Democrat leader in the legislature selected by Mayor Daley.

Mike, like Dan, proved his worth over and over again by his legal and political skills, making allies at every turn. He developed one of the strongest state parties for the Democrats in the nation and certainly make the Democrat Party in Illinois a force to be reckoned with due to his efficiency, energy, and savvy. He was a tireless worker, never counting on anything but his own hard work and attention to detail. He hired young staff who were exceedingly bright and energetic.

I always felt proud to know these two bright, honest men. They attended my wedding to Maureen and I attended their weddings to their wives—Shirley to Mike and Mary to Dan. The three of us got together for lunch on a weekly basis for many years, learning from each other. Mike was particularly interested in our ideas, thoughts, viewpoints, and beliefs. He was raised as a very parochial Irish Catholic from the southwest side. He learned much from his father, the local ward superintendent, who died shortly before I met Mike, but his schooling was only in Catholic parochial schools. He knew I was a Jew and Dan an Italian Protestant. He soaked up knowledge.

Dan and I were curious as well and we all shared our lives openly with the others. We talked about our athletic ability or its absence, how we went through stages of being taken to the husky section for clothes for a few years, how certain childhood friends never interacted with people different from themselves. My relationship with Dan and Mike has always been enriching. We have all been mutually supportive, and to this day, I fully trust and respect both Dan and Mike. Maureen joined us for lunch once after we were engaged to marry. She told me how she marveled that we each listened attentively to each other without any interruptions and then would give our own opinions which might be entirely different. We all showed each other respect and deference. Years later, she would sometimes ask me to listen to her and the children as I would listen to Mike and Dan.

Career Development

Mike was a great positive force in helping advance my career at every stage. He never sought anything from me in return. I remember an incident a few years after I retired from the bench, when I was already serving as a neutral doing mediations and arbitrations as well as weddings and was quite busy. I was walking

Dan Pascale, Michael J. Madigan, Michael S. Jordan, Maureen Lynn Jordan, and Shirley Madigan

through the back corridor on the top floor of the Aon Building to meet a bride and groom before their wedding ceremony, when I noticed Mike in a room with an open door. He was sitting with his press secretary, Steve Brown. Steve had helped the Democrat candidates for judge I ran with in 1984. We hired several publicists. I felt very comfortable with Steve since I had served as chair for all of the judges running on the same Democrat ticket.

My co-chair in 1984 when I ran was Michael Getty. In spite of his keen insights and intelligence, he was defeated in the Democratic primary and I became the sole overall chair with sub-chairs for the candidates running suburban-wide, (our suicide squad), and our city-wide candidates, (our sure winners). Getty had been an aide to Mike in the legislature and was parliamentarian of the Illinois House of Representatives before my cousin, David Epstein, assumed the role. Mike Getty ran again two years later, in 1986, listing himself with his middle name Brennan (his mother's maiden name), a clearly Irish name, helping him to garner the needed winning votes. Ballot names were important.

Getty's father had been the Cook County Public Defender for many years but that name was not magic, like an Irish name.

I told Mike and Steve that I was early for a wedding I was scheduled to perform and asked what brought them to the Aon Building. Mike said the governor was signing several bills passed in the last session of the legislature and they were waiting for one bill to be signed with the attendant publicity since he had been the main sponsor.

A moment later, Governor Rod Blagojevich entered and Mike started to introduce us. The governor was dressed in a conservative blue suit that fit him perfectly, his hair brushed and combed professionally without even one strand out of place. I saw no wrinkles in his clothes except the required crease on each pants leg as he stood up sharply with photogenic posture. He was fresh as a daisy with a wide smile showing his pretty teeth. Blagojevich acknowledged that he knew me and I told Mike that he had appeared before me years before he became governor when he was practicing criminal law. He had felony cases in front of me when I sat in the Skokie courthouse—Municipal District 2. Years before he did not have a "body man" attending him and looked more human and not like the mannequin he had become.

Mike told Blagojevich, "You know, Jordan is doing arbitration and mediation and it would be excellent if you got him some cases to hear." Rod said that sounded like a good idea. He asked for my business card, which I gave him. He and the young man with him then departed, telling Mike they would be ready for him in about two or three minutes. Mike told me not to count on anything since everything with Rod is based on value to him. I was, of course, grateful to Mike, even if our governor would never fulfill his promise to help. When I gave the governor my card, he passed it on to his "body man" to put in his pocket. Among other things in the aide's pockets were Rod's comb and brush so he would always look pretty. He did not want anything in his pockets to make him look fat or out of shape. Later, when he was indicted, I suspected he may have wanted room in his pockets to put payoffs. When he was incarcerated, he could no longer tint his hair to look dark, so grey became visible, showing his age. I left to go to the wedding as Mike and Steve left to join the governor for the dog and pony show.

A few years later, Rod's failures let my son Jeff down even more than his failure to recommend me for any arbitration or mediation cases. Jeff was not only disappointed by our governor but betrayed. Jeff had the plan of becoming a forensic scientist working for the state police as a criminal science investigator in their CSI unit until he earned a career pension. Jeff had a degree from DePaul University in Interdisciplinary Science with high honors as well as a certificate in criminal justice. He was a perfect fit for the state CSI job with the state police. He thought that after 20 years with CSI he could retire, live off his state pension, and then start an organic farm, knowing he would have the security of the state pension. He had interned on an organic farm in Michigan the previous summer as part of his baccalaureate program and felt working on an organic farm would fulfill his dream after giving service to the state.

Jeff went through all the hurdles for the CSI job. He was required to go to Springfield for the final interview. We drove together and stayed the night in a hotel in Joliet to have a head start getting in on time for the afternoon appointment. As we arrived in Springfield, a major snow storm was building in intensity, but the interviews went ahead. All went well. We had hoped to see Mike in the capitol building, but buildings were closing early due to the developing storm, with heavy drifting and blinding snow. The capitol building had been remodeled at great expense over an extended period of time and had just been completed. Mike had said we should see our tax dollars at work since it was beautiful. He had arranged a tour for us. The visit at the capitol building was not to be. The driving was miserable, but Jeff got us back home safely, sometimes having to follow in the ruts of large trucks making a path for us. After the challenging, and—I thought—death defying trip, we found that Jeff did not make the cut.

We learned from sources, not Mike, that the selection process Jeff went through was a sham. Payoffs were made and those hired were first made interns to give the impression of hiring those with experience. Blagojevich's later impeachment and removal from office was appropriate and overdue. I applaud Mike for his part in overseeing the process as Speaker. The Governor was selling everything for a price. Jeff was the tip of the iceberg with his treatment unknown to the public, press, and prosecutors. The shameful governor was selling support for the Children's Hospital in Chicago by demanding contributions to him, selling a US Senate seat after the election of our U.S. Senator, Barack Obama, as President of the United States, and other despicable actions that were designed to profit Blagojevich personally.

I also found out that my cousin, David Epstein, who had been on the Illinois Court of Claims, appointed to successive terms by two prior governors of the opposite party—Republicans—had been dumped by Blagojevich, a Democrat. No money to him meant no job. I saw how the governor's corruption hurt everyone; and I saw how it hit hard at home—particularly hard. I will never pardon or commute Blagojevich in my mind as Donald Trump did with his written paper using and abusing his presidential powers. I see Mike as a public servant acting to rid the public of bad actors even when the bad actor comes from the same political party. As I write this paper, I realize that my friend Mike has been accused of serious offenses. I not only adhere to the presumption of innocence in the law, but have confidence in Mike's innocence based on my knowledge of his character and sense of decency.

The New Boss Enters

Finally, I got to meet my new boss, Allen Hartman. I saw a fast-moving stout man in a dark suit going into his office. His hair was combed back neatly. He had a slight smile but I could tell he was a serious man who was thoughtful and pensive. He greeted me with a warm handshake and offered me a seat in his small office. Most of the offices were the size of his office. He shared the space with his secretary.

Like all of the other offices in the law department except that of the corporation counsel and the first assistant corporation counsel, the partitions between the hallway and adjoining offices only went from the floor to about three and a half feet high. The top three feet of the partitions were made of plexiglass with full visibility. There was no privacy.

My boss seemed rushed, but he was clear regarding his expectations for honesty, diligence, and care. I was reassured with the smile on his face. After meeting with Allen Hartman, I came to know a very hardworking bright man who was a stickler for details. He taught me early on that I needed an identity. Was I going to be signing off on formal legal opinions to city officials and in letters to lawyers and other stakeholders as Michael Jordan, Michael S. Jordan, or Michael Stephen Jordan? I should be consistent. A name was important. Spelling, punctuation, clarity, and precision were important considerations for a lawyer.

He took me to an office only two cubicles away from his own. It was occupied by an elderly man neatly dressed and very well groomed. I shook hands with this dapper man, Maurice Handlesman, who was in his 80s. Allen pointed to the empty metal desk near the doorway and said it was now mine. I would use the metal file cabinet near the window for storage of my assigned files. Allen's secretary would help me get supplies and introduce me to the support personnel. Dan was actually the one to show me around and introduce me to all the people.

I met the secretaries in the steno pool and was introduced to their supervisor, Marge, who would assign any work I had to one of the others. I met the receptionist, Jayne Byrne, who would take my calls whenever I was out. She could pick up every call on the floor. She would leave us messages on folded paper on her desk with our names on the outside so I needed to look for my name each time I returned to the office from court if she did not tell me herself. I also met the lady in charge of reimbursements. I was shown where each division of the office was located on the fifth and sixth floors, told who was in charge, and what they did. I was shown the copy machine on the sixth floor and shown how it works. Eventually, as technology allowed for **better accounting**, I learned to use a digital key that recorded the date, time, and the number of copies made using that key. I learned how to dictate over the telephone so a secretary could later type from my dictation. I learned how to use a disc as well and of course could still dictate to a secretary directly. Without computers I would often get the evil eye from a secretary when I told her that a letter or word had to be changed since the entire page usually had to be typed over again and changing the carbon copies was problematic. We usually made several copies of each document. Every lawyer had a name plate on a shelf at the entrance to his or her cubicle, so by walking the isles, I could learn the names of the lawyers. I had no such help with the secretaries.

About a month after I came to the General Counsel Division, I saw Ray Simon's secretary in the hall and she said she had something for me. I dropped by her office and I was handed a black plastic base and a black plastic piece to slide into the base and place at the entrance of my cubicle. I was now officially in business and identified as belonging. The nameplate said: "Michael S. Jordan." I had chosen that form of my name and have used it ever after in my professional career except on the judicial retention ballot, where I deleted my middle initial S.

While I served under Allen, he consistently found the time to monitor all my written work, since it was the office policy for every document leaving the office from our division to be reviewed by him before being issued by the Corporation Counsel, whose signature was on all documents in addition to mine. When Allen assigned me a new matter, he told me of his expectations, what resources were available to me, and who in the office had experience with similar matters. Allen was generally a great teacher. On occasion there were times he asked for research on a subject but did not tell me which side of the issue I should take. I realized that he wanted to know the other side's case support as well as our own. Sometimes I did not know where my research would lead until I saw something in the newspapers that looked like it involved all of the issues I researched. Sometimes I learned that Dan or someone else was doing the same or similar research. Clearly, Allen did not trust that any one of us would find everything he wanted. I knew that I could never accomplish what Dan discovered in a short period of time. While we had a small library in the back of the office near the bathrooms, we often went to the large law library in the Civic Center. I got a library card for my use there although I rarely took out any book. I merely looked up cases, read them in the library, and abstracted the cases. I also found it was a quiet place in which to study or write. I often saw Allen reading books for his own personal research. He did everything in addition to assigning and supervising all the lawyers in our division.

At various times there were between 18 to 23 lawyers assigned to the General Counsel Division that Allen supervised. He also had his own case load and rendered advice to various city officials. Years later, I learned that the Corporation Counsel relied on him, the first assistant Richard L. Curry, and the head of appeals, Marv Aspen, for advice and counsel, strategy, and tactics. In the beginning I learned the strengths and weaknesses of all of my colleagues, usually asking Dan to guide me. Dan never led me astray. There were some with whom I only exchanged pleasantries but never asked for advice. Some were in specialized areas I was not yet working in so there was nothing to ask of them yet. After a short time, I found that new hires were asking me for advice. Allen also assigned others to assist me on some cases and put several law clerks under my supervision at different times. I enjoyed all of my responsibilities.

I was temporarily assigned to an office in the basement of the Civic Center with several other people designated as staff. I served as legal counsel to a committee created by the administration to review the zoning laws of the city—the Zoning Review Committee. The mayor appointed a real estate developer, Harry F. Chaddick, as chair, with others in the zoning community involved, as well as a representative from the city council. There were fewer than a handful of staff. I diligently studied the zoning ordinance and its many parts while having the feeling of being back in law school. I was my own teacher. During meetings, Allen was always there to give the committee advice. That is when I learned from the master. I learned that before Allen was brought to the city by Ray Simon, he had worked for a zoning lawyer who represented many municipalities. Allen had much practical experience. After several months, proposals were made by the Zoning Review Committee to the city council and approved. I was returned to my regular functions and later saw some of the other staff working in other departments I encountered. They were on temporary assignment as well. I was now better able to represent the city on zoning litigation now being assigned to me.

One of the perks of that detached assignment was giving me the opportunity to meet the 7th Ward alderman whose staff member was assigned to the committee. He often offered me a ride home, since he and the staff member traveled to South Shore, while I lived on the way in Hyde Park. It was great, and a nice friendship developed with these two Republicans.

The Lay of the Land

The offices of the law department of the city were located on the fifth and sixth floors of city hall at 121 North LaSalle Street. My office was down the hall from Allen's office, which was not far from the offices of the Corporation Counsel and his First Assistant with their secretaries in a room outside their respective offices. The Corporation Counsel's office had a private entrance to the mayor's private office with the mayor's other staff and offices filling much of the center of the fifth floor of City Hall. In the back of the fifth floor offices of the law department, not far from the washrooms, was a circular metal staircase going up one floor to the remaining offices of lawyers in the department. This inner stairway was in addition to the public stairway outside the office and the public elevators. I found I had to go up to the sixth floor regularly since the copy machine was located there. On the other side of the fifth floor offices, away from the General Counsel Division offices, were the lawyers in the Appeals Division and the Land Acquisition Division. On the back of the fifth floor offices were the lawyers in the Public Utilities Division. On the sixth floor I found the Tort Division and the Building Code Enforcement Division. On the sixth floor out of the main office were additional offices for the Ordinance Enforcement Division. Of course, I knew that the traffic division, where I started, had offices at traffic court then housed at 321 N. LaSalle Street in a red brick building immediately north of the Chicago River with a clock tower at the top. That building was infested with rodents and bugs. I found it safer to take my serious business to a second floor washroom where many fewer rodents found their way.

When Ray Simon resigned to go into private practice and the first assistant Richard L. Curry replaced Ray, Allen was promoted to first assistant corporation counsel. Allen was replaced by Benjamin Novoselsky, who had been assigned to the Tort Division but was more freelance, representing the city in most all federal litigation. He had also been special counsel for several city agencies and the Illinois Medical Service District on the west side. Ben taught me practical trial techniques in federal court and was a great friend. I tried matters with him and learned from a master. Ben was the age of my father. His son, Henry, had been in my law school class and was working in the Appeals Division of the office. Later, I learned that Henry had married a cousin of Maureen's, so we were all family.

Ben had a long thick white mustache and reminded me of the Parker Brothers Monopoly game figure in his looks. Ben always showed a lot of bluster but he was a sweet dear man. One day we tried a case together in federal court and he told me he was going to stumble and mutter, but he was ok. He said a young lawyer opposing us would have an advantage with the jury unless we made them think we were less able. He would be an old over the hill lawyer and I was his young inexperienced assistant. The jury would have as much sympathy for us as they would for the lawyer we opposed.

When Ben became an Associate Judge in 1973, Brian Killgallon succeeded him. Brian had been in charge of the Torts Division responsible for tort actions filed against the city. Brian taught me the art of settlement negotiations, his forte. Brian was a lawyer and an engineer. After I left the office and became a judge, and a short time after Brian became General Counsel, the Mayor tapped him to serve as Executive Director of the Public Buildings Commission that managed all city facilities. Mayor Daley was head of the Commission. Brian remained there until shortly before he died.

After I left the Corporation Counsel's office, the General Counsel Division was divided into segments. It was no longer easy or routine for people like me to have a diversity of case types assigned. It would be unusual to be assigned liquor prosecution, zoning cases, human relations issues, employment cases, federal civil rights litigation, prosecution of police officers at the police board, defense and prosecution of extraordinary remedies and chancery matters seeking mandamus against public officials, as well as opinion writing, counseling to the city council committees, service as staff counsel for the Zoning Review Committee, and other responsibilities I had been given that made me a perfect candidate for judge. Many of the lawyers were placed in a building outside of City Hall. I was fortunate to be in the right place at the right time with the right people.

My First Office Mate

That first day after visiting with Allen Hartman in his office, after he assigned me to a cubicle just a couple of offices away from his, I got to know the man in his 80s who was very tall, unbent, and dapper. I came to know Maurice Handelsman in the last year before he died. Although he had no known medical problems, he died the night of his retirement party. Morrie, as I called him, was a former Assistant United States Attorney. He was well educated and well spoken. He was assigned to represent the Chicago Board of Health and the Chicago TB Sanatorium. He frequently received calls and gave sound advice immediately based on his experience, or he quickly looked up the appropriate ordinance in the Municipal Code. Morrie had no hobbies and no family in Chicago. He had been divorced for many years and his daughter lived out of town. Upon retirement, he no longer would have to come downtown and visit with the friend who drove him, not have to shave and dress in his fine clothes or see many people and get to flirt with all the ladies. He had nothing to look forward to once he retired. While he had several pensions that he would get to support himself, the job of coming to and going from work was more important.

Later in life, whenever friends would tell me they were about to retire, I would ask them what plans they had for their future. What would they be doing each day? Some friends told me of elaborate plans and I wished them well. Others told me that they would figure it out or decide later, once retired. I told them of Morrie and challenged them to decide upon specific activities they would engage in each day before retiring.

Over the years in the office, I was assigned a couple of other offices that were near other lawyers having the same assignment, such as Barry Greenburg and Richard Kaplan. I enjoyed all of those lawyers that I worked with. My only issue was remembering a new telephone number each time I was relocated, but since they were all in order and since I knew my previous number and I was one office further away, I just raised the last number by one digit. It worked!

I remember working with Henry Weber, a lawyer in the General Counsel Division on a zoning case defending against the property owners' claims that they were entitled to a special use or zoning variance and it was improperly denied to them. One day Henry came in and said their pleadings were amended and he was now named as an additional defendant with the City since they claimed he was responsible for holding up all approvals. I agreed to represent Henry and took over the case. Henry was the first lawyer I had represented. Henry told everyone in hearing range that I got him off the hook when we won. He was happy and delighted. I worked hard since I felt I could easily be sued as well for no greater reason than doing my job as a lawyer, just as Henry had done his job as a lawyer. That case may have firmed up my image in the office. It sure did not hurt. I had my first malpractice case with the claim of abuse of power.

Making Connections

When I was assigned to represent the Chicago Commission on Human Relations, I came to know the executive director, Jim Burns. We traveled together to Hartford, Connecticut, to represent the city at a convention consisting of civil rights agencies. I was there as legal counsel and Jim as the executive director. Within a short time, we became good friends.

Years after the meeting, when Jim learned that I was applying to become a judge, he was very supportive and introduced me to a lovely lady, Amelia Sharpe, who he knew was friends with many judges. Some were Hispanic, like her, but others were not Hispanic, such as Judge Eugene Wachowski, clearly a Polish gentleman. She took Maureen and me to dinner with Judge Wachowski and his lovely wife where I met him in a relaxed environment. Judge Wachowski was then the acting Chief Judge of the Circuit and the Presiding Judge of one of the largest components of the Court, the First Municipal District.

Amelia was dressed elegantly, was soft spoken, had no detectable accent, and was clearly at ease with herself. She spoke and acted in a way that made others comfortable. She found discussion points that made it easy for all to connect. I thought to myself as the conversation progressed that here Maureen and I were with the acting chief judge of the Circuit Court of Cook County, one on one, with a limited number of campaigning days ahead. He would have little time to dine with all the candidates. I was put into a special place and this was my time to show my best. Judge Wachowski was at his peak in power, charm, and intellect. I was blessed.

Although many years later when Judge Wachowski was assigned to the County Division and served as a retired recalled judge into his 90's, he ruled on sensitive election cases, but he did not have control over the largest unit of the court and he no longer had staff. When we met, he had it all! The day after our dinner, Judge Wachowski introduced me to his administrative assistant, Francis X Poynton, an associate judge, who made countless calls on my behalf urging judges to vote for me. I sat across from him in his office as he made call after call. I wondered why people would listen to him or be persuaded by him, but realized he spoke for Judge Wachowski and the judges on the other side of the telephone knew that. He had a delicate tea set and offered me tea as he made his calls. I felt like I was inside a formal reception in another time and place. He retired from the bench on December 31, 1978. Fortunately, he was in the right place at the right time to help my candidacy. I can only assume that Judge Poynton also helped another candidate in my group of inductees, John Bowe, since his father, Augustine Bowe, had been the Presiding Judge of the First Municipal District before Judge Wachowski and Judge Poynton had worked for him as well.

Jim Burns also suggested that I contact each of the members on the Commission on Human Relations. I followed his advice. The members included the who's who in Chicago society in management and labor, civic affairs and law, news, and public action. Without exception, all agreed to lobby the nominating committee and later to contact judges they personally knew on my behalf, since I was the lawyer for the Commission they served. The members of the police board that I appeared before also helped me. The membership included the head of the largest land title company, Chicago Title and Trust, the CEO of the largest gas company, and a leader in the Teamsters Union.

The hearing officers I presented liquor and license cases in front of were eager to help me as well. In fact, one of the hearing officers, Peter Fitzpatrick, was not only one I appeared before, but also a mentor, a teacher, a guide, and political adviser. He sponsored my admission to the United States Supreme Court with Justice Glenn T. Johnson. He helped me through the process of getting bar association approval to become a judge. When I first met Peter, he was probably in his 60s. He and his wife Alma had 16 children. He spoke slowly, almost with a stutter, to say the right words. He was so very careful and thoughtful. He listened intently and spoke few words. I learned to pay close attention to those few words since they were usually important gems to learn by and act upon. He was balding and what hair he had was white. He had a warm charming smile. I could see how he would connect with a jury with the charm he displayed. I knew he had many responsibilities to fulfill, but he always had time for my questions. He modeled perfect listening and responded perfectly with deliberate thought.

He had been on the judicial evaluation committee of the Chicago Bar Association and had just ended his term as the President of the Illinois State Bar Association. He told me the sort of things that are looked for in an application and interview and who my audience would be. He taught me about body language as an aid in conveying my thoughts during my presentations. He advised that when I fold my arms, I appear to be resisting and distant, but when leaning forward with hand cupped on the table before me, I looked open, receptive, and available. On his advice, I listed lawyers I litigated against in my assigned cases, considering a balance in different areas to show my diversity of experience, and I also listed women as well as men, young and old, and persons of different religions, races, and ethnicities to show I was even and fair to all. Peter was a treasured friend and resource until he died.

Peter Fitzpatrick was also the Chairman of the Human Relations Commission, where he heard and took my advice and counsel as the agency's lawyer. He also tried cases in the federal courts, like me, and saw me in action just as I saw him. At the end of a day when I prosecuted liquor and license cases in front of him at the City Hall hearing room—usually two to five cases a day—he would critique me, asking why I called witnesses in the order I did or why I introduced evidence through one witness and not another. I strived to master the skills of a trial lawyer with help from a pro. Even though he had 16 of his own children, he found the time to mentor and train me. I felt like he was another father to me—one of several I have already referred to and others I will talk about later.

In addition to Peter Fitzpatrick at the liquor and license commission, the other hearing officers I appeared in front of included a former state senator. The brother of an administrative assistant to the mayor was another. His brother became the 49th Ward Democratic Committeeman and then Illinois Attorney General. That hearing officer was in the private practice of law. Another hearing officer, Morgan F. Murphy, Jr., had a father who was a member of the Chicago Police Board. I knew both father and son. That hearing officer later became a U.S. Congressman from the south and southwest side of Chicago. I believe they all put in a good word for me. Two of the hearing officers were also so very gracious, giving me wedding gifts that we have used for over 50 years. These generous men were great friends.

Starting from Scratch

I knew only a handful of the voting judges. I had to meet all the judges and meet those I had not previously met. I had been told it is useful for friends of mine who were known by the judges to introduce me. In the years since November 1966, when I became a lawyer, I had made many friends in the office I worked in—the Law Department of the City of Chicago—as well as persons I represented as a city lawyer. I had represented the Chicago Commission on Human Relations, appeared before the Chicago Police Board, represented the Chicago Zoning Administrator and appeared before the Zoning Board of Appeals. I appeared before the hearing officers for the local liquor control commissioner—the Mayor of the City of Chicago—and represented him and his decisions at the License Appeal Commission and in the Circuit Court. I had worked as legal counsel to the zoning review committee chaired by a prominent real estate developer who was close friends with the mayor.

I kept no secrets and was quite transparent, telling all in the law department that I was applying to be an associate judge. I told the lawyers in my division of the law department as well as those in other divisions. I told the secretaries and clerks as well. To my great surprise and delight, many volunteered to help, saying they were friends, neighbors, or relatives to voting judges. I felt it was like a tag team match where different allies took me into different chambers. Some had connections to ward committeemen who had helped some of the judges get elected and agreed to ask them to help me. It was great! No matter what someone's position is in life, he or she has value as a person and has friends and family. No person should ever be ignored, since any one person could be the one who saves the day and perhaps the world. During my years on the bench, I always felt responsible for keeping the faith with all of those men and women who had supported me and had faith in me.

I found that another lawyer in the General Counsel Division, Bob Mackey, had also applied to become an associate judge, but I believed with the number of openings and the fact that he was much older than me, was from the northwest side while I was from the south side, was Irish Catholic while I was Jewish, and had case assignments different from mine, it would not divide our assets and allies. I always spoke favorably about him and I trust he did the same for me. We both made it! He became a full voting Circuit Judge only four years later in 1978.

Most of the contacts I had knew the judges in the Civic Center and walked me over there. City Hall occupied one half of a larger building shared with the County Building, with entrances on all four sides—Randolph, Washington, Clark, and LaSalle Streets. City Hall was on the LaSalle Street side with many of the city's offices, and the County Building was on the Clark Street side. The County Building housed many of the offices of the Cook County government. The mayor on the fifth floor of city hall and the president of the Cook County Board on the fifth floor of the county building could easily walk across the floor with no barrier separating the two buildings at that level. Mayor Daley never made that journey, unlike the President of the County Board George Dunne and his predecessors who walked over regularly.

On a nice day we took the elevator in City Hall going from the fifth floor, where my law department offices were located, to the street level, and walked out of the Clark Street side of the Cook County building and dodged traffic, crossing Clark Street in the center of the street going east to enter the Civic Center building. The Civic Center building occupied half of the block bordered by Randolph, Dearborn, Washington, and Clark Street, with its imprint being along Randolph. On the south side of the Civil Center on the rest of the block was an open plaza, later to be the site hosting a major piece of iron sculpture by Pablo Picasso. There was a small pool of water as well as stone benches. Some believe the adornments were added to minimize the space available to protestors. The available space, however, was significant and was used for major celebrations, festivals, and speech making.

Pablo Picasso, a Spanish artist, was selected to build the massive piece, which was fifty feet high and weighed over 160 tons. It was commissioned in 1963 and unveiled on August 15, 1967. The untitled piece has become a world-wide icon and source of pride for all Chicagoans.

On a cold or rainy or snowy day we could take the escalator in the County building at the ground level near Clark Street to the pedestrian way under Clark Street to reach the Civic Center's basement, passing the office of vital statistics, and take the escalator up to the ground level and then take the elevators in the correct elevator bank going up to the designated floor. The pedway continued through the Civic Center under Dearborn to the CTA rapid transit subway station and then proceeded east to the State Street CTA rapid transit subway station. The walkway continued east into old Marshall Fields Department Store, later to become Macys, before passing outside the department store east to the main public library of the city and on to the Illinois Central Railroad station at Michigan Avenue, where the pedway ended. The main public library became the Cultural Center and a new main library headquarters was built at the south loop at Van Buren and State Street. A branch of the pedway also went south from the Civic Center to the Brunswick Building at Washington and Dearborn. That office building later became an annex of the County Building. One could go a fair distance underground in inclement weather using the pedway and other buildings as cut throughs, such as I did when I had legal business in the federal courthouse at Dearborn and Adams.

When I went to the many other buildings, such as 26th and California, the Juvenile Court Building, branch court buildings, and suburban courthouses to solicit the votes of Circuit Judges, I was on my own. There were fortunately many calls made to judges in those places. My father told me he would make himself available to drive me to any location. He could stay in the car and wait until I was finished. We had no cell phones to use to communicate, but whether he needed a washroom or something else, he was always there when I was ready. My father was great and made my schedule work. I can't imagine any of the other candidates had someone as devoted to them as my father was to me. He would then accept my chatter or my silence when I was thinking. He merely asked for the next stop. My father helped me reach many of my goals in life by being present, saying little but doing much. I love him for his kindness not just to me but to my children and wife. I also learned that sometimes the best person to know is not the one who is constantly boasting about his accomplishments, but the one who does the job and does not seek praise and adoration. While my father would always take pride in my accomplishments, he had to know the great part he played in my successes. He taught me dependability and reliability by his example. My father never swore or used any profanity. He was courteous to all and had no bias or prejudice. He was always early. He was always dressed in a suit and tie and well groomed. From my earliest memories, I always knew he was near and his hand and arm were there to protect me. Whenever he applied the brake when driving, his arm swung out to keep me from moving forward into the dashboard. He was my seat belt before there was such an item in cars. He loved me and protected me always!

While I was on the run, I still had cases to cover, although the other lawyers in my office, graciously covered for me when they could and freed my time up for my campaign. Thank you's go to John Virgilio, Tom Heneghan, Richard Kaplan, Ken Cortese, Barry

Greenburg, George Keane, Henry Webber, Charles O'Connor, and a few others. There were some matters I could not hand off and I had to attend to those matters personally. Somehow, it all worked out and I saw all but a handful of judges. I did not even try to reach Judge Boyle since he was ill. I did not want to intrude, not knowing him or his illness. A couple of other judges were unavailable due to vacation or illness as well. I had to revisit several judges on many occasions since they were often in conference, on the bench, or away. It was frustrating, but I finally saw most of them on my third or fourth visit. Perhaps they voted for me based on my persistence.

Speaking of John Virgilio, I think back at the many jury cases we tried together in federal court. I still hear myself telling the jury in my opening remarks, "I am Michael Jordan and with my partner John Virgilio, we represent" the current client. In defending police officers accused of excessive force or false arrest I would tell the jurors not to exclude from the jury deliberation room the two best friends they will need—common sense and human nature. They will be guides to get you through the challenges you face as jurors. I told them about the fairy tale story of Goldilocks and the three bears and how things can sometimes be twisted upside down. The person who trespassed, broke into the house, and wanted to use the homeowner's beds, chairs, and porridge became the heroine. The plaintiff in our case is also trying to have you perceive him or her as innocent, but he or she is the wrongdoer and should not be rewarded. The policemen, like the bears, were only living life and doing their jobs. Now the criminal wants to punish the policeman rather than face any consequence for his or her crimes. The story worked since I lost only one of the many jury trials I was assigned.

Sage Advice

When I became a circuit judge and noticed a judicial candidate for associate judge enter my courtroom, I called for a recess in the proceedings and invited the candidate into my chambers, knowing the challenges facing the candidates. In fact, during the period when candidates were circulating during my judicial years from December 1984 until my retirement in December 1999, I would announce to the lawyers and parties in my courtroom that I would be taking short recesses to interview judicial candidates, a very important responsibility of my job, and asked for their understanding and forgiveness to allow me to do so to insure the betterment of the court system.

I kept in mind the sage advice I received from Glenn T. Johnson, a lawyer I met while I was in law school. Glenn gave me the insight that there are two types of lawyers. Those who admit they want to be a judge and those who don't admit they want to be a judge. Hearing this, I concluded that just about every lawyer at some stage in their career wanted to be a judge. As the years passed after I entered the practice of law and I began telling myself that I could do what this or that judge was doing and maybe do it even better, I found I was starting to realize I wanted to be a judge. Since, at first, I did not realize my desire, I did not admit it to myself or others, but eventually I saw I wanted it and began sharing my desire with those close to me, like Glenn Johnson. When we spoke, he always spoke lovingly of his children and then a grandchild. I recall that Maureen and I gave that granddaughter a small rocking chair as a gift. He and his son were ever grateful to us for thinking of sending a gift for his granddaughter. I have to thank my very thoughtful wife, Maureen.

Successful Classmates

Some of my law school classmates were helpful to me down the road but I found my college fraternity brothers were particularly helpful. One man was Dennis Carlin, who was a semester ahead of me in college and at DePaul Law School. By the time I transferred to DePaul, he was one of the editors of the Law Review. He helped me onto the staff and solicited me to write an article. He clearly advanced my career as I was now able to list my law review service and published article on my resume as a means of showcasing my accomplishments. Later when he became the managing partner of a large law firm and after I retired from the bench, he referred cases to me, recommending me as a mediator or arbitrator.

Denny's parents were in the Chicago parents' club for AEPi members at Madison. I had joined the fraternity. In the spring of each year, we enjoyed a weekend when the parents came up and gave a song and dance parody show to the delight of all. My parents made some long and lasting friendships during the meetings and rehearsals for their shows. While few, if any, of our parents had gone to college, they truly enjoyed this experience of friendship and camaraderie.

Denny's father was in show business as a producer, so he became the director of their shows. During the summer, he presented several plays at Melody Top Theatre in Hillside, Illinois. Each opening night when the newspaper critics came to review the newest play, he invited all of the AEPi families with dates to fill in the audience. He treated us. He wanted to avoid any empty seats. While I enjoyed all of the shows, we were expected to lead the applause and laughter in a spontaneous and appropriate way to help the critics realize how great the show was and to speak ravingly about the first act during intermission so the critics could hear the positive buzz. I sure did learn about marketing. Mostly, I had a great time. My dear friend, Al Lipton, and I would be in one car with our dates and our parents would be in another car with each other. Everyone was happy.

After I left the bench, another fraternity brother, Allen Lapedos, a former assistant United States Attorney, referred cases to me from his large law firm. A pledge brother of mine, Michael Reiter, who became a managing partner of his firm, also recommended me as a mediator and arbitrator to his partners and associates. Still another fraternity brother, John Simon, who was a year behind me at Madison and at DePaul Law School and had risen to head of the Civil Division of the U.S. Attorney's Office and later became a managing partner at another large law firm, Jenner and Block, was instrumental in having several cases referred to me to mediate. John became a president of the

Chicago Bar Association. He later was appointed to serve on the Appellate Court and was elected to a full term of ten years. His father, Seymour Simon, was a public official as well having been a Democrat Committeeman from the 40th Ward, the alderman, a county commissioner, the president of the Cook County Board of Commissioners, an Appellate Court justice, and a member of the Illinois Supreme Court from Cook County.

The legal career successes of each of my fraternity brothers from Alpha Epsilon Pi bestowed benefits on me. When I decided on AEPi with Al, I never dreamed of the later dividends it would yield. I also had several positive interactions with members of my law school class, especially when I was a judge.

3 ENTERING THE FRAY

Judges Get Dirty Assignments

One of the least favorite assignments I had in my first year on the bench was night bond court at the old Chicago police headquarters, located at 11th and State. The building had most every domestic variety of insect and the choice of rodents was plentiful, but it was the hours that I deplored most. I was assigned to be on duty in person from 8:00 PM to 4:00 AM for seven nights to set criminal bonds and issue search and arrest warrants. No prosecutors or public defenders were assigned. I dealt directly with the police.

Police officers and their informants were my constant petitioners. Rarely did I see any lawyers, but on one occasion, the valedictorian of my law school class appeared before me. Startled, I said to him, "I have to be here, but why are you here?" He said that he, too, had a command performance since the client was a favorite of one of the people he had to answer to in his job. I figured it was not his wife and did not want to ask more questions. He was dressed in a suit. I had only my judicial robe over a white shirt and tie with wash pants. I did consider that the client had ties to the community, that someone thought enough of his worth to hire a lawyer for him, and that the lawyer was excellent. I set a fair bond in light of the facts and circumstances. What I set seemed to satisfy all concerned. I don't think I saw my classmate again. The robe I wore was an abandoned robe I had found in one of the judicial chambers at traffic court that I knew would be perfect to use whenever I was working in a filthy bug infested environment. This assignment was perfect for that shabby tattered robe.

After each of my nights at bond court, I stripped off my clothes outside the doors of my apartment before entering, due to the creatures I might be bringing home with me. Since it was the shag of the night and the neighbors in the four other apartments on our floor were probably still asleep, I felt fairly comfortable stripping out in the hall. The greatest concession to modesty was to strip in the small area next to our garbage cans at the back entrance near the rear elevator, where only one other neighbor's door and ours opened. By arrangement, Maureen left the chain off our door and had a plastic bag for me to stuff my clothes in.

After my almost 26 years of service on the bench, when I was hearing labor and employment grievances involving the Chicago Police Department and the local branch of the Fraternal Order of Police, I had a case involving the safety of working in the building at 11th and State due to the presence of exposed asbestos. I held that until the city remediated the exposed hazardous materials, management was in violation of the contract as well as in violation of federal OSHA provisions. Within a few months of that ruling, both parties informed me that my services were no longer required in resolving their discipline and contract matters. I suspect that management told the union if they fix the problem, that money will not be available for monetary benefits for the rank and file. Several years later, the entire building was demolished. It must have been cheaper to have a tear-down and move headquarters to 35th and Michigan Avenue on the south side in Bronzeville than to remediate an old building with more problems than the presence of asbestos. I came to the conclusion that sometimes truth gets in the way of maintaining the *status quo* and a nice job. Truth to power here lost me a job.

Thinking of my adventures as a judge while living at 1606 East 50th Place in Hyde Park, I recall a brief assignment to fill in for another judge who was regularly assigned to a branch criminal misdemeanor court at the area police station at 51st and Wentworth near the Dan Ryan Expressway. He was either sick or on vacation. I was quite busy that day, but always took several breaks so the state's attorneys, public defenders, and clerks could have a bathroom break or meet with people. I called home to see what our young daughter was doing. When I called, Maureen told me that even though we had a 10th floor apartment, she could hear shouting on the street and saw our janitor chasing someone and yelling "Help, call the police, thief!" Within a couple minutes, the chase stopped with the police arriving and catching the person our janitor was chasing. Maureen gave me the colorful blow by blow narrative and commentary.

Later, I asked Maureen if the man being chased had a red jacket, white gym shoes, was about six feet tall and was White. She answered yes on all accounts. I told her I had set the bond. The young man had come from the north side to steal and probably then convert his gains into money to get a "hit" from his drug dealer.

For several years after going on the bench, wherever I was assigned, whether it be traffic court or some other place, I would sometimes get a call from Gene Nesgota, an administrative assistant and coordinator in the First Municipal District, who worked for Presiding Judge Eugene Wachowski. Since he knew I lived in Hyde Park, he would call me to go to the south side branch courts. I was sent to either the misdemeanor courtroom at 51th and Wentworth or the adjoining preliminary hearing courtroom for felonies. I was also sent to another courtroom at 61st and Racine for misdemeanor hearings and preliminary hearings of felonies. The third south side courtroom building was at 89th and Exchange in South Chicago, where misdemeanors were heard. Going to each of these venues gave me a chance to appreciate the history of our court system before those courtrooms shifted years later to a consolidated facility. Each year that passed with more and more judges of color, there was less and less likelihood of having White judges assigned to those facilities. I knew it was always best for the community to see persons who reflected the community sitting on the bench.

The building at 51st and Wentworth was newly built and fairly comfortable. My former boss, Ben Novoselsky, was one of the first judges assigned there as was another friend, Ben Edelstein. I found that the numbers' racket was still strong in that part of the city, unlike in other parts, and the same attorney represented all of the defendants whether they be charged as betters or bet takers. I learned that the so called "Jones Brothers" were in charge on the street and not part of the so called "Mob."

I saw the building at 61th and Racine change for the better. The first summer I was asked to fill in for a judge on vacation, I noticed the oppressive heat and learned there was no air conditioning. It was sometimes devastating. The next summer I was there to fill in, things had changed. Air conditioning had been installed. I was comfortable and did not even think of the temperature inside or out. The building came of age in a great way, improving the administration of justice.

The building at 89th and Exchange in South Chicago was ancient but air-conditioned. The courtroom had been an all-purpose courtroom in years past for civil and criminal matters arising in the far southeast side of the city. My infrequent visits to the lockup revealed to me a dungeon-like environment with little light. While the court room had continuous large windows bringing in sunlight, the basement had none.

On one occasion when I was assigned to 61st and Racine, I did reflect a segment of the community. I saw that a complaining witness at a preliminary hearing was Dean Lieberman, a man who had attended South Shore High School a couple of years after me. He also attended the University of Wisconsin in Madison and joined my fraternity, AEPi. He was the victim of an armed robbery in his father's electrical appliance store. He had the courage to testify and point out the defendant as the man who pointed a gun in his face, demanding all the money in the cash register. I had not seen Dean for over 12 years and, unfortunately, have not ever seen him since. I don't know how much longer he or his father continued the business in the Englewood neighborhood, but I knew, if it were me, I would need nerves of steel.

Once when I was at traffic court on the bench, I was summoned to come to see the supervising judge, Richard F. LeFevour, who later became a convicted felon, who told me that Gene Nesgota wanted me immediately at 89th and Exchange, where the sitting judge failed to show due to illness. LeFevour may have been a supervising judge, but he knew Gene ran the show to be sure all courtrooms were covered.

I said I did not have my car with me. I had taken the bus downtown. He arranged for a police car to take me at high speed to the South Chicago courthouse where I was already 50 minutes late. Upon arrival, I saw people filling every seat and standing in the halls and on steps going down to the street. I was told a police car would take me home when I finished. I was grateful for the rides, but was always uncomfortable when I needed to be in a car with an officer who was a smoker. Fortunately, the problem did not occur all that often. There were almost no female officers.

Usually, Gene would call the night before he needed me when a judge reported illness. If someone's vacation was coming, he gave me much earlier notice. I learned that I needed to have a judicial robe at home for times when I received late notice. I had to figure out how to get my robes back where they belonged and to have something for note taking and a required name plate. It sometimes was awkward and it looked funny for me to be carrying a robe and other materials on the Jeffrey Express CTA 5A bus going downtown. On occasion, when I knew I had plans downtown or Maureen needed the car, I suggested that perhaps we should not answer the telephone. That was in the days before Caller ID. I figured Gene would have to go on to his next judicial officer "victim." But we always did answer the phone and told Gene of any plans. He knew when I finished a case in the Daley Center, unlike many other judges, I would call him and let him know I was available for him to send another case. Maureen thought I was a sucker while others had an extended afternoon break. I saw it as getting experience.

On one occasion when I received a call the night before to go to 89th and Exchange, I drove and left my car in the judge's reserved parking space. At the end of the day when I returned to my car, I saw a parking ticket on my windshield. I went back into the station house to the District Commander's office and asked why I was ticketed. He quickly apologized and said the officer, knowing Earl Neal, the elderly judge regularly assigned, would not have a car seat in his car, thought my car was that of a trespasser. He said he would have the city non-suit the ticket. It was fine in the end.

Being almost 15 years younger than Judge Neal's son did create problems for me. The son, Earl Neal, was a lawyer who had been a condemnation lawyer with the city when I was there. While I really did not know the father, I came to know his son as a fine bright gentleman. Earl served a term as an elected trustee for the University of Illinois. I remember he was on the dais for an event and somehow Maureen was seated next to him. He had a long conversation with her and they came away as friends. I was seated at one of the many tables on the floor. Neither Maureen nor I remember how she got on a dais with Earl Neal instead of me, but she truly enjoyed the evening.

At the time Earl Neal was law partners with Cecil Partee. Their families lived in the same two-flat around 50th and Michigan Avenue on Chicago's south side. Partee was a state representative when I was in law school writing my law review article on the need for better insurance industry regulation. He gave me a lot of background information about the problems and possible solutions. I found him to be very intelligent and he became a good friend and ally in the future. I gave credit to him for his help in one of my law review articles.

For a short time, Partee also served as head of a major city department and found it necessary to fire some unproductive employees. By chance, I ran into him a few days after the newspapers noted his action of firing several city employees in his department. I asked how he could do so knowing that each of them was a precinct captain and political worker for the Democrat Party. He said it was easy. If they were not good as city workers, they were probably not good as political workers either. He agreed with the saying that good government is good politics and good politics is good government. I clearly felt comfortable asking him the question and he was not insulted and did not feel challenged. He knew I wanted to learn from him.

He moved from the State House to the State Senate and later was elected the president of the state senate. He became the Cook County States' Attorney. He told me he was raised in the south and when it was time to go to law school, he was refused admission to every school in the state. When he complained, the state offered to pay his tuition at any school he was admitted to attend. He chose Northwestern University College of Law. He remained in Chicago after he passed the Illinois bar examination and had an illustrious career in Chicago. I remember at his funeral knowing the truth of the many laudatory comments said about the good man by so many in attendance. He was a model of community service, competence, fairness, and duty. As a Black man, he was the first to fill many of the roles he had. He also served as Democrat Party committeeman from the 20th Ward of Chicago until he became State's Attorney. Since he believed that the two positions posed a conflict of interest, he stepped down from the political position upon entering the office as prosecutor. His ethics were always above reproach. Partee saw people based on their qualities and not based upon their race or religion. I saw him as a great friend whose memory I will always cherish.

When he was States' Attorney, he could no longer practice law in a separate law firm. His former partner, Earl Neal, formed his own law firm dealing almost exclusively with land condemnation law. He hired a high school fraternity pledge brother of mine, Michael Leroy, who later became his partner, and another lawyer, Richard Friedman, who also grew up on the south side and had gone to the University of Chicago Laboratory High

School. They had both worked in the city law department with Earl while I was there. Mike was in condemnation with Earl and Rich was in appeals. The law department was a real incubator for many talented lawyers.

Mike Leroy and I had met in the second semester of our freshman year of high school when we both pledged the Schmegglers Fraternity. I attended South Shore High School and he attended Hyde Park High School. We didn't live that far from each other. I was at 75th and Essex and he was at 69th and South Shore Drive. One day, we decided to play golf together at the Jackson Park Golf Course operated by the Park District— now the site of the President Barak Obama Presidential Library. Although I had gone with my father to drive golf balls at a golf range and also went to miniature golf parks to putt, I was terrible. There is no other way to describe my lack of ability. I had awful eye-hand coordination. Mike was very patient with me, but he never ever called again to play golf. He was a good judge of events and would not be abused again by me at least! I took multiple strokes for every one of his. My good company could not overcome my lack of ability. Years later, as we were approaching the age of 80, Mike said he never enjoyed golf and never played with anyone. It had nothing to do with me. I beat myself up for no good reason. Not everything is about me!

Experience Acquired

While I was practicing law for the city in the General Counsel Division, I was asked to abate a nuisance. There was a house of prostitution posing as a massage parlor that I was expected to close. I worked in tandem with lawyers in the States Attorney's office and filed a complaint seeking an injunction in the Chancery Division. At a certain point, we anticipated that a hostile witness would invoke the 5th amendment against self-incrimination. We would use the power of the states attorney's office to ask the judge to grant the witness immunity so that he would be compelled to testify or face contempt charges. We succeeded and secured his testimony, making our case and win-

Cecil Partee at my installation as a Circuit Judge Monday December 3, 1984. As the seats in the room are filling, Partee is seated close to my family on the left. Behind the unknown man next to him is Lucia Thomas, a judge from the 4th Ward.

ning the injunction abating the nuisance. The figurehead owners and the actual mob owners were not happy. I bring up this case since it made me a man of interest in the family. My father-in-law usually had little interest in the subject matter of my cases, but when he discovered I was working on a case dealing with a house of prostitution and the mob, he came to court with one of his brothers to hear the testimony from prostitutes and clients. Most of the clients were undercover police. He had newly found respect for my work from that point forward.

I would see high school, college, and law school classmates as well as other family and friends when I practiced law and later when I was on the bench. Sometimes I felt it best to say nothing when someone from my past came in front of me as a judge on minor cases in traffic court. Once when I was assigned to hear minor traffic court cases, I saw one of my high school biology teachers, who looked very nervous. There was no officer to testify against him, so the case was dismissed for want of prosecution. I think he was too nervous to notice that his student from about 17 years ago was the judge. I said nothing to embarrass an already nervous man. More likely, he had never taken notice of me in high school or never dreamed I could achieve this position as his judge.

One day while sitting in the courtroom hearing forcible entry and detainer (eviction) cases, I saw my brother-in-law step up with his mother-in-law. My brother-in-law, Sy Pearlman, was a lawyer, of course, but he was practicing in a large accounting firm and told everyone that he did not practice law. I had to recuse myself since I could not hear any case of his no matter who he was representing. The matter was sent to the presiding judge to transfer to another available judge. I told my wife that evening that I got to see Sy with his mother-in-law, Millicent. My wife was quite surprised and disappointed that Sy had not told us he represented close friends and family. He thought we would never know, but as others would learn, I could pop up anywhere at any time.

On another day while assigned to traffic court, I saw a high school classmate, Gary Wild, step up to represent a client in an auto accident. Gary probably represented the person on his personal injury claim. I told both sides that if they agreed not to testify against each other, both cases would be dismissed, but if they choose to testify, they could both be found guilty and find their insurance rates rising, not just for being in an accident but also for being found guilty. Both sides agreed not to prosecute. That was the result in most cases where the policeman came to the scene after the collision.

Gary was a kind and decent person who I had a chance to visit again in our roles as members of the North Suburban Bar Association. I served on the Board of that bar association and was given a first-time award for service. The award was in the name of the first executive director, Lee Blustin. Gary became the president a few years later; and an award has been given in his name, since he died at a young age because of being radiated for ear, nose, and throat issues as a child.

The two main pediatric practices in Hyde Park and South Shore, those of Dr. Joseph Calvin (my doctor) and Dr. Maurice Rosenblum, were each affiliated with now shuttered Michael Reese Hospital. When there was an ear, nose, or throat problem in the late 1940's, the answer was more often than not to radiate the patient. I was one of thousands who were radiated. I got sore throats often as well as ear infections, and had been snoring. My loving sister, who I shared a bedroom with, turned me in to my parents, who took me to the doctor, who referred me for the treatment. I don't know who turned Gary in, but he was one of the many boys my age who had the treatment. Unfortunately, he was not as lucky as I. He died from the radiation with cancer of the thyroid.

In 1966, towards the end of my last year of law school, I received a "recall" notice from Michael Reese Hospital telling me that I needed to come to the hospital to receive a radioactive dye for a scan and be tested to determine if my thyroid was cancerous because of the treatment I received as a child. I asked if in 20 years the radioactive material might be found to be more toxic than the radioactive treatment done to me as a young boy. They said it was safe. I asked if that wasn't the same reassurance given to my mother when she took me for this procedure to inhibit my snoring. The hospital personnel claimed everything was fine now.

After much soul searching, I took the test. At that time, I had no sign of cancer of the thyroid; however, they suggested I see an endocrinologist for annual testing. I have been going regularly ever since, watching a nodule on my thyroid grow and shrink—usually grow! Two times I have needed needle biopsies that are not pleasant. My first biopsy was by a masked man who never identified himself and said "whoops" as he had the needle in my throat. My wife was present in the procedure room and told him to step away and not to touch me anymore since he had his chance and blew it. With a needle in my throat, I was unable to speak and was so very grateful Maureen had come into the room and protected me.

The last time that I faced a needle biopsy, I fortunately had a great doctor, Robert I. Silvers, a diagnostic radiologist at Highland Park Hospital, who had a perfect touch and told me everything he was about to do. I saw the difference between an incompetent person and a great doctor. I have been fortunate each year with my status. Gary and several other people I know who were radiated died of thyroid cancer in spite of the fact that thyroid cancer is supposed to be slow growing and easy to detect. I have always believed in science, but generally believe that longitudinal studies are necessary. Jumping ahead to the present with COVID-19, there are exceptions to long-term studies when a plague is overtaking the world's population.

Another friend from the south side was Marty Solomon, another precinct captain in the 4th Ward. He was actively involved in B'nai B'rith during his lifetime. He and his wife, Darlene, moved from Hyde Park to Northbrook, where they raised their son and daughter. He died young as well with thyroid cancer after being radiated as a boy. Both Marty and Gary gave so much to the community. I have always missed both of them.

When I received my recall notice, Simon Pearlman, a classmate in law school who became my brother-in-law, also received a recall notice. Although he grew up on the north side, his mother had taken him to Michael Reese for radiation treatment as well. His thyroid was removed, requiring him to take Synthroid to provide the thyroid hormone. He lived many years afterwards. I suppose we are the lucky ones, with me going annually for an ultrasound and doctor visit. It has been over 55 yearly rounds with co-pays and the anxiety of awaiting the test results. Medical science can be a blessing and a curse.

My mother-in-law, Eve Pearlman, and my brother-in-law, Simon R. Pearlman

4 PERSONAL LIFE

A Story of Attraction at First Sight

Sometimes things are pure coincidence, or perhaps, meant to be. When I transferred from law school in Madison to law school in Chicago, I was placed in a section where I made many friends. One friend was Simon Pearlman. I sat next to him often. During the year, he had taken and passed the Certified Public Accountant exam. His family threw a party to celebrate his accomplishment. He invited me to attend with a date. The next morning in school, I asked Sy who was the beautiful girl in the blue dress with alluring blue eyes at his party. I said I saw her across the room and would love to take her out if she was available. He said that was no girl; that was his sister.

    He said he did not know if she was dating anyone, but he would find out. The next day he said she was not dating anyone special. I asked for her number, which he gave. He said it was his parents' telephone number. I called and made a date and began my trips north on weekends, eventually marrying Maureen. If I had stayed at Madison, I would have had to find another way to meet this beautiful girl I saw across a crowded room. I did not see others in my class at the party, so Sy has always been in my heart as the reason and cause for our meeting. Even if Maureen resents her brother for bringing me into her life, I will always love him. I firmly believe that my transfer to DePaul University Law School and then becoming friends with Sy was *bashert* in that it led me to meet Maureen.

As years passed and Maureen and I went to many different places, I came to realize that I was not the only one to take notice of her beautiful blue eyes. I remember being in an elevator where an older woman told Maureen her blue eyes were so very beautiful. A waitress, a shoe salesman, a teacher at a parent-teacher conference, and the wife of a judge were among the many people, usually women, who spoke of their observations. I can only guess how many others censored their observations for fear of sounding sexist or inappropriate. I am so proud that I gave voice to the obvious before anyone else said the same. If someone else had given the compliment in my presence first, my statements would have fallen flat.

I always enjoyed the fact that Sy and I had common friends and acquaintances and instructors from law school as a frame of reference. I realized that as much as Maureen and Sy are different, they possess in common some qualities that attracted me to both. When I sometimes challenge myself about a belief in God, I conclude that only the power of God put all of the coincidences in play to create our relationship. Those with faith base it upon different pillars. The opportunity I had to meet Maureen was the pillar for me!

5 WORKING FOR WHAT YOU WANT

Get the Votes

Of course, my parents and wife knew I had to make contact with all of the voting judges, and so they told everyone they knew. To my amazement, a number of family and family friends knew several judges and communicated with them. Every call or letter was appreciated. I believe the calls and letters were effective, since many judges I solicited told me that a friend or relative had called and had already gotten them committed to vote for me. My 13th Ward friend Mike called a few of his closest friends in my support and let the mayor know he strongly supported me.

To my surprise, some of my cousins, including second and third cousins like Peter Lisagor, a childhood hero of mine, and his brothers and sister, knew judges. Peter had been the Editor-in Chief of the Stars and Stripes military newspaper during World War II. It had the largest readership and circulation of any newspaper in the history of the world, then or now. After the war, he became the Washington Bureau Chief of the Chicago Daily News. He regularly appeared on CBS's *Face the Nation* and NBC's *Meet the Press*. A journalism award was created in his name and several top journalists each year are presented the now prestigious Lisagor Awards.

Peter Lisagor, my cousin and childhood hero who had been Editor-in-Chief of the Stars and Stripes Newspaper during World War II

Peter's brother Jack contacted a recently appointed judge he knew from childhood, the former alderman of the 50th Ward, Republican Jack Sperling. I met Sperling when he was an alderman sitting on the Judiciary Committee of the Chicago

City Council. I was assigned to give legal advice on a proposed amendment to an existing ordinance regarding bar maids in licensed liquor establishments. I received criticism from Alderman Leon Despres of the 5th Ward, since I supported the administration's position backing a clearly sexist position. Sperling whispered to me to ignore Despres since he was merely playing to the press and I was merely doing my job. I reported policy; I did not make policy for the city.

I always appreciated Sperling's encouragement and support. I never knew if he knew of any connection to me before he got my cousin's request for him to vote for me. I saw that allies could appear at any time from any place. I was later to learn that enemies could as easily appear as well. I still don't see Despres as an enemy. He was merely expressing his own strong opinions on a subject and did not want my position to go unchallenged. I also learned that I must always separate attacks on me personally from attacks on my position or client. Again, every event and interaction could be an opportunity to develop my character and skills, or it could become a trap to entangle me. It was always my choice. I actually disagreed with the policy I espoused. My client was Mayor Richard J. Daley and the city that employed me. He set the policy; I merely advocated his position as a lawyer. It was not illegal, unconstitutional, or immoral for me to articulate the city's position and it certainly did not violate the code of conduct I was sworn to observe as an attorney.

Despres vs Holman

I came to understand that Despres consistently opposed most anything proposed by Richard J. Daley and his administration. Since Alderman Claude W. B. Holman consistently supported Daley, Holman was seen as Despres's antagonist, to be defined not only as wrong, but as evil, racist, an Uncle Tom, and other labels useful in his *ad hominem* arguments. I realized that Despres's methods demeaned him and diminished the power of his arguments. For one so admired by the press and independents, he was not the role model I wished to emulate. While I thought I would not allow him to be my mentor, with maturity, I understood he was great at guiding me away from foolish and tantrum-like conduct he was demonstrating.

When I came to Judge Sperling's courtroom to solicit his vote for me as an associate judge, I saw a huge crowd. I identified myself to one of the deputy sheriffs in the courtroom. The deputy went over to the judge while he was on the bench and after a few whispers, he returned and told me that he was voting for me and I could move on to see other judges. I nodded to the judge and he nodded back as I left with great appreciation to him and to my cousins.

Another cousin, Paul Zabrin, had died, but his widow, Rita, remained in touch with my mother, even after she remarried. Rita told my mother that her brother, Sidney Steinman, was the ward secretary to Eddie Barrett, the county clerk and a Democratic ward committeeman, and she would have Sid put in a good word with Barrett to get him to make a few calls. Rita also said another relative of hers was an aide to 31st Ward Alderman Thomas Keane, later to be indicted and convicted for other unrelated misdeeds. They would ask him to help me as well. My cousin Rita had a lot of pull. Alderman Keane's sister had been an investigator on a slip and fall accident I handled in federal court. Adeline Keane also put in a good word with her brother as did his nephew, Michael Keane, with whom I worked.

I was fortunate my father had used Rita's husband Paul as our insurance broker until Paul died and that my mother stayed in touch with Rita. In her later years, Rita always spoke of her grandchildren with tremendous pride, saying one was a social worker, one was an actor, and the other was a spy. Her daughter constantly reminded Rita that we are not allowed to say that he is a spy and blow his cover. He is an employee of the State Department.

Before his retirement, my cousin, the spy, told Maureen and me that the Chinese and Russians presently know his real position since he rose to a level where he was no longer covert. He also reassured us that no important secret would be given to any president like Trump who might monetize the information or release it inadvertently and harm our national security. On the one hand everything had to be disclosed to our president, but on the other hand, we are patriots. Extended family can be helpful; and in my case was truly connected.

One of the lawyers in my office, George Michael Keane, was so very kind to me. He called his father, a member of the tax board of appeals, as well as his uncle, the alderman and Democratic party committeeman of the 31st Ward, to voice his personal support and request their help. He also took me in to see several judges. Another lawyer in the office, Judy Landesman, not only called her father, a judge, but asked him to contact other 31st Ward judges as well as Alderman Thomas Keane, who had supported him. Alderman Keane must have gotten so many requests about me that he was impressed.

While Keane may have been convicted for his bad acts, it was clear to me that he did many good things as well. He was a strong supporter of Jerome Torshen, a lawyer who worked on the staff of John Paul Stevens when he investigated the Illinois Supreme Court decision dealing with Theodore J. Isaaacs. The investigation resulted in the resignations of two corrupt Illinois Supreme Court Justices, Ray Klingbiel and Roy J.Solfisburg. They were accused of corruptly accepting stock from the Civic Center Bank and Trust Company of Chicago (CCB) at the same time that litigation involving CCB was pending at the Illinois Supreme Court. In the case, *People v Isaacs*, the Supreme Court upheld the dismissal of criminal charges against Isaacs, the general counsel of CCB. The two justices obtained CCB stock shortly before ruling in favor of Isaacs. Isaacs had been Governor Otto Kerner's revenue director.

One of the many friends in the law department that I enlisted for help was a great trial lawyer who had been in the Building Violation Division before coming to the General Counsel Division. Tom Heneghan was very politically savvy. After the death of an incumbent, he served as an interim Democratic Committeeman from his north lakeside ward until a permanent candidate was selected. He took me to several judges he knew, but one in particular stands out.

Judge Kenny Wendt was a former leader in the legislature before becoming a judge, and Tom was very helpful in his campaigns. Wendt was easily persuaded to not only vote for me but to also solicit votes for me from other judges he knew. He made a couple of trades, promising to vote for other candidates they supported if those judges he spoke to would vote for me. I strongly believe he got votes for me. For some judges, he was their leader in the legislature and they were conditioned to following his lead.

I was so very pleased years later when Wendt's daughter, Mary Jane Theis, became a judge. We served on several bar association committees and section councils together and she was always logical, well-reasoned, and knowledgeable regarding the law. Her advancement to the Illinois Supreme Court was not surprising. I believe she has been doing a great job and is a reflection of her late father's attributes. On November 14, 2022, she was sworn in as the fourth female Chief Justice for a three year term.

Years later when I ran for circuit judge, Tom enlisted his friend and then law partner, State Senator and President of the State Senate and Oak Park Democratic Committeeman, Phil Rock, to help me. He discovered I had either omitted or not signed a form needed to be on the ballot in 1984. He had the document delivered to me by messenger and flown to Springfield in time to save me from myself. Phil had become the chairman of the state party and was a great friend. Tom was the best. I have gratitude for both Tom and Phil, each of blessed memory. They each contributed to others in many ways without seeking notice or fame.

Another Lesson Learned

Another lesson I learned was that no one should ever be ignored and no one should be distanced as too powerful or learned for me to converse with and trust. Every person is important to engage with! I observed a lawyer, Sydney Marovitz, the brother of Federal District Court Judge Abraham Lincoln Marovitz, who I met as an adversary over liquor license cases at the city's liquor and license commission. He served later on the Park District Board, and a park on Lake Michigan at Belmont is named in his memory. At his funeral I heard that he engaged everyone, whether in high or low station in life, perceiving everyone as his equal. His brother was similar, saying that every day one must do a good deed, a *mitzvah*, or the day would be wasted. He tried to make a new friend each day. As he grew older, he said his friends from years ago were sick and dying and if you make a new friend each day, you will be enriched with friendships until your last day. I always considered both brothers as my friends and learned much from both of them. They both acknowledged getting their values from their parents—mostly their mother. They were fine exemplary public officials coming from the Chicago Jewish community and growing up on the west side in the old 24th Ward, then led by Jacob Arvey, who served as chairman of the Cook County Democratic party in the years preceding 1948.

Judge Abraham Lincoln Marovitz was a man of truth. The year before my run for associate judge in 1974, where I prevailed, I had asked for the judge's support when there were five or six vacancies for associate judge. I knew he was influential having been the Presiding Judge of the Criminal Division of the Circuit Court of Cook County before ascending to the federal bench with an appointment by President John F. Kennedy. Before he was a judge, he served as a state senator in Illinois with Richard J Daley. They became close allies. He swore Richard J. Daley into office as mayor each time he started a new term. Judge Marovitz told me he would be pleased to support me in the future. He admired me, having had me appear before him several times in federal court, but he was "riding a different horse" this time.

When I learned he was backing my then boss in the General Counsel Division, I was very happy. Ben Novoselsky was another one of my mentors. His son Henry was in my law school class and worked in the Appeals Division of the Law Department.

Henry married Debbie, a cousin of my wife. Ben was my father's age and was a seasoned trial lawyer. When I had been assigned to try federal cases, Ben introduced me to several of the federal judges, who all seemed to like and respect him. I tried personal injury cases filed against the city based on diversity grounds, but more often defended civil rights actions involving police officers and other city officials. I also defended city ordinances under constitutional attack. Ben introduced me to all of the federal judges and set me up for success. Fortunately, he was selected and became an associate judge in 1973, allowing me to be the next Marovitz "horse" to ride.

Many of the federal judges I appeared before, appointed by both Republican and Democratic presidents, supported me and made calls to state Cook County judges they knew and allowed me to list them as references when I filed my bar association applications. After my selection was announced, I had to withdraw from each of my pending cases and have other lawyers in the office substitute for me. It was a fantastic opportunity to say thank you for helping me get votes, but especially for modeling what a judge should be. I enjoyed my appearances before most of those judges, but not all. I learned that the method of selection, appointment versus election, does not guarantee quality. One can find great judges coming to the bench by both election and appointment and some very bad judges coming both ways as well.

Judge Marovitz was always pushing for a settlement and did not want matters tried in his courtroom unnecessarily taking up his time. I had a particular case on his call where my client was a police officer sued for using excessive force. The person he apprehended resisted arrest and injured the officer in the process. I decided to take the unusual step of filing a counterclaim on the officer's behalf so he would not lose the chance of seeking recovery for his injury.

When Judge Marovitz suggested during a pre-hearing settlement conference that I give the plaintiff some money, I said the plaintiff deserved none but should pay for my client's injury. The judge said since he was friends with the mayor, he would ensure that the police officer got what he was entitled to from the city and I should not worry. I resisted that attempt, believing that both the judge and the mayor were up in years and might not be around to help my client. Of course, both the judge and the mayor were both younger than I am today.

That evening, Judge Marovitz was speaking at a Hadassah meeting attended by my mother-in-law. She went up to him and asked if he knew her son-in-law. He said he certainly did. Michael Jordan was a stubborn man, not listening to him and being unwilling to settle a case. Later that evening, my dear mother-in-law told me she met Judge Marovitz, who felt I was stubborn. I said I had an obligation to my client and could not be pushed, even by a federal judge. I did not ever expect I would get lobbied on a case by my own mother-in-law. I learned that it's sometimes hard to maintain independence. I would learn later that many judges failed the test of real independence, as revealed during Operation Greylord.

Two judges that I held in the highest esteem were Philip Tone and William Bauer. Both were Republicans who were fair to me and my clients. They both served on the trial court and later on the 7th Circuit Court of Appeals. Besides being role models on the bench, I saw each of them at bar association functions and realized that a judge does not have to hide under a rock. I always thought of Judge Bauer as a great teacher. After learning that I grew up on the south side of Chicago, he told me that he also grew up on the south side before he began his legal career in DuPage County, where he was the prosecutor and judge. He then moved into the U.S. Attorney's office for the Northern District of Illinois, becoming the U. S. Attorney before becoming a federal district judge and finally becoming an appeals court judge. He was the chief judge of the 7th circuit before taking senior status. His was a long and splendid tenure.

Judge Tone always showed his calm and even demeanor and was never ruffled. He was scholarly and easy to understand. I was at ease with him since his kindness always showed through.

I was happy to see him at receptions and meetings of the Northwest Suburban Bar Association. He was proud of his son Michael, who became a well-respected trial lawyer. I was greatly saddened when I learned of his passing.

Protections Provided

Another federal judge I appeared before was Joseph Sam Perry, who had a lengthy tenure starting with his appointment by FDR. Judge Bauer took his seat when Perry took senior status. I knew Perry as a kind man. I had some well publicized cases before him. He always kept the temperature down with his humor. One such case assigned to me was to represent Chicago police officers. They were city defendants who had been assigned to the states attorney's office and participated in the raid that resulted in the deaths of several Black Panther Party members.

The motion practice in that case consumed hours upon hours of my time. I needed extensive secretarial help. Other lawyers in the office were being shortchanged by my needs and deadlines. The Corporation Counsel then was the former first assistant under Ray Simon, Richard L. Curry. He was a great boss who was very supportive of my needs. He asked me how long I estimated I would need a secretary for the work and I gave my best estimate of about four to five months. He decided to get a temp from an outside agency and she was great. The other secretaries were so very happy to find out the pressure was off them and they all treated her well.

I think Judge Perry respected my timely and well-prepared briefs. He did not always rule with me, but he followed and accepted my major arguments most of the time.

At a certain point after the explosion of motions was behind us, he summoned me to his chambers and told me of an opening in the court system for a quasi-judicial officer. He asked if I might be interested. He had already checked it out with Mayor Daley, which was a great surprise to me. I told him I was interested if he thought I could handle the job. He said not to count on getting the position since a majority of the executive committee of the court were Republicans and when it came to appointments, many considered this to be political patronage and would only support a fellow Republican. He wanted to have a candidate in the race. I suppose I was his horse. Nothing came of it, but I learned a little of the inner workings of the Court and of his affection for me. I realized, too, that Judge Perry's judicial clerk was not in the position for just a year or two, but was a career clerk he had trained and could rely upon.

Judge Perry told me that due to a hearing disability he acquired, he wore hearing aids. I knew this since they were visible to me and at times would buzz. He said when a particular long-winded lawyer would ramble on, he would turn the device off so he could better concentrate on orders he was preparing for other cases. He turned the hearing devices on again when he saw the lawyer getting ready to sit. He was a character.

When I became a judge, I realized it was better to stay in my chambers after the court session to do the paper work than get a reputation for not paying attention. I had already heard that Judge Perry would turn off his hearing aid on occasion. I was thinking then that there must be other ways to deal with the verbose lawyer. I later set time limits or interrupted to let the lawyer know that I understood his point the first time he made it, but certainly the second or third time. I gave a few moments to allow the other side to say they were objecting since the lawyer was repetitive. Then, all I had to do was say, "Sustained, move on!" There were always lessons to learn. Judge Perry was a kind and gentle teacher who showed his willingness to be my mentor and supporter in my career.

When the pre-trial pleading motions were completed and before it was time to set the matter for a trial, I went into the Corporation Counsel, Richard L. Curry. He had always been supportive, not just with the extra secretary when I needed one, but in other matters. I had a case defending the mayor, where I needed to interview his press secretary, but each time I tried, I was rebuffed. I went into Mr. Curry's office and explained that Mr. Earl Bush would not speak to me.

Curry called him on the phone and told him Mike Jordan is my guy and he is representing us. If my office is going to help the mayor in this matter, you must answer his questions. Mike will not hurt you or the mayor. He is your lawyer. Bush gave me the information that helped me dispose of the case with no harm to anyone. Dick Curry trusted me and I trusted him. He gave me pay raises as my responsibilities increased. He assigned me clerks and younger lawyers to train or mentor and they assisted me. I enjoyed his trust and the opportunities he gave me.

I was at the crossroads in the Black Panther case, Calvin vs Conlisk. Calvin was the lead plaintiff and Conlisk was the Superintendent of the Chicago Police Department. Several of the police employees had been represented by outside counsel and had developed a good attorney-client relationship in companion criminal matters against the city and county officials involved in the December 4, 1969 raid on the west side of Chicago who were being charged with obstruction of justice. I had no such personal relationship with the police defendants since our case had been at the pleading stage for such a long time and the discovery in the other case was being utilized. I acknowledged that I thought it was a waste of city resources for me to get up to speed on the factual issues where the outside counsel, Carmine Volini, was well informed and capable, probably possessing more trial experience than I had.

I must have made convincing arguments adding that for myself personally, I was then the President of the predominantly Black 4th Ward Regular Democratic Organization and did not want to embarrass Alderman Claude Holman, since this case had stark racist tones. If someone else in our office took over the case, there would be a lot of learning to do. Normally I have one file for each case. This case already had six or seven thick files. There was a lot of material. There were many intricate legal issues I had developed, but none on fact issues. I believed the master of the facts was Volini.

Curry agreed. Volini was hired. I hoped that someday I might meet Volini but he died March 1, 2001 before we ever met.

When word got out that Curry was having the outside counsel take over this case, the newspapers excoriated Curry. A well-read popular newspaper columnist, Mike Royko, wrote a series of articles on the case pointing out that Curry was a cousin of the mayor and, therefore, had no intelligence—which was the farthest thing from the truth. Royko claimed this was an effort to enrich Volini, who must be a good friend of Curry's. Curry took all the heat and never once disclosed to anyone that I made the request for his actions. He never brought it up to me in any way. Volini had worked for the city law department in the early 60's so it is possible Curry knew him, but I was the activating force triggering the use of outside counsel.

Richard Curry went on to become a judge on the Cook County Circuit Court and served well in that position. I admired him and respected his courage. When he died. I attended his funeral. I felt it was my obligation. I was the only one from the office at his funeral except for Dan Lynch from the southwest side, who was originally a clerk and then lawyer who later took on a high position in the Cook County Assessor's office before he become a judge. I believe Dan Lynch had been hired by Dick Curry and never forgot that act. When Ray Simon had attended the funeral of Allen Hartman he told me there that he always relied on three men while he was the corporation counsel: Richard Curry, Allen Hartman, and Marv Aspen. I knew he respected Richard Curry so he may have had other obligations that kept him away. I felt fortunate that I was able to attend and pay my heart felt respects to a man of valor.

At Dick Curry's funeral I reflected on another one of his acts. There was a large baking company, National Baking Company, that owned a building housing its factory, where it was suspected that the fire prevention system of ceiling water sprinklers, required by city ordinance and state law, was not operational. Curry told me he believed the judge in building court was not giving the matter the attention it deserved. He wanted me to meet with the chief fire prevention inspector and visit the site and then organize a case. I saw the obvious. Water sprinkler pieces were pushed into the ceiling tiles to give the impression of having a fire suppression system present and operating to reassure the employees, but, in fact, none were connected to any piping or water source. It was a death trap!

I was to appear in court and substitute in as a Special Assistant Corporation Counsel rather than being assigned from another division of the office. I had to demonstrate that the sprinkler heads were not connected to any piping but merely stuck into the ceiling tiles. Had there been a fire, there was nothing to suppress the fire and many employees' lives would be endangered. I was charged with protecting hundreds of lives at National Baking Company. In court, I was polite but forceful and appeared more powerful than I was. We got the job done. Curry was happy with me and I did a great deed, a *mitzvah*! I remembered the Jewish teaching that if you save even one life, it is like saving the universe. Dick Curry put me into responsible positions exposed to many people who would help me get my goals fulfilled. May his memory be a blessing.

There was a federal judge that I will not name who had been a Circuit Court Judge in Cook County and who usually ruled with the side that was last to speak. After he ruled on a motion, the losing party would ask him to reconsider and would offer another argument kept in reserve or would repeat the same argument. Often, he would then reverse his decision. There was never an end to the litigation since he was not ever definite. I learned that a good judge must invite all the argument possible, but once a ruling is made, the judge must preclude further argument. On the other hand, I would never be so rigid, that I would not objectively consider a written motion to reconsider based on new facts or law or a mistake on my part. Flexibility and humility were essential ingredients of a good judge, but not being a willow branch waving in the wind.

There was another federal judge who had some idiosyncrasies. He tended to drink to excess after his wife died. I was advised to avoid any pre-trial conference with him in the late afternoon or I would be asked with my opposing counsel to join him in his chambers for a few drinks. I always provided good reasons why the late afternoon times would not work for me. He was fair to me and my clients until another event took place—his son was arrested by Chicago police following a drug raid.

After his son's arrest, my arguments were discarded and rejected although previously the same arguments were accepted and followed. I told my supervisor and we went into the Corporation Counsel to decide what to do. We agreed that although the judge had previously been neutral or even favorable to our positions, he was no longer fair and impartial to the city and its clients.

I was authorized to take a rare action of seeking to have him recuse himself from all pending and future city cases. He rejected our request and things got even worse. We made a record in each case as motions arose. It was a difficult period for me and the office. He eventually eased up and I will never know if he saw how biased he had been or if someone he listened to had a quiet and sober conversation with him. I know my supervisor tried, but failed. I can only guess that the mayor may have called him to express his good wishes for some holiday, but I will never know.

Another federal judge I appeared before, who was unpopular in the public eye, taught me many things. Julius Hoffman was seen by most as an old grouch, which he was, but he was more. Although he wanted perfection as he perceived it, he really wanted attention to detail. After a lawyer from legal aid and I hammered out a fair and just consent decree on a challenged municipal ordinance and its application to a taxi cab driver, Judge Hoffman sent us back a couple of times until we crossed the t's and dotted the i's as he wanted. I represented the city vehicle license commissioner, James Carter, and my adversary represented the cab driver affected by the ordinance. Eventually the judge signed on to our decree and it became binding on the city. I saw that Judge Hoffman did not want his name on a document that was not letter perfect.

On the other hand, before commencing a jury trial before him where I represented two policemen, he strongly recommended that I settle the matter. That case was the only jury case I ever lost. Afterwards, he told me that he could tell that the Jewish and Arab policemen had nothing in common except corrupt motives. He and the jury saw what I could not see. I realized that he had a sense of people most others reviewing his career would ignore. I learned that a judge sometimes is best when he steps away to see the whole picture. Julius Hoffman's quirks went too far in the criminal trial of the men who tried to disrupt the city during the 1968 Democratic Convention in Chicago. The 7th Circuit Court of Appeals criticized his methods and actions, reversing his orders. The newspaper editorialists and cartoonists referred to him in many different demeaning ways. I could still see his good attributes as well as those not so good that were the headline makers.

During the 1968 Democratic Convention in Chicago there was a Host Committee and its staff from Illinois and the National Democratic Committee and its staff. Tickets for admission were strictly guarded and two people were in the room with the tickets at all times so that they could distribute those tickets fairly to each state delegation. Before the distribution of the tickets, the two men guarding the tickets began to visit with each other, learning they were both from Chicago. After they told what wards they were each from, they realized one represented a Chicago Congressman who was chair of the Illinois Host Committee and the other represented another Chicago Congressman representing the National Committee. They each called their principal bosses and were told to bring the tickets to a particular place where they were equitably divided to everyone's satisfaction. There was no reason for the great tension to continue with the discovery and distribution of the tickets. One of the two congressmen later told me the story.

6 STEPPING UP FOR GREATNESS

My Opportunity to Change History

There was a lawyer in the General Counsel Division, Charles O'Connor, who, among his other assignments, represented the Chicago Commission of Human Relations. One day he came to me and said there was a new case filed at the Commission that might be up my alley. He could prosecute the case and move it forward, but for me it might be more significant and meaningful.

I asked what he meant and what the case was about. He told me that a wealthy Jewish man, William Samuel Sax, President of the Exchange National Bank on LaSalle Street in Chicago, claimed that he and his wife were being denied the opportunity to buy an apartment in the co-operative building at 209 East Lake Shore Drive, since there was a quota restricting Jews.

I said I wasn't even sure where that building was located. He said the building was a few doors east of the Drake Hotel. He gave me the facts, as alleged, and they seemed interesting. I knew he was no bigot refusing to prosecute other bigots and said I thought the case would interest him as well. He said it did, but it would be better for me down the road. If I took this case, I would have to take on the entire assignment of representing the Human Relations Commission.

After a discussion of what that might entail and my agreement, we went into our boss, the General Counsel, Allen Hartman, and he agreed. Allen told me later that this might be a very important matter, to give it great attention, and come to him with any issues or problems. I would have to establish that the building had imposed a ten percent quota for Jews and that a Jewish resident, Joseph Regenstein, was responsible to serve as the gate keeper, selecting those Jewish families meritorious enough to gain entry and deciding which of the other families should be rejected.

I learned that Peter Fitzpatrick, the hearing officer at the liquor and license commission I appeared before, was the chairman of the Commission and would be quite helpful. The more I learned, the more motivated I became. I looked around the office and saw other capable Jewish lawyers and wondered why Charlie picked me. I was always grateful to him, since that assignment let me meet many helpful and influential people who carried me on my way. The case was reported widely, as far as New York; the news of the case was carried in the *New York Times,* prompting relatives and friends there to take notice and contact my parents.

I came to understand that the members of the board of the building co-op were powerful makers and shakers in the Chicagoland community. One lawyer on the board, James A. Dooley, became an Illinois Supreme Court Justice. Another lawyer, Charles A. Bane, was nominated by President Richard Nixon to the Seventh Circuit Court of Appeals, based in Chicago, to fill the vacancy of Justice Elmer Jacob Schneckenberg, who had died. Bane claimed he withdrew his nomination to spend more time with his family and to support his law firm, but President Richard M. Nixon withdrew his support of Bane at the request of Illinois senior U. S. Senator Charles Percy, based on a few reasons, including Bane's involvement in the 209 East Lake Shore Drive co-op board's antisemitism, when allegations involving this discrimination became known. The Schneckenberg vacancy ultimately went to John Paul Stevens, then positioned to be tapped by Nixon's successor, President Gerald Ford, to be the next justice on the Supreme Court.

I elected to depose each member of the board to put them on record as to their individual reasons to vote against Sax's admission to the building. Sax and his personal lawyers had asked me to rule out any reason connected to his running of the bank, since that would invite a full audit by the federal regulators. Sax was personally represented by senior counsel Edgar Bernhard and his associate, Nathaniel Sack. They would assist me in the prosecution of the Board, but since I was counsel to the Commission, I was the lawyer of record at any of the proceedings. I welcomed their background, legal knowledge and support. By coincidence, Nathaniel Sack, a Southsider, was known to me as Nick. Although he went to the Harvard School for Boys high school, he too had joined Schmegglers Fraternity. I knew that taking the depositions would delay matters and risk exceeding the 30-day limit imposed on us by the ordinance. Yet, I also knew that the request of the complainant was important. It was determined to be more important to expose the board's scheme to impose the antisemitic ten percent quota system than to be able to impose any monetary penalty.

The depositions from each member of the board achieved the admissions that their actions had nothing to do with the operation of the bank. Further, they all admitted that there was a scheme to maintain a ten percent quota restricting Jews in the building, with Joseph Regenstein being the gatekeeper. My proof at any hearing would be easy with these admissions.

Many years later, I wrote a review of a book by my high school classmate, Ken Manaster, regarding U.S. Supreme Court Justice John Paul Stevens. My review was published in the *Chicago Lawyer Magazine*. Justice Stevens's service on the Court was possible with the withdrawal of the Charles A. Bane nomination because of Bane's complicity in the scheme to discriminate. Here is my review of the facts and circumstances encapsulated in that book review.

"The secret of success in life is for a man to be ready for his opportunity when it comes"—Benjamin Disraeli

With his retirement notice submitted to the president, the illustrious career of John Paul Stevens, an outstanding justice of the United States Supreme Court, comes to an end at the close of the term ending in the summer of 2010. Scholars of the law as well as others will write many articles and books regarding the man and his impact on American jurisprudence for years to come.

The intention of this article is to share some personal insights as a result of finding myself near the sidelines of history when I was a young lawyer. I was drawn close to a set of events that may have been a catalyst for a fine Chicago lawyer, John Paul Stevens, to have the opportunity to ultimately rise to the U. S. Supreme Court.

In 1968 I was working as an assistant corporation counsel in the General Counsel Division of the Law Department of the City of Chicago representing the Chicago Commission on Human Relations. That agency was in place to fight discrimination. The president of the Exchange National Bank, a Jew, believed he was denied permission to purchase a cooperative apartment at 209 East Lake Shore Drive on the gold coast of Chicago based solely upon his religion. The Chicago Commission on Human Relations received his charge and after an investigation by the Commission staff that reported to the 15 commissioners appointed by the mayor, it was determined by them that there was merit in the charge. The commissioners, as I recall, were unanimous in voting to authorize a complaint be lodged against the 209 E Lake Shore Drive co-op board by the Commission.

It was my responsibility to prosecute this and other complaints pending before the Chicago Commission on Human Relations. Unlike the many other pending cases, this complainant had private counsel. His able counsel came from the well-regarded law firm of D'Ancona & Pflaum and included a senior partner, the late Edgar Bernhard, and a junior associate, Nathaniel Sack. It was my responsibility as counsel for the Commission to direct and pursue the matter. I was grateful for the opportunity to consult with these fine lawyers and benefited from their wisdom. I ultimately developed a relationship of trust with them and the complainant.

The complainant made it clear to me that for him to continue with the matter he wanted me to pursue sufficient discovery to determine that no co-op board member voted to exclude him from the building due to any reason other than his religion.

I agreed to a plan whereby I would depose all members of the co-op board to learn the reason for their votes dealing with his application for residence in their co-op building. These were all prominent members of the community. One later became a justice of the Illinois Supreme Court. One was a major benefactor of a great university in our city and contributor to a hospital and museum. His name is found on wings of buildings around the city. The other board members were similarly situated.

As the discovery proceeded, I was convinced that the evidence showed that the one Jewish member on the co-op board was assigned and willingly accepted the task of insuring that a ten percent religious quota was not exceeded for Jews in the building. It was our opinion that the entire board condoned this practice of exclusion based on religious discrimination including the Jewish board member.

The complainant was a strong supporter of the senior senator from Illinois, Charles Percy. Percy had recommended that President Nixon appoint a lawyer living in the building to fill an opening on the Seventh Circuit Court of Appeals. The complainant prevailed on Senator Percy to withdraw his support for this nomination due to that lawyer's participation in or acquiescence in the discrimination at his residence. The lawyer unsurprisingly asked the

President to withdrew his nomination in October 1969 just before his confirmation—claiming he had a need to spend more time with his family.

The vacancy on the 7th Circuit Court was again open as the scandal of 1969 involving the Illinois Supreme Court concluded. Allegations had been made that a criminal case involving a motion to quash all charges reviewed by the Illinois Supreme Court may have been fixed! An investigating commission was established that appointed Chicago anti-trust lawyer John Paul Stevens as its legal counsel. Stevens made his mark as a fair and skilled lawyer for that commission created to determine if any members of the Illinois high court did anything improper reviewing and upholding the quashing of the criminal charges placed against Theodore Isaacs, Governor Otto Kerner's Director of Revenue, charged with receiving kickbacks.

We know that shortly after his noteworthy efforts on behalf of the investigating commission were completed in July 1969 and two Illinois Supreme Court Justices resigned in August of that year, John Paul Stevens was appointed by President Nixon to the still open Seventh Circuit position. Judge Stevens served admirably on that Court for several years and earned the attention of President Gerald Ford who took the high ground placing this man of character and integrity on the high court when a vacancy occurred rather than merely attempting to satisfy political expedience.

Justice Stevens' proven record on the intermediate court was his opportunity to demonstrate his worth. Had the resident of 209 East Lake Shore Drive retained Senator Percy's support, President Nixon would likely have placed that man in the position on the Seventh Circuit Court rather than John Paul Stevens. Historians might well ask if Stevens would have been selected for the high court without his service on the Chicago based court where he received accolades from all.

Justice John Paul Stevens was ready for the opportunity when it presented itself and Steven's sterling record gives value to the memories of Percy and Ford.

I have purposely avoided the names of some of the persons referred to above but historians may easily fill in the blanks. Among those I will mention were some of the able young lawyers Stevens enlisted in his investigation of the integrity of the Illinois Supreme Court decision regarding Isaacs. As a matter of coincidence, Nathaniel Sack, who worked on the 209 East Lake Shore Drive case, was one who also served as an assistant to Stevens in the investigation of the Illinois Supreme Court and the integrity of the Isaacs' decision. Stevens assembled a fantastic team of young and promising lawyers. This team also included Kenneth A Manaster, who became an expert in environmental law and a law professor at a prominent law School in California. Stevens also appointed the late Jerome Torshen, a brilliant trial lawyer to his team.

Professor Manaster wrote a beautiful book on Stevens published by the University of Chicago press in 2001: *Illinois Justice—The Scandal of 1969 and the Rise of John Paul Stevens*. Justice Stevens graciously provided a foreword to that book. I had the pleasure of reviewing that book for the *Chicago Lawyer* magazine giving the book a rave review.

Years later, my classmate Ken Manaster gave me a call asking for some help. He said that the Public Broadcasting Service was doing a documentary on the rise of Stevens, starting with his investigation into the conduct of the Illinois Supreme Court. The producers wanted to tape Stevens in the ceremonial courtroom in the Daley Center that he had used for his investigative hearings. Ken asked if I could help facilitate the process. I agreed, knowing there would be several obstacles. We needed permission from the Chief Judge of Cook County Circuit Court, Timothy C. Evans, to use the courtroom. I knew the courtroom had a heavy docket and was a busy space. The request for a taping time was not early morning before a court call or lunch time or late afternoon or evening but was at 1:00 PM to 3:00 PM at a busy time during the afternoon motion call. Another courtroom had to be used for the afternoon with adequate notice to appropriate persons including the Presiding Judge of the First Municipal District, the judge assigned to the room, and the clerks, sheriffs, and attorneys. I also had to secure Supreme Court permission for cameras in the courtroom that was not common in Illinois at the time.

I called and spoke to Judge Evans and framed this as a request I was making on behalf of Supreme Court Justice John Paul Stevens. He quickly consented, understanding that this was something the justice wanted. He agreed to make all necessary arrangements with the court personnel. I then called Justice Lloyd Karmeier, then a justice on the Illinois Supreme Court. Lloyd was always accommodating to me and was on this occasion as well when I asked for permission for television cameras in the courtroom to reenact the hearings prosecuted by Stevens in the late 1960's. He secured the unanimous consent of the entire Court. I notified Ken and the filming went ahead. I appeared at the taping session and visited with the Justice and his daughter. I found when the program aired in Chicago that the producers listed me in the credits. If I did not know I was in the credits, I would not have known since they flew by on the screen at warp speed.

I had seen Justice Stevens before, when he was honored by the Chicago Bar Association and given an award for his lifetime of service. Yearly, the same award is given to other worthy candidates in his name. My good friend, Justice Michael B. Hyman, knowing my 209 East Lake Shore Drive Co-op story, which affected Stevens's nomination to the 7th Circuit, asked me to write an article to be placed in the honorary brochure being distributed at the presentation. I wrote the article and it was in the program. I attended with my son, Jeff. Jeff had two heroes in public life: Senator Russel Feingold of Wisconsin and Justice John Paul Stevens, based on the high ethical conduct these men displayed in their public lives. Jeff and I were able to take a picture with

Justice Stevens. When I later went to the Public Broadcasting Service's taping, I took along the picture of Justice Stevens with Jeff and me and asked for his signature. The signed picture is prominently placed in my son's living room. When Justice Stevens died, it was a tragedy not just for his friends and family, but for the nation, since he brought truth free of politics to the high court.

Justice Stevens learned in his earlier investigation involving the Isaacs Illinois Supreme Court decision that, many times, justices would go along and not register a dissent to give a united front and at times a justice would join the majority rather than concur with another opinion, showing their reasoning was different from that of the majority. In the *Issacs* case, Justice Walter Schaefer, an honest man, did not dissent or even write a concurring opinion. Justice Stevens felt this was a disservice when clear precedent was necessary to truly understand the earlier cases. It was necessary to know that the reasoning was not uniform and that other views prevailed. Stevens rarely failed to voice his views in dissenting or concurring opinions, clearly voicing his positions in detail. He did so on the 7th Circuit and on the Supreme Court, based on his close examination of the Illinois Supreme Court and the practice in the *Issacs* case.

When I was the lawyer assigned to represent the Human Relations Commission, I had the opportunity to recommend lawyers to serve as hearing officers, usually for fair housing cases, but for other matters as well. My good friend Glenn Johnson had introduced me to his law partners before he became a judge. Some of these men were also former presidents or officers of the Cook County Bar Association. I believed that Blacks should have the opportunity to serve when they were qualified. I recommended several, and all of them served beautifully before they became judges.

I gave them a chance to see if the neutral judicial role was a fit for them. It enhanced their resumes and gave them ammunition when they appeared before the other bar associations rating judicial candidates. They all served on the bench with distinction, so I am proud of the role I played in their careers. It was a wonder that I could help those much older than me. I was supported in this effort by Jim Burns, Peter Fitzpatrick, and Claude Holman. Helping someone get even a part time job was very fulfilling for me. When I received help to get on the bench, I knew it was a benefit not only to get help but to give help. Thereafter, I tried to help as many worthy people as possible, especially after I became an elected Circuit Judge. Every person, no matter their station in life, can be like a step in a ladder to help others rise higher.

Honorable Michael S. Jordan Retired Judge of the Circuit Court of Cook County, Illinois and Honorable John Paul Stevens, Retired Judge of the 7th Circuit Court of Appeals and Retired Justice of the United States Supreme Court

7 RECOGNIZING THE SUPREME POWER

Gratitude

In my 1974 competition to become an associate judge, I will never know what number of votes I got from the voting judges and what actually motivated them in voting for me. I don't know if it was a call from a friend or an examination of my resume or my interview. I believe that everything done was necessary. I learned that you have to work for something if it's important. Nothing is accomplished alone. It takes a community to make success. Luck comes to those who work hard. Tests are easy for those who study. There are a lot of cliches to express my thoughts.

I remember Maureen asking me how I would express my gratitude to the almighty for my upcoming position. I called the rabbi who had married us and who officiated at the services on the occasion of my becoming a Bar Mitzvah at B'nai B'zael Congregation at 76th and Phillips in South Shore. Rabbi Ephraim Prombaum gave me a prayer that has been used by Jewish judges, which, translated into English, is as follows:

May it be thy will, O Lord my G-d, that no offense my occur thru me and that I may not err in a matter of law and that my colleagues may rejoice in me. And that I may not call the improper proper and the proper improper. And my colleagues may not err in a matter of law and that I may rejoice in them.

I was thinking of what else had brought me to this place, figuratively and actually. I had joined a fraternity in college, Alpha Epsilon Pi, that in my mind shrunk the campus of over 17,000 students to a more manageable size. I felt I was in a cocoon protected in so many ways. At its peak, the fraternity had about 110 members with 38 living in the house at any one time.

We had a speakers program, and in my junior year, I was in charge. I invited professors to dinner at the house on a Wednesday evening when we had our best meal, and the professor would speak after dinner. I recall inviting Dr. Phillip Mosse, a history professor I had for a class. The university later named a program in Jewish studies in his name. Another professor I invited was Dean Rudacelli, a dean in the College of Letters and Sciences, the largest division of the University. I took his class in psychology statistics. He was interesting to hear and was well received at the fraternity house.

At my graduation from college, as I crossed the stage at Camp Randell Stadium in Madison with thousands of graduates, I saw that Dean Rudacelli was one of three or four officiants awarding the diplomas. As I approached, he took my diploma and handed it to me with a big smile and a warm handshake. The four-year college experience was reduced to a one-on-one personal relationship. I felt special. Thereafter, I always felt there must be a way to find my place and feel comfortable everywhere. I recall too that for a year, I was song leader in my fraternity. I would not be in the crowd, but I would be in front as we serenaded the sweethearts who were pinned or engaged. I learned that I could be up front and show myself and lead.

Still earlier, while I was in high school, I joined an AZA, a Jewish boys' organization sponsored by B'nai B'rith. The unit I joined was called Barney Ross AZA. It was named for a prize fighter, a boxer. Later, in the corporation counsel's office, I shared a cubicle with Richard Kaplan, the nephew of Barney Ross. We both prosecuted liquor and other licensed businesses believed not to be in compliance with the law. I also joined one of the many southside predominately Jewish fraternities, Schmegglers.

Schmegglers participated in football and baseball competition, joined with sororities for parties, and sponsored either a fall opener or spring closer dance, raising funds for a selected charity. We had weekly meetings on Sunday afternoons following either the baseball or football games. Football was played at the midway in Jackson Park near the University of Chicago. The baseball games took place at various elementary school play yards. The many fraternities were centered around activities designed to give each member a fuller experience by being involved in charitable endeavors, participating in sports, having social events, and getting members to meet new people and older members who could give guidance. I saw that, similarly to AZA, the fraternities helped boys develop into young men.

Every year one fraternity, Eta Lamb, gave a dance called the Sing, in which other fraternities entered into a singing and marching competition. For Schmegglers, one or two members composed the songs around a theme, and then the members got together once or twice a week to learn the songs and practice the entry and exit. We were fortunate that the family of one member, Howie Pizer, allowed us to use their apartment in Hyde Park regularly for practice. His father was a lawyer in practice with a couple of other lawyers, including Sid Marovitz.

At the end of the weeks of practice, as the Sing approached, we used a ballroom at the top of an apartment building in Hyde Park, the Powhatan, on 50th Street near Lake Michigan, lived in by another member, Jim Spear. Jim's father was head of circulation for the *Chicago Sun Times*. Jim passed away as I was writing this part of my story.

Our regular weekly meetings took place at the homes or apartments of the members on a rotating basis. Some apartments were small, but a few were huge—perhaps palatial. I was impressed by the apartment of brothers Dale and Ralph Pinkert in Jackson Park Apartments. It was the first opportunity I had to see a two-story apartment within a high-rise building. The apartment of Joel Rubin at 5000 S. Cornell was the penthouse the size four smaller apartments on other floors below. About the time I graduated from college, my parents moved into that building on the lowest floor. Another house in Hyde Park, on the block where I used to live, was the home of another member, Tom Horwitz. He had a ballroom. We used it for a party that I remember well, since we had a hypnotist and I was one of the five subjects. I do not think I was under his spell, but I tried to cooperate.

Joel Rubin's family owned the Morrison Hotel and was quite generous to many charitable groups, but especially Jewish charities, reducing or eliminating charges to use the ballroom for their events. The Morrison Hotel building was torn down to create space to build the Civic Center for court and government office expansion in the early 1960s. The Civic Center was built and completed in 1965.

Most of our other parties were in the beautiful basement recreation room of the Meitus home at 67th and South Shore Drive. Richie Meitus's family graciously welcomed us for many parties. The Meitus family owned the Superior Match Company, a successful company until the 1980s, with the prevalence of cigarette smoking. Richie was in my pledge class. He went to the University of Chicago Laboratory School for high school with pledge brothers Steve Bishop, Art Ginsburg, and Dave Kraines, while I was at South Shore. Mike LeRoy was at Hyde Park. Emmett Greenfield was at Bowen and Donald Hork was at Hirsch High School.

Steve Bishop later went to the University of Wisconsin at Madison and pledged AEPi when I did, but decided he did not like it and dropped out. Howie Pizer and I both went to Madison and initially agreed to room together, but Howie knew I was into pre-med then and he was going into business. He decided we should each find someone going into our own fields. I accepted his judgment, but I selected Al Lipton, who was going into business as well. I never regretted my choice. Al ultimately became the managing partner of a boutique law firm and did well. His father, Harold, was also a lawyer with his own firm.

Howie Pizer became very successful, joining Jerry Reinsdorf, who was a ZBT as an undergraduate at Northwestern. They both went to law school at Northwestern, where they met. Howie joined Reinsdorf, who was taking over the Chicago White Sox in 1981 and the Chicago Bulls in 1984, and their home arenas. Howie became Reinsdorf's vice president. When Maureen turned 40 years of age and I wanted to take her to see a Bulls game, I called Howie and told him I wanted to celebrate Maureen's birthday. He told me he would arrange for two great seats and that it was his pleasure to do so. At a break in the play, we saw a message flash on the screen, "Happy Birthday, Maureen Jordan!" There was an uproar from the crowd, who believed it was the star player Michael Jordan's family. Howie made Maureen feel quite special.

Not everything in life costs money. Friendship goes a long way. Howie had married his high school sweet heart Sheila, and we were together in Madison again for our 50th reunion. I sat at the AEPi table and adjoining us was the ZBT table with Howie and Shelia. When we were called to the front to receive our half century pennants, Shelia told me to smile as I received mine since she was taking a picture of me. Shortly after, Shelia and Howie sent me the picture. Howie and I had attended other important events together as well, such as getting our certificates on admission to the bar of the U.S. District Court for the Northern District of Illinois and later for the 7th Circuit Court of Appeals. Our respective histories were not identical, but there were several intersections.

Mentors and Guides

My family of origin: My father Benjamin, me, Michael Stephen Jordan, my sister Gayle, and my mother, Sally

My loving sister Gayle is cuddling our cousin David Epstein and me

I had no idea when joining any group that many of the members would become so successful in life and would be so generous to me when help was needed. I reflected upon the people in my life who gave me attention, helped guide me, and mentored me before I even knew the meaning of the word "mentor." In addition to those in the groups, some were my closest relatives, such as my father and my sister.

My sister Gayle was almost seven years older than I was. Growing up, I saw many pictures of her holding me as an infant or playing with me. I know my father had to be the one taking the pictures. As I grew older, it was my sister who encouraged me to play with others. She suggested places to go and people to see. Getting older yet, she asked a high school friend to ask his younger brother, who was then president of Schmegglers, to invite me to join. I went to the invitational dinner at Ho Cows Chinese Restaurant on South Water Street at the beginning of my second semester of high school.

I was invited to join and I have friends from that group even today. In 1958, after my sister became a young bride, she moved to Little Rock, Arkansas. She invited me to visit in the spring of 1959, before I graduated from high school. I spent a fun week with her and my brother-in-law, Jerome J. Landy. I enjoyed water skiing while she and my brother-in-law were in a power boat. She fixed me up with dates and also hooked me up with boys to hang out with during the day. She found the time, although she was in her last months of pregnancy with my oldest nephew.

I visited them again during the summer and was present when she went into labor. I went on rounds with my brother-in-law, who was the chief surgical resident at the University of Arkansas. I even scrubbed in for a radical neck dissection, but I grew bored after a few hours and wandered into another operating theatre where a hysterectomy was in progress. I decided that summer that even if I might be interested in medicine, I was not going to be a surgeon. I was not yet considering law, even though my father and others I knew were all practicing. Jerry's brother was a practicing lawyer in Miami who appeared to be enjoying the practice.

What eventually took me away from my thoughts of becoming a doctor and turned me toward becoming a lawyer was a realization that evolved over several years. While in Little Rock, besides shadowing my brother-in-law, I took a course in Speech at Little Rock University. I did well in the speech class and saw that when given a factual scenario to discuss and an opportunity to study the subject matter, I could speak coherently with little effort. My practice in speech making later helped me prepare my court presentations. I realized one must always be aware of his audience, have a purpose, know the time limits, speak clearly and with sufficient volume, pace oneself to connect with the listeners, and have my ideas organized. I also audited a course in Literature at Little Rock University. Since I was an entering freshman and the class was a second-year course, I could not take the course for credit.

During that summer of 1959, the Arkansas Governor, Orval Faubus, was taking strong measures to maintain segregation in the public schools. Blacks wanted to integrate the schools, including Central High School in Little Rock. There were daily peaceful demonstrations. I remember one day seeing the demonstrations and stopping to observe and being careful not to be arrested, since that would have put a blemish on my record. Government action was interesting to me already. Later, in law school, I learned that I would have to go before the character and fitness committee for a report of good character to become a lawyer. Had I been arrested for disorderly conduct or some other offense, I would have had a lot of explaining to do. I was mature enough to be concerned with consequences even if they might be in the distant future. Maybe I learned from my senior high school prank with the library books after I escaped unscathed. I was not going to tempt fate a second time.

8 THE FORMATIVE YEARS

College Begins

Weeks later, I was up at Madison as an incoming freshman with my roommate, Al Lipton, both of us coming from South Shore High School. In our last semester of senior year of high school, after we decided to become roommates, we began getting to know each other better. We jointly decided to go through fraternity rush. Al and I were not sure we would join, but we decided we would have the chance to meet a lot of new people if we went through rush.

We both wanted to concentrate on the Jewish fraternities. Neither of us felt particularly Jewish, but we both strongly identified culturally as Jews. There were four Jewish fraternities of about thirty-six fraternities in all, but the Interfraternity Council's rules required everyone going through rush to visit at least six different houses. We heard that the house next door to AEPi was a Frank Lloyd Wright building, so we picked that one to see the inside. It was a great experience. It looked small on the outside, but the house went down a hill towards Lake Mendota for four floors. The appearance of being small was deceptive. The members recognized from either our looks or our words, (certainly not our names), that we may have desired a Jewish fraternity. They said that if we were looking for a sixth house to fulfil the

IFC rule, they suggested going to a particular house, which we did, and we found a friendly reception. We were impressed with the honesty. Since they understood what we were looking for, we did not see any bias on their part and they did not accuse us of bias either. In the fall of 1959, the standards, mores, and values were quite different from those of 15 or 20 years later.

Of the four contenders for our consideration, we each perceived independently that two were composed of friendly, welcoming guys who we thought we would be quite comfortable to be with. In each house we knew a member a year or two ahead of us from our high school. One house was closer to campus and the housing arrangements looked all right, but they had fewer than 20 members. The other house was a further distance from the campus and classroom buildings, the housing looked comparable, but the membership was 75-80 members. I believed that in the larger house we would have more of an opportunity to find compatible individuals while in the smaller fraternity the odds would not be as great.

We both agreed on the house with the larger membership and hoped they wanted us. The other two fraternities were not our cup of tea. The members seemed either more materialistic or only interested in sports rather than studies. We were happy that the house we wanted, Alpha Epsilon Pi (AEPi), wanted both of us. There was a match. I do not know what either of us would have done if only one of us were accepted. Our friend from high school in the smaller house, Lenny Malkin, was very disappointed. I had met both Lenny and Bob Kaufman, who was in AEPi, at the same time at Hebrew school. Both knew each other from Hebrew school at B'nai B'zalel and, of course, from high school. They were ahead of me in school by one and two years, respectively. Until Bob died, I had stayed in touch with him. I saw Lenny regularly over the years as well, since he became a lawyer and an associate in Al's law firm. Al had an annual party on July 4 for his law firm and clients. I was always invited and Lenny and his wife, Robbie, were always there.

Becoming a Judge

For the first few weeks at college, while Al and I were going through rush, getting used to our classes, and finding a rhythm, we connected for Sunday dinners with a couple classmates from South Shore—Pat Henig (Hartman) and Rose Michael (Lewis). We shared our new experiences and emotions with each other as accepting friends.

Pat later married Marshall Hartman, her youth advisor in her synagogue, who became a lawyer in the public defender's office in Cook County. He was assigned death penalty cases and appeared before me on a few cases. Marshall was later instrumental in getting Governor George Ryan to suspend the death penalty in Illinois. Marshall had argued numerous cases before the Illinois Supreme Court and also before the United States Supreme Court, resulting in the guarantee of counsel for children placed under arrest. At his funeral in late September 2021, his family spoke with pride regarding his accomplishments that benefited all of society. Maureen and I attended by Zoom. Due to COVID-19, we could not attend in person.

Rose married a member of our high school class, Sherwin Lewis, who became a doctor specializing in obstetrics and gynecology. The president of our student council, Ken Manaster, told me that Sherwin delivered one of his children, and Sherwin's twin brother, Shelly, who became a rabbi and served as a Jewish chaplain in Vietnam, officiated at the naming ceremony for the child. Ken said he was tied to the Lewis twins. They all attended Rabbi Shelly Lewis's synagogue services in northern California. Ken was a law professor at Sana Clara Law School, primarily teaching environmental law but also teaching torts, procedure, and other courses. Ken became quite close to Supreme Court Justice John Paul Stevens.

After those first few weeks at college, we each found our way; we all realized that while we were all there for each other, we would not need to have dinner on a Sunday evening to prove it.

The relationships I had in college in the fraternity have continued to this day. As Al and I expected, some of the persons would become our close friends and some relationships did not blossom. I kept my distance from a few I did not like. That was the benefit of a large membership. We pledged with 36, and of those, 28 became members the next semester. We really did not know them as we were all going through rush, but many became our closest friends. The upperclassmen basically selected our pool of friends. It all worked out well. We could pick and choose who to room with in later semesters in and out of the fraternity house.

At the time we pledged and for many years after, fraternities in Madison had a significantly higher grade-point average than that of other students on campus. There was an environment in most of the fraternities that encouraged adherence to the rule of law, leadership training, participation in cultural and political events, and general socialization with both other men and women. Housemothers and chaperons were always listed with the university so that proper conduct could be monitored. Identification with one's fraternity assured proper conduct as well to increase the value of the name and not to diminish that name.

Al and I decided to move into the fraternity house our second semester and we were allowed in. We went into one of four triples. Our third roommate had lived in the fraternity house before rush, and to this day, I don't know how that happened. He was from the Bronx and was about ten months older than we were, so when we moved our belongings from our boarding house to the fraternity house, he was able to rent a car for the day to move our things. Al and I were still 17 years of age and too young to rent a car. I was 17 almost my entire first year until April 7. Al was two months older than I was.

Our first semester, Al and I roomed at a boarding house that was owned by Mrs. Calloway, a lovely widow. She had fluffy white hair, a bright smile, and a friendly voice. We learned of an available room from the prior occupants, Bob Lerner and his roommate, both from South Shore, who were in Al's AZA. They were moving into the ZBT fraternity house, so we knew the room was available. It was the largest room on the second floor.

There was only one other smaller double and a single room on the floor. In the attic was one other single room. We all shared one small bathroom that had a sink, shower and toilet. We couldn't take any unnecessary time with all the customers.

Although we only paid for the room and not for meals, when Mrs. Calloway learned I had a fever and stayed in from class, she brought some food up for me. Al also brought me some food from the fraternity house. I did the same for Al one day he was not feeling well. Bob Lerner later went to law school at Wisconsin and was hired as a teaching assistant for my legal writing class. He was a great student qualifying to teach and he was a great teacher. I slept in his bed and learned from him. How many students can say that openly?

Al and I got into the habit of studying up on Bascom Hill in the classrooms in various buildings, where it was much quieter than in the Memorial Library. We would go with pledge brothers. Harvey Schiller, Wayne Schwartzman, Al, and I all studied hard. Harvey and Al tended to get A's. I never knew what Wayne got. I was always elated when I got a rare A. I usually got B's.

Harvey was a pre-med from a suburb of Milwaukee. He became a pathologist in Seattle.

Wayne also came from a suburb of Milwaukee. He was bright also. In our freshman year, he was in the Integrated Letters and Science Program for accelerated students. The students in the program all took the same classes, which were determined by the program's advisors. Wayne went on to form a company that manufactured goods. He lived in both Wisconsin and Illinois until his retirement. He then moved to California and has played pickle ball in his 80's with another fraternity brother, Rick Tenser, who moved to California after serving as a neurologist in Hersey, Pennsylvania. He was affiliated with the university there, where he was head of the department for many years.

Al went on to the University of Chicago Law School, worked for the legal aid clinic affiliated with the University of Chicago, and later joined a good law firm, became partner, and later the managing partner. He dealt with estates and tax planning. All of the friends that I studied with became quite successful.

Many years after college, after my daughter, Eliza, had been seriously injured in a motor vehicle collision, in which a huge truck hit her car, I called Rick Tenser regarding her nerve damage. While we had not spoken for many years, it was as though it was only yesterday. He was so very helpful and kind and gave us guidance and support. He was the same friend who led me through my psychology statistics problems with ease. He assured us that our daughter would have a gradual recovery. Rick's prognosis became reality over the year. Every year now, Eliza celebrates her survival and recovery by giving thanks to the Almighty in a brief ceremony for prayer where she invites close friends and family.

I took Rick to dinner when he came to Chicago for a meeting of neurologists from around the nation. He stayed at the Palmer House Hotel and was shuttled to meetings at McCormick Place. We have continued a telephone relationship ever since. There was another time Rick and his lovely wife, Janet, came to town and Maureen and I took them to dinner. Rick has his children and grandchildren in California to show him love and support. He still travels east where Janet's family gives him more of the same. Rick and I continue to exchange stories of AEPi's that we each see or speak to.

Immaturity at College

Towards the end of the first year of college, a few weeks before final exams, the fraternity had an end-of-the-year party, where we rode in buses to a resort for a day of swimming, followed by dinner and dancing in formal attire. There was liquor available at the pool. I was offered an orange juice drink spiked with vodka. It was hot outside and I enjoyed the cool drink. After a few drinks, I was a very happy person, but quite tired. Al and some others took me to a room and I was put in bed. My date was accompanied by others for the dinner and dancing. I missed all the pictures. My tux and I stayed in the room that was used by about six to eight others to change into and out of their tuxes. My date, Vicki Schwartz, also from the south side of Chicago, was told I had taken ill. I never got into my rented tux, although I had paid for it. Obviously, I returned my tux in perfect condition.

On the bus ride back, I had sobered up, but unfortunately was sick to my stomach. The bus had to made a short stop to allow me to regurgitate. My date certainly had evidence that I wasn't feeling well. I told her I had too much to drink and apologized to her. I later thanked everyone who kept her occupied and entertained.

Later in life, I retained some understanding of the destructive power of alcohol and drugs, trying always to help and not judge those with issues. I sent many young people to various programs to help them. I did not have a need to punish them, knowing how drunk I had been when I was protected by friends. Not everyone under the influence is as fortunate as I was when I was just 18 years old.

I am happy to say that years later, Vicki and her lovely husband, Mike Turoff, and my wife and I had several opportunities to socialize. We had dinner together and enjoyed each other's company more than once. My behavior was greatly improved since I was sober. I learned that more than a sip of alcohol is not in my best interest. When people insist, and they do, I say my sponsor would strongly object. People drop it then.

Vicki and I met when she and Rachel Friedland, students from Hyde Park High School, joined students from South Shore on our high school trip to Washington, DC. Rachel and Vicki were close friends with Julie Goldschmidt, a South Shore student, who was on the trip. Julie later married Bob Schlossberg, who was two years ahead of us at South Shore. Rachel, Vickie, and Julie had all been in the choir together at a Reform temple, Beth Am. Rachel's father was the rabbi there. In high school I dated all of them. I liked them all. I don't think Julie dated Bob until college or after. I had taken Julie to many of my high school fraternity parties. She could probably describe Richie Meitus' basement better than I could. We had some fun times together.

Years ago, when we were adults but had little experience with death up close, I attended Rachel's *shiva* and saw Vicki and Julie and their husbands. We were all so very sad when Rachel passed away at a young age.

Mike Turoff was the managing partner of his large law firm and was kind enough to refer several cases to me for mediation after I left the bench. Bob's firm also engaged me to mediate some matters and to arbitrate some through the Financial Industry Regulatory Authority.

I recall a big confusing weekend my freshman year. I invited Julie, who was going to the University of Michigan, to come to homecoming weekend in Madison as my date. I had two tickets for the Friday night homecoming show at the University Field House. She came and stayed with Pat Henig and Rose Michael in the Gilman Residence Hall. I realized it was a mistake. Her trip was long and her arrival was delayed. She missed the homecoming show. I left the show early at the intermission to await her arrival. In those days there were no cell phones, texting, or e-mailing, so we were both flying blind! I took a cab to the train station and waited for more than an hour in the cold damp station. I finally heard the roar of the train and the sound of its whistle. I went out into the cold fall air hoping to see her coming off the train. Finally, I saw her with her bright smile. I ran up to greet her and take her suitcase so we could get one of the few disappearing cabs, allowing her to get to the place she would be staying and beat the clock before girls' curfew, which was fast approaching.

Unfortunately, our pledge class decided to pull a pledge prank that weekend and we ended up going to Fond du Lac, Wisconsin, for the night by bus and returning with little or no sleep. Al's parents and my parents had come up to campus and we sort of missed everything important. Our parents kept one of their rooms at a Madison hotel so that Al and I could sleep in quiet for a few extra hours that Sunday. Julie went back without seeing me as much as I had assumed we would. It took me a few days to catch up with my sleep. Happily, I knew that Julie had some quality time with her closest girlfriends, Pat and Rose, and maybe Vickey and Rachel, so all was not lost in this lost weekend. I was just a catalyst for her visit. Vickie and Julie have always been forgiving. I developed a love for all of them.

In the late Fall of my freshman year, a few weeks after homecoming, I went back to Chicago to attend a big dance given by Schmegglers and a sorority that had been in the planning stage the previous year, when I was a high school senior. I thought I would enjoy myself more, but I saw that I had moved to another world and my return was inappropriate. Mike Kamerlink, who was a year behind me in school, was the chairman of the dance. He went to Hyde Park High School. He put together a great event. A lot of money was raised for a worthy charity. I took as my date someone I had taken out before who was a year behind me in school and was a senior then.

Mike Kamerlink and I connected years later when we all lived in Glenview and belonged to the same synagogue. The woman he married was a divorce lawyer who appeared before me when I was in the Domestic Relations Division of the Court, from 1982 to 1987. Mike and his wife, Lydia, moved to Florida when they both retired. He always loved boating and can do that much more than while in Chicagoland, with a more limited season. I learned it is best to soak up all one can, but then move on and live in the present. The joys of yesterday are best lived in memories, not by going back as an outsider.

One of my fraternity brothers in Madison, Arnie Levy, was interested in politics, and he set in motion the opportunity for the fraternity to take part in the mock United Nations, with several of us as delegates. He also entered the house in the 1960 Mock Democratic convention as the Missouri delegation in favor of favorite son Senator Stuart Symington. These activities were a fun way to learn about American politics and civics in a very practical way.

Arnie later ran for state representative in Illinois, and several Chicago AEPi's helped him in his losing campaign. I believe he would have been a great legislator if he had won. I realized that

I had an interest in politics as well. Even in the fraternity, I ran for office and finally became the vice-president, elected the end of my junior year to serve the first semester of my senior year and sitting on the board of governors where all decisions were made regarding the governance of the chapter. Arnie had served as president the semester before. Years later, Arnie and a pledge brother of mine, Howie Weisman, organized annual and semi-annual reunions in the Chicago area. We even had a big one in Madison for spouses and attended a football game and had a big dinner.

In my senior year at Madison, I saw that a Chicago alderman was coming on campus to make a speech on politics. I was able to attend and kept in my mind that I would look him up when I was back in Chicago. The Alderman was Leon Despres from the 5th Ward.

Career Plan Change

During the second semester of my junior year, I was taking my last pre-med science course—comparative anatomy. I found it very difficult to learn and memorize all of the bones as was required. I dropped the course and called an end to any future medical career. In my freshman year, I had signed up for a course to learn the origin of Greek and Latin medical terms. It was given by my pre-med advisor, Mr. Howe. Within the first week of that semester when I could still drop this one credit course, I found that learning all the prefixes and suffixes was a challenge for me, as was taking a language, French, which was part of the pre-med curriculum. I should have realized that memorizing details was not my talent and given up medicine then. I persisted with the dream until my senior year when, after consultation with my parents, I took a wide variety of courses, including a few in business to see if my interests lay in that direction.

I thought of the possibility of dentistry, with all of my science courses under my belt, so I contacted Northwestern University's Dental School in Chicago to see what was required. I was told to take a written test and also a chalk carving test. I couldn't study for the written part, but I did practice carving chalk. Every piece I carved fell to pieces but I kept trying for several days, hoping for the best. I seemed to understand the written questions and felt I did well but on the practical chalk carving my chalk broke, as it did when I was practicing. I hope I carved out enough to pass.

I was invited into the dean's office at the dental school at Northwestern. He said I scored well into the ninety per centile score on the written portion and would know just what to do; but based on my inability to carve the images using the chalk, I would not be allowed into the school since I would destroy the patient's mouth. I decided not to apply to any other dental school, since I believed the dean. I assumed I would never return to that place again—until I did about a year and a half later when, Michael Vold, one of my fraternity brothers who I had roomed with the beginning of my junior year at college, asked if I could come to the dental school to serve as his practice patient for an exam and cleaning of my teeth. I agreed to help him, and luckily for both of us, he received the grade of A for his work on my mouth. Mike and I are still in touch and speak and see each other.

About 15 years after becoming a dentist, Mike went to law school and developed a specially practice in law while maintaining his dental practice. He prosecuted dentists at the state regulatory agency on professionalism for a few years on a part time basis and then began to represent dentists before the agency and dentists named in malpractice actions. Mike consulted patients as well as an expert witness. He represented dentists buying and selling practices. He even referred a dispute involving the sale of a practice to me for mediation. I learned something again: if you can't serve in one capacity, you might serve in another. I would not be a dentist, but I could be a great patient earning an A for a friend, and years later I could help resolve conflicts for dentists.

Since I could not yet decide what I wanted to do, I again consulted my parents. My father, a lawyer, suggested that I seek admission to a law school to learn critical thinking, logic, argument, and other skills that would be a great background for any job I might wish to pursue. Since I could not think of any better choice, I agreed and took the standardized entrance exam. I told my current roommate, Philip Charles Ravid, who was a business major. He said he was considering staying in Madison to work on his MBA there. I decided that we could continue rooming together if I applied and was accepted in Madison at the law school, which I knew was a great school.

We were both accepted to continue our education in Madison, in the Business School for him and the Law School for me, and we cemented our agreement to room together another year. We roomed together for five semesters and rarely had a disagreement and never had a fight. His program was for one year. Mine was for three years. That summer I had committed to work for my brother-in-law on behalf of his company, Germfree Laboratories, traveling to college campuses in New England and Canada with the company's chief salesman to demonstrate the company's line of equipment, including animal boards used for animal research, isolator units used to perform research in a safe environment and to treat burn patients and avoid infection, and a few other items.

I read all the brochures and learned from the salesman as we traveled, and I became an expert. At least, that is how I wanted to appear. A number of PhDs and many graduate assistants and researchers asked me questions as though I were an expert, and I heard myself giving reasoned answers. I remember my brother-in-law saying that, if I didn't know an answer, to take the name and number of the questioner and write down the question. Tell them we would get back to them. Each night I asked the salesman what I didn't know and also asked Jerry what neither of us knew. Each day, I could answer more questions than the day before. This trip was a practical way to learn. I learned how to learn and that had to help me in school as I continued my education.

While I was on the traveling trip for Germfree, an apartment for my first year of law school in Madison had to be found. Phil agreed to look and when he thought he found something acceptable, he went to see it with my parents and my oldest nephew, David. David was then seven years old. Phil told me David was cute and David said Phil was nice. They were destined to see each other again at my wedding to Maureen a few years later, when Phil stood up for me and David and his younger brothers, Keith and Craig were also in attendance. In fact, Craig, then about age five, led my grandfather up the aisle. My grandfather couldn't see well and would not listen to anyone, but he followed the lead of his great grandson Craig, to everyone's delight.

First Year Law School

I had taken out a lot of girls in college, with dates just about every weekend except during exam periods, but I had many fewer dates in law school. I was intimidated by about five classmates who always seemed to know the answers to all of the professors' questions. Others tried to answer, but their answers were not always accepted by the professors, or a professor would say, "Close but not exact." These five students were never wrong. I felt I had to study harder and harder and re-read passages in cases and review my notes multiple times. I was never too sure of myself. At the end of the first semester when my grades came in, I was not sure if the number grades were good enough. In civil procedure, I received a 96 so I felt confident there; but the other numbers were ambiguous to me. I did find out the following fall that I had done remarkably well and I will get to that shortly.

The year I attended law school in Madison was like a fifth year in college. The law school building had just been torn down. The old building had been a fixture on campus for almost a hundred years. All that was left was the adjoining library with some offices. Each class was held in the surrounding buildings on Bascom Hill. There wasn't the time between classes to visit and get to know my classmates. We spent the time between classes walking to the next building and, as the weather became colder, we spent half of the time putting on and taking off autumn or winter gear.

I could not find any classmates from Illinois. I realized that, unlike the class ahead of me where there were several Chicago area students, none existed in my class. I learned that the following class would have a few Chicago area students, but my class had only me. The professors taught the majority and minority views on subjects that tended to highlight California, New York, and Massachusetts law, with other states, like Illinois, only sprinkled in on rare occasions. When the national leading cases were not used, or federal cases not employed, Wisconsin cases were featured.

It was understandable to feature Wisconsin caselaw since that is where we were and where most of the students lived and would live out their careers and their lives. Moreover, those graduates of the University of Wisconsin Law School and Marquette University Law School in Milwaukee, upon graduation, would be admitted to the state bar without needing to pass a bar exam. If I stayed, I would either have to stay in Wisconsin to pursue my legal career or pass the Illinois bar without the advantage of learning the Illinois law on a regular basis. At the end of the year, when Phil confirmed he was getting his MBA on time and would be pursuing a job in Chicago, I had to make my plans for the next year.

I realized that even if I wanted to stay in Madison, I had not made close enough friendships with any classmates to ask if they wanted a roommate. I knew I wouldn't want to be alone without a roommate. I feared I would be going down a dead-end street with no good future after graduation in two years. I did not know then that a fraternity brother of mine had spent the year working on a master's degree and would be going to law school in Madison. In fact, he roomed with another fraternity brother a year ahead of us who was from Milwaukee. They were friends with another Chicagoan who was a year ahead of me who I came to know better in Chicago years later when our daughters went to high school together and he was appearing before me when I was on the bench. Whether it was for the best or not, I decided to transfer to a Chicago area law school.

Religious Education

In many ways, I am my father's son. He cared about practicalities and was very efficient and methodical in how he worked and handled tasks. When we lived in Hyde Park, he joined the Reform temple across the street from where we lived at 917 East 50th Street. I loved the music there in the Reform temple—K.A.M.—Kehilath Anshe Maarav. K.A.M. had a huge building and the temple attracted families from all over the south side.

Children were carpooled in for Sunday school and other programs. On Sunday mornings and other times, our quiet street was very busy with happy sounds. I merely had to walk across the street. I went there for Sunday School and for monthly cub scout meetings in the evening. My Hebrew School classes were a few blocks away at another Reform temple, Isaiah Israel, since the two temples had a joint program. I went to Hebrew school the last year we lived there before moving to South Shore at the end of the summer of 1951 when I was 9.

In the 1970's, K.A.M. and Isaiah Israel merged and moved into the building of Isaiah Israel. The K.A.M. building was sold to the organizations of Rev. Jesse Jackson Jr. for use as Operation PUSH for prayer and political purposes.

I was happy with the program at K.A.M., loving the Bible stories, singing Zionist Israeli songs, doing art work, participating in plays, and generally having a great time. Hebrew school was not as enjoyable. I had to learn the alphabet letters of a new language; and it was hard for me. I walked the two and a half blocks by myself, and soon after the fall classes started, when the time changed, I found I was walking home alone in the dark. The kids in the neighborhood all knew that the house at the end of 50th Street at Ellis that I had to pass was haunted. I felt I was risking my life to learn the Hebrew alphabet and that I was making a tremendous sacrifice. I did not want to sound like a coward, so I told no one. You may be among the first to learn this secret I was ashamed to share. In the spring, I knew I was safe, since it was again light when I returned from Hebrew School. Everyone knew that ghosts did not show themselves during the daytime.

When we moved to 7524 South Essex Avenue in South Shore, my father said we were joining B'nai B'zalel, at the corner of 76th and Phillips, which was across the alley behind our apartment building and down the block. It was the closest place to affiliate. Now we would be going to a Conservative Synagogue. When I was enrolled in Hebrew School and tested for fluency with Hebrew, I was told that rather than being in the second-year class, Bet, I would be starting over in the first-year class, Aleph, since I did not know enough. I had spent that past year in Hebrew school with no benefit.

Fortunately, I found I was in the same class with several classmates from Myra Bradwell Elementary School who became my best friends: Larry Lichtenstein, Lawrence Weprin, Ronnie Opper, and Billy London. Others in the class were all very nice as well. The point is, my father did not care about Reform, Conservative, or Orthodox Judaism, he merely wanted to affiliate and for me to attend any Hebrew School to prepare me for my Bar Mitzvah—something he missed when he was my age. When he was approaching the age of 13, his poor family moved from Philadelphia to Chicago. There was insufficient money to send him to Hebrew school in Philly or Chicago. He felt we were Jewish and really did not care about denominations.

My father was a great influence on me. He taught me that I could learn from anyone in public school or religious school regardless of denomination. I expanded that to Orthodox later. He showed me how a place of prayer is also a place of learning. I saw that first in a very literal sense when I came home from college during vacations with exams hanging over my head and needing a place to study. I found refuge at the synagogue where the rabbi allowed me to use a quiet room to study when our apartment was too noisy for me with a lot of holiday activity.

Later, as a young married, my wife encouraged me to continue my studies and become actively involved in our synagogue. We had joined a Conservative synagogue, Rodfei Zedek, at 5200 South Hyde Park Boulevard., close to where we lived in Hyde Park, at 1606 East 50th Place. I joined their Board of Trustees and came to know Rabbi Ralph Simon and Rabbi Emeritus Benjamin Daskal. I sat on the board when we hired Rabbi Vernon Kurtz as the assistant rabbi.

I began taking courses. One course given by both Rabbi Simon and Rabbi Kurtz dealt with ethics and morality and used the book *The Ethics of Our Fathers*. The class lasted for years and was taught in the Hyde Park synagogue, but also downtown in various locations. I learned much from these fine teachers even after we moved from Hyde Park to Glenview.

When there were multiple services, my wife and I enjoyed going to the service led by Rabbi Daskal, who presided over the auxiliary service, since he provided enriching stories regarding each prayer, sharing their origin and giving the background. I realized now that this was not quite the beginning, but the continuation of my spiritual, cultural, and ethical education to take with me into my secular life. My father had set the tone to be open to all and my wife urged me forward in the development of my character.

When Maureen and I attended Rodfei Zedek as young marrieds and especially after I became a judge, when I felt it was my responsibility to actively involve myself in the Jewish community, we heard Rabbi Ralph Simon say to all of the men that we must all be romantic and, therefore, have some candlelight meals. If we have it on Friday night and the woman says a prayer, it would be followed by a perfect Sabbath dinner. If we already did that, we should consider having a little wine or juice and say a blessing and have a fuller and more meaningful Sabbath dinner. We began the rituals and continue today.

His point was to do a little more than whatever we were then doing. It would be romantic for husband and wife, but show we loved the Almighty as well. He spoke about having a sukkah of our own if we could, although it was fine to use the communal sukkah at the synagogue. After we moved to our own house in Glenview, Maureen learned that Craftwood Lumber Company in Highland Park had sukkah kits priced inexpensively to encourage people like us to buy and use them.

We did buy a sukkah kit and, with the help of friends and family, put up the sukkah on our patio each year. We called Rabbi Simon the first year, and he was delighted. He said he would love to come and see it. We invited him and his wife to come with the cantor and his wife. It was a lovely evening. They were proud of us and we were so happy to share our sukkah with them. I will never forget that evening and the happiness.

Dinner in our sukkah with my cousins, the Zabrins. Shown are Amy, Mary holding Eaon, Nancy, me, Steven, and Kyle. Not shown are Doug, Maureen, Eliza, and Jeff.

We invited many friends who had never been in a private sukkah. On certain nights when the weather was good, it was great with the stars above. When it became windy and rainy, it could be necessary to move back inside. With Maureen's encouragement and hard work, we shared lovely times with many friends and family for over 40 years. Maureen was always my inspiration and I often had to be pushed to put it up. In the years approaching my 80th birthday, I found it more than I could handle. We have the materials, but they sit in our garage. I don't know what we will do with the many tinker-toy like pieces when we finally move and downsize. We entertained many of our non-Jewish friends in the sukkah or inside the house if the weather did not cooperate with us being out in the sukkah.

To this day, I attend either in person or by Zoom lessons, classes, and lectures given by several rabbis who are great teachers. I have attended the lessons by Rabbi Moshe Solavechik, a descendant of numerous learned rabbis. He usually focuses on the portion of the week with each year bringing a new prospective, in tune to the events of the day.

Maureen and I regularly attended the lectures by Rabbi Daniel Moscovitz, given in the home of friends. He helped create several Chabbad Shuls in the Chicago area, including one in Northbrook, which we would attend. Later, after his death, his son Meier took responsibility, and we have taken courses from him and gone to his services. Sometimes, we have attended the courses of other Chabad rabbis, including Rabbi Yochanan Posner, whose parents had hosted our daughter when she was becoming observant. I found out later that Rabbis Meier and Yochanan were study partners. They, like Chabbad rabbis around the world, were teaching several six-to-eight-part weekly courses on various stimulating subjects and topics, some of which even gave me continuing legal education credits or gave my wife social work credits. It was a win-win situation, and we had the chance to meet many old and new friends in a learning environment. Some of the lessons truly aided me in my legal challenges as a judge and later as a mediator. I learned that all education can be transferred. What I learned in the spiritual world could be used in the secular legal world.

I think back now to another relationship I made in the Law Department of the City in the General Counsel Division. In the cubicle next to mine was a lawyer, Michael Small, who I soon learned was an Orthodox rabbi. He showed me how he could navigate both the religious and secular worlds. He was completely observant of all religious rules. He would take a break before sundown to say his prayers in the corner of his office at the window. He took off on all religious holidays. The food he ate was all appropriate for his observance. He was a tremendous influence in my life and became a source of inspiration and guidance for my wife and daughter as well.

Rabbi Small had several assignments, but one that took up a lot of his time was the prosecution of police officers violating their responsibilities as officers. I was brought into his observant religious world when I received an invitation to the wedding of his oldest daughter. At that wedding most men sat separate from the women, but he had Maureen and me at a table together with a few other members of the office. Some were not Jewish. Years later, he told me that the restrictions tightened so at another wedding he hosted, the women and men were separate at the ceremony, the meal, and the dancing.

I experienced at his weddings the joy, customs, traditions, prayers, and true celebration that accompany a Jewish wedding. Judaism and religion were more than just ritual, religion, spirituality, and education; Judaism was also joy with singing, dancing, laughter, and happiness. It was much more than learning another language. Judaism had revealed itself as life itself and a source of joy.

Maureen and I spent many evenings at Rabbi Small's house with his family. He became the major religious advisor to my daughter. His wife, Chaya, born in Europe and raised in Shanghai, China, was an inspiration for hope and joy. She called Rabbi Small her Yankee Doodle Dandy, since he was born in the USA, the son of an Orthodox rabbi. He took over his father's schul, and after his own death, it was the responsibility of his oldest son to maintain the synagogue.

My father had set me up to move along and learn from and develop friendships with Jews of all denominations. My father opened me to people of other faiths and colors as well. He liked everyone—especially the people I liked.

The point of observing my father's choices of houses of worship being proximate to our residences was a lesson for me to find a law school to attend that had a location that did not pose a challenging stress to attend. I ended up at DePaul University

College of Law. It was an easy ride downtown on the bus or Illinois Central Railroad from the 51st Street station, a couple of blocks away from our apartment.

Loyola University Law School required an additional trip through downtown Chicago that would add at least a half hour in each direction. I ruled out nearby University of Chicago. I doubted that I would be admitted, but the prime reason is that I perceived it to be too theoretical. I ruled out Northwestern due to it being even further than Loyola. At the time I thought that John Marshall Law School, which only recently in 2020 became part of the University of Illinois system, was a proprietary school owned by the Republican State Representative for our district, Noble Lee, as less than stellar. Likewise, Kent Law School, where my father attended, was not then as attractive as it became later when it became part of the Illinois Institute of Technology. As a result of my thinking, I applied only to DePaul and was accepted. I did not know it then, but a few years later I would be going to John Marshall after I graduated from DePaul to attend graduate law school.

9 SURPRISE! SURPRISE!

Front Page News—Babysitter Becomes Judge

The day that news broke on the selection of 13 new associate judges, Maureen had a dentist appointment downtown. Since her appointment was during the lunch hour, I told her I could take over responsibility for our daughter, Elizabeth, while she was at the dentist. She brought Elizabeth to me with her bottle and other equipment. Everyone in the office who saw her gave her a few "coochi coochi coos." While I was holding her, I received a call from a *Chicago Tribune* reporter asking me to comment on my selection. I said I had not heard or known of my selection. The reporter asked if he could come to my office for an interview. I agreed. No sooner than I hung up the phone, a *Chicago Sun-Times* reporter was on my line asking to interview me then. I tried to focus on his questions with Elizabeth on my lap. Before I knew what was happening, I saw flashbulbs going off. It was a photographer from the *Tribune* who caught me holding Elizabeth while I was being interviewed by the *Sun-Times*. There was a press office on the second floor of City Hall and I was on the fifth floor. It took less than two minutes to get to me using the elevator.

Within a few minutes and seeing the flashing bulbs, my dear friend Rabbi Small came in and offered to take Elizabeth a few feet away to his cubicle. She would see me through the glass that separated our separate cubicles and was happy with him so I gratefully agreed. I tried not to say anything improper. In those few moments Rabbi Small and my daughter bonded and began a life time relationship. She not only was comfortable with him but grew to admire his wisdom and advice.

To my utter amazement, early next morning, before I left for work, I received a call from my father-in-law who was so very proud. We already told our parents that I made it and were busy thanking everyone who helped. He opened the front door to his apartment to take out the garbage to the chute near the seventh-floor elevators and saw the front page of the *Chicago Tribune* delivered to his neighbor across the hall, facing him and showing a big picture of his granddaughter and me. He could not have been happier and wanted me to know how happy he was. When I got to work, I already had more messages than I could imagine. One of the calls was from a Jewish judge who was outraged. He said I should not seek such publicity. It was improper. Furthermore, when I was asked about my age and said that I hoped to help reduce the backload, he felt that was critical of all judges not working hard enough. I apologized to him and promised I would not allow such an event to repeat itself. He calmed down and congratulated me.

I realized that my coverage brought me too much publicity. While I did not seek the publicity, it came my way in a totally unexpected way. It also brought out jealousy, envy, and hatred. A headline "Babysitter on The Bench" gets a lot of attention with a calm and happy 16-month-old infant on the front page. It was hard for anyone to ignore my success. Elizabeth was cute and adorable for all to see.

When Maureen returned to the office after her dental appointment, she asked how things went. I told her I was soon to become a judge. I said it would take place on April 1, 1974. We had a lot to do in the meantime—me especially.

10 WHERE DO VALUES COME FROM?

My Father Helped Me Help Others

When I was ending my last year of law school, a friend that I met through the 4th Ward organization got in trouble financially. When I obtained my law license, but had no experience at anything, my father helped me steer this friend through bankruptcy. The friend was Henry Davis, but his friends called him Stinky. I never learned why he took on that nickname. Henry referred to himself as colored, the most positive reference to his race that he heard when he was growing up. I told him the more modern or politically correct term was negro or later Afro-American or Black. He was a creature of the past. I felt very comfortable discussing things with him. My father accepted him because I did. He had a job as a building inspector. With his money problems, I knew he was an honest man.

    I also had my father help me by representing a Black pharmacist, Cal Smith, who was wrongfully charged with a serious traffic offense. He was acquitted. Later, when he ran for state representative in our district, my parents hosted a reception in their apartment for him so the people in our part of the ward could meet him. That was done because I liked him. He won and served well with our other state representative, James A. McClelland, a lawyer. Jim's brother-in-law was an assistant U.S.

Attorney and his father-in-law was the first Black general in the U.S. military. These men were fine, as were their families that I met through the 4th Ward Regular Democratic Organization.

When I was a boy, my father took me to the Hyde Park YMCA to swim, he took me to a golf range to drive golf balls, we went to see major league baseball, and we went for car rides for ice cream. Sometimes, I found us walking into to a toy store and he told me to pick something out to buy. It wasn't even my birthday! He just wanted me to be happy. In a restaurant, if he saw I truly enjoyed a dessert, he would order another for me. When I played with my toys as a boy, he would join me on the floor to play as well. I tried to do all of these things with my daughter and later with my son. My father modeled behavior I would follow. One girlfriend of my daughter said her father never got on the floor. Elizabeth said she thought that was sad. You couldn't play with your father unless he got down on the floor.

When my father had a massive stroke before he died, I had a chance to spend private time with him and told him while he was hooked up to tubes and wires and unable to live on his own that I missed his physical love for me, but thanked him for the time and support he gave me and my children by his example and his financial help. I enjoyed his company.

My father spent a lot of time with my two children when they were each small. He got on the floor with each of them. My wife and I would kid our son saying that when Grandpa Ben took him to the bank in Skokie to make a deposit, Jeff liked the deposit slips with an image of a Native American. He wanted as many as he could have, so my father grabbed all he could and gave them to Jeff. A few weeks later the bank went out of business. We said that since no one could now make a deposit, the bank failed. We quickly told the truth that they merely merged with another bank and did not need those deposit slips. If Jeff didn't get them, they would probably be thrown away. Jeff knew his grandfather would give him anything even if it closed the bank.

My father was a great mentor but not the only family mentor. My mother's father, Hyman Kritzer, Grandpa Hymie, was a brilliant man. Unfortunately, his eyesight and hearing were inadequate to his needs. As a young man he had read the Russian classics, probably in Russian, and maybe some later in English. By the time I was old enough to have meaningful conversations with him, I realized that he had not read the literature we discussed for 40 years. He retained a memory of many details that he had absorbed years earlier. I knew when I read something I did not always remember it a few weeks later, but my grandfather remembered everything from much earlier periods of time.

Grandpa Hymie spoke of the economy and politics and political parties. Grandpa spoke of the struggles of the poor and oppression by those like the Czars. Grandpa spoke of the dangers of communism, socialism, and fascism. Extremism was problematic. What he did was give life to my social consciousness, my awareness about government, the need to participate in society. I discussed his words with my father who said that sometimes to avoid a leader or a party having or attaining and keeping too much power, it was good to vote for the political party not in office. In a two-party system, it is good to shake things up. The new people will hopefully keep the good programs but eliminate the bad. Society will move ahead. If only those principles were applied today.

My sister tried explaining from her perspective that the Republicans tended to favor the rich corporate interests and the Democrats tended to protect the poor and minorities. I came to identify as part of a minority, and felt I wanted to root for and later become a Democrat. I came to understand that when I was born and for quite a few years after, our alderman in Hyde Park-Kenwood and then our alderman in South Shore were Republicans. Each would later be replaced by Democrats who were Black.

My political mentor, Claude W. B. Holman, was the black man who replaced Alderman Abraham H. Cohen in the 4th Ward, and Alderman Nicholas J. Bohling's 7th Ward line of succession was to be Black in short order as well. My mother let me accompany her when she went to vote, and I saw how easy it was to vote and soon realized how important it was for everyone to vote. It was every citizen's right and also their duty. No one would ever have to urge me to vote; I would vote on my own volition whenever the opportunity was present.

My grandfather was not just an influence on my interest in politics and public service; he influenced others, including my cousin, David Epstein. My mother's sister Esther had a son one year younger than I, and his family lived in my grandparent's apartment for several years in the same building we were in, but around the corner. My cousin David and I were always together with another neighbor, Warren Weisberg. David and I would hear the same messages from Grandpa.

David also became a lawyer and, shortly after he was admitted to the Illinois Bar, was hired by the Illinois House Democratic leader John Touhy to be a member of the Democratic legislative staff. A few years after the Democrats took control of the House, David was named Parliamentarian and worked for Speaker Michael J. Madigan. After serving on the Democratic House staff for a few years, David left for private practice until he was appointed by the Republican Governor to a vacancy on the Illinois Court of Claims, where he continued serving under two governors. Disgraced, impeached, and convicted Democrat Governor Rod Blagojevich ended David's term as a judge. David continued his private practice and later became the County Administrator for estates where the heirs were not apparent.

Another relative worked on the Republican side of the isle with Republican House leader George H. Ryan, who later became Secretary of State and Governor before being sent to prison. The cousin, Arthur Harrison, was a legislative aid to Ryan and later served as legal counsel to the Department of Corrections when Ryan was governor. David and Arthur served in Springfield at the same time. Arthur's mother and our mothers were first cousins on our mothers' mother's side. Arthur, of course, knew our grandfather as well.

Another cousin on our grandmother's side worked in Springfield as well for a few years. Alan Feingold, still another cousin whose mother was the sister of Arthur's mother became a lawyer also and he was made a hearing officer for the Illinois Department of Pollution Control under a Republican administration. These cousins are all cousins of my famous cousin, Peter Lisagor. Politics and public service was a thing in the family. Coincidentally, in the 27-unit apartment building David and I grew up in lived a family whose daughter, Jill Swislow, years later married and moved to the far northwest suburb of Elgin, where she became a Republican State Representative. Maybe our early discussions rubbed off on her as well. Jill Zwick and David were long-time friends since both were in Springfield together for a number of years.

Perhaps since there were so many of our relatives in government, it was hard for us to avoid each other. I was assigned to pursue a case involving the City of Chicago before the State Pollution Control Board. The other party was represented by a law school classmate of mine, John Ward. My cousin Allen Feingold was the assigned hearing officer. I told John Ward and he had no objection since he felt the hearing officer only made evidentiary rulings and the Board would make the decision. We told Allen, who agreed to serve with no objection, agreeing that he had little discretion. Since we both followed all the rules of procedure and evidence, Allen did not have to rule on anything. We all did our jobs without tension and enjoyed each other's company. While I represented the City of Chicago, John's father was a city department head dealing with contracts for and purchases by the City. We were all conflicted, but none of us had a bias. At the time, none of us saw how anyone else would perceive the appearance of conflicts. This case was one where we learned the practicalities of full disclosure, the presence of a conflict, and the absence of bias.

The Family Secret I Did Not Know

My father shared with me that when he was in law school at Kent College of Law (now part of the Illinois Institute of Technol-

Grandpa Hymie - Hyman Kritzer

ogy), one of his law professors urged all his students to run for office to participate in the political process. The office suggested for my father was alderman. My father did not tell me, but I have come to believe that he changed his name from a long ethnic sounding name to Jordan in the 30's while still in or just out of law school. He helped change the names of his parents and six siblings, all younger than he and before any were married.

Growing up, I never knew that the family name was anything other than Jordan. I can't even correctly pronounce or spell the original name. I doubt when I later went into public life and ran for judge that I would have been received as well with my true unpronounceable and unspellable name. My father may have been motivated for himself, although he never achieved any public office, but his actions certainly made it more likely for me to win with such a beautiful name as Michael Stephen Jordan.

My name is bland. Someone can like or dislike me for no reason other than who I am. I have never hidden who I am. I take off for the Jewish holidays. I am a member of the Jewish bar association, Decalogue Society of Lawyers. I am a member of the Jewish Judges Association and have been since it formed about ten years before I left the bench. I list my affiliations in all my listings for arbitration or mediation panels and I did the same when subject to peer review by the many bar associations seeking appointive and elective judicial positions. I was known in 1974 as one of two Jewish candidates who made it as an associate judge. The other was former State Representative Bernard Wolfe.

When I was selected as an associate judge by the voting judges, it appeared to me that they maintained a balance reflective of the community. In addition to placing two Jewish judges, there were two Republican judges, two Black judges, some Irish judges, some Polish, Italian, civil and criminal practice lawyers, some private practice lawyers, and some public office holders. Every part of the larger community got a piece of the action.

My wife was very aware of the perceptions and observations of others and felt that I had an obligation then and thereafter to see myself as representing the Jewish community on the bench.

We always maintained a synagogue affiliation. I involved myself in the Decalogue Society of Lawyers and served on the board and in other capacities and attended their functions. I took off on Jewish holidays and went to synagogue. I made it as a Jew and I should reflect that fact. I knew I had strong support from every other community, so I worked hard to be fair and even to all. I learned that foreign nationals from around the world would find themselves in my courtrooms and I was to show no bias to anyone.

I thought back to a summer in law school, when I worked as a clerk in the Probate Division of the Circuit Court, learning all of the many functions of the employees in the office. Towards the end of the summer, I was assigned to the courtroom of Presiding Judge Robert Jerome Dunne. He had quite a political pedigree, with a mayor and governor in his family years ago. Among his responsibilities, he reviewed the distribution of funds to minors. When he learned the money would be sent to a communist country behind the Iron Curtain, he held up the release of those funds, believing they would go to the state and not the minor. When a minor was in the US, he would tell the child, if old enough, that the money should be used for their education and not something frivolous. When they acquired an education, they had a tool in their tool box for life that could not be taken away from them. I learned that a judge can use his or her social consciousness in the exercise of the judicial responsibilities. It would always be possible to put each case into a larger perspective.

Judge Dunne was on a committee of the Circuit Court dealing with the plans for construction of the new civic center courthouse. We were in the county building. All of the downtown courts would move to the new court house to be first known as the Civic Center, where I would become a judge one day in the future. He discussed the need for ceremonial courtrooms and courtrooms for trials without jury boxes and those with. I had a mini-lesson in the making of a new court system and facility. It was quite interesting.

I also had the opportunity to meet other deputy clerks from various parts of the county who were of different races and religions. I was transparent and acknowledged that I was from the 4th Ward and was a precinct captain. I told how I was going to law school and this was a summer job for me. I may have acknowledged that the summer before I had worked in the Estate Administration Department of the Continental Illinois National Bank, one of the largest banks in the country. It is now Citibank. I had prepared inventories, annual accounts, and final accounts for filing in the court. Now I was on the receiving end, accepting wills and other papers after people died. While assigned to a courtroom, I learned the words to administer the oath to witnesses, a task I performed for many years after as a judge. When I was back in law school taking my estates and trusts course, the subject seemed very useful and practical. Years later when I was soliciting votes from judges, Judge Dunne's nephew was a voting judge. I told him my positive recollections of his uncle. A year later, I was assigned a chambers next door to his for a few weeks while another judge was on vacation. I became very comfortable visiting with him.

11 MINDGAMES

Thoughts Before Being Sworn into Office and Dangers to Face

Bugs, Guns, Guillotines, Insults, Bombs, and Neo-Nazis

As I was preparing my mind for my swearing in as a judge and the reality of what that meant, I know now what I did not know then what was going to happen to me. It would be little things but big things as well. While my memory is still with me and without suppressing the painful, I reflect on some of those events. There was the reoccurring problem of being assigned to insect and rodent infested places. Most people think a judge assumes a lofty role but don't realize that we are sitting in places where the criminally accused have lice, roaches, and other creatures in their hair or clothes and some of those things don't stay put. They migrate. I was riding on a bus going home from work and I saw a roach. I looked around to see who it came from and realized I was the most likely subject. I had one judicial robe that never entered the house. I would sometimes change clothes outside, as I did when I had night bond court at 11th and State. Once we moved to Glenview, we had a garage where I could strip in relative privacy.

One day in a misdemeanor branch court at 89th and Exchange in South Chicago, I saw what seemed like a parade of roaches marching across my bench while the court was in session! I summarily sentenced them all to death without trial before the clerk could call the next case. At that same courtroom on another occasion, I had the good fortune of looking up as a prisoner was brought before me from the basement cellblock. He passed the clerk's file cabinet and quickly pulled out the metal file divider before the clerk or sheriff's deputy could do anything. As I said, it was lucky I was watching, so I ducked when he threw the metal plate at my neck. It missed me and went crashing to the floor behind me.

I was not guillotined that day, so I had life yet in me. I referred him for a psychiatric exam before deciding if he would be held in contempt or have additional charges placed against him. On another day when I was assigned to that courtroom, the public defender said there was a prisoner in the lockup who was quite agitated and that it might not be safe to bring him upstairs into the courtroom. The prosecutor, the public defender, the court reporter, and I all went down to see him with a sheriff's deputy. We conducted our business, all thanking the public defender for her professionalism and regard for everyone's safety.

Unlike 89th and Exchange with only one courtroom for misdemeanors from the police districts around that courthouse, at 51st and Wentworth there were two courtrooms: one for misdemeanors for the police districts around that courthouse and another for preliminary hearings on felonies for a greater part of the south side. I was assigned to each room on various occasions. One day at 51st and Wentworth a male defendant was brought before me, and I could see lice jumping off his head. I felt my stomach churn and the hair on my arms move. I saw I was moving my chair further away as I quickly gave several orders. The hearing was abbreviated and steps were taken quickly for hygiene and to protect the environment of the courtroom. I checked all of my clothes before resuming the bench and slowly ran my hands through my hair as I looked at my image in the mirror in the chamber's washroom. I looked into the sink to see if anything fell in, but fortunately, I was good to go. When notified that the room was ready, I continued the call with gratitude to the cleaning crew and the risks they take.

When I was assigned to preside over domestic relations cases between 1982 and 1987, I had many experiences, but none so chilling as one involving Hutchie Moore, a former Chicago policeman going through a divorce. His wife was represented by a fine young lawyer, James Piszczor, age 34, but Moore had no desire for a lawyer. He was *pro se*—that is, representing himself when I tried his case. He had been injured and needed a wheel chair. I did not know his son had shot him. Each time the case was before me, he was in his wheel chair with a blanket covering him. On the last day I saw them, after finishing the testimony, I made my rulings dividing the couple's property, including the police disability pension and their house. The lawyer for the wife was instructed to prepare the decree. I signed the decree a few days afterwards, after finding that it included all of the provision as I directed, including the provision that if Hutchie Moore did not convey his interest in the home to his wife, then I or any judge sitting in my stead would be authorized to sign the deed on his behalf.

On October 21, 1983, about a month after the decree was signed, the lawyer for the wife brought the matter into the post judgment courtroom to enforce that provision. Judge Henry A. Gentile, age 63, of blessed memory, was sitting that day hearing post degree matters. It could have been me or anyone else in the Domestic Relations Division, but it was Henry's fate. When he asked Hutchie Moore if he was going to sign the deed, Hutchie Moore said no. Judge Gentile then announced that he would sign on his behalf as my decree provided. Hutchie Moore then said no again and pulled out a loaded gun from under his blanket and shot the judge in the temple, killing him on the bench, and then turned the gun on his wife's young lawyer wounding him mortally in the stomach and chest. Two unspent bullets remained in his gun's chamber. Hutchie, however, was satisfied and just sat back waiting to be arrested.

A judge sitting next door, Robert Cusack, heard the commotion and sounded the alarm. The unarmed sheriff deputy in the courtroom had dived for cover protecting herself. She did nothing to help Judge Gentile or the lawyer or to subdue the shooter or take his gun. Other deputies raced in and did her job. It was clear that Judge Gentile was dead—he fell over to the side—but the lawyer was still conscious. He managed to go across the hall to the men's washroom where he was found by paramedics. As he was being removed from the building on a stretcher to a waiting ambulance, a television crew in the lobby of the Daley Center picked up his image and voice saying, "Tell my wife I will be all right." He died shortly thereafter in the hospital after a failed surgery.

James Piszczor's infant child would never know his touch again or his embrace. I attended Judge Gentile's wake and saw his open casket. As I looked inside, I saw myself lying there and shuddered. I felt a tear pass from my eye down my face. I gathered my composure, straightened my clothes, corrected my posture and moved over to the family and expressed my deepest sorrow to each of them. Henry had left home that fatal day going to a job most people think of as one to strive to have, but he never survived to make it home. He would never see his 64th birthday.

Hutchie Moore was taken to 61st and Racine where, years earlier, I had heard preliminary hearings for felonies where bond was set. He was indicted by a grand jury and tried in the criminal courts at 26th and California. Moore was found guilty by a jury of his peers and convicted with a judge out of Cook County presiding, since the judges in Cook would appear to have a bias. I would hope any judge would have a bias to punish one who had assassinated a sitting judge merely doing his job and fulfilling his professional responsibilities. Moore was sentenced to a life term. Moore died in prison November 9, 2001. The day I learned that he had died in prison was a day my wife, children, and I felt a huge weight lifted. I took a deep breathe, and sat down to reflect. We did not know if he felt he had an unfinished agenda to take my life, since I was the one who entered the order awarding the marital home to his ex-wife. While I did not seek his execution, I welcomed the news that he could no longer pose a threat to me or anyone else. I spoke endlessly about the news and realized how upsetting it was for his name and the news to re-enter my mind.

After this shooting in the courthouse, I became a strong advocate for metal detectors in public places like courthouses. I went in to see the Sheriff of Cook County, Richard Elrod. I advocated for metal detectors for all courthouses. He said it was too expensive. He said he heard I had bad mouthed his deputy who was assigned to the courtroom. That criticism was clearly his focus. I said she did absolutely nothing to prevent this tragedy before or after. She was useless. I would never want her assigned to a room I worked in.

Dick Elrod and I had both served in the law department of the city years before. He was head of the Ordinance Enforcement Division. During the Days of Rage, on October 8, 1969, he and a couple of his assistants were working with police officers downtown to advise on arrests of demonstrators. Dick saw one demonstrator who appeared violent, but instead of having police officers act, Dick tackled the man, Brian Flanigan, and injured his own spinal cord in the process causing permanent injury.

From that day on, Dick needed help and care for his most mundane body functions. His momentary act caused him permanent injury as well as suffering to him, to his lovely wife, Marilyn, and to their children. Mayor Daley had extreme sympathy for Dick upon learning of his condition. Besides being a lawyer in the city's law department, Dick was a Democrat state representative from the 50th Ward on the far north side. Daley knew Dick's family, who had been prominent Democrats when on the west side of Chicago years earlier.

One of the Mayor's administrative assistants had a card and a tape recorder for any staff who were so inclined to offer messages of support to Dick while he was in the hospital and at the Chicago Rehabilitation Center. No one judged him for what had happened. We all knew he would have a rough time in the future. After he was elected as sheriff, he had sufficient staff to render him needed assistance. He stayed in office as sheriff for about 12 years, until he was defeated, and then became a Circuit Judge assigned to hear personal injury cases in the Law Division of the Court.

In the early days of the unified court system, elected judges were almost always assigned a personal bailiff. That practice ended in the late 60's and early 70's, but due to Dick's special circumstances, he was assigned a personal bailiff to help him. There were no complaints from anyone, including the media, since all knew his tragic story. He served well as a judge. I spent some time with him in 1998 in Reno, Nevada, at the National Judicial College, when we each took a class in mediation. He was assisted by a close friend who also took the course.

I know Dick believed what he said when he told me it would be too expensive to have 24/7 metal detectors. He did agree to have them in place in the Daley Center from 8 AM until 3 PM each day. I told him someone intent on killing a judge or anyone in the building could enter after 3 PM without being checked. He would go to a bathroom and place a gun into a toilet water reservoir. He could then return the next day and go through security and be cleared. He would then go into the same bathroom stall and retrieve the gun. He was free to go on a rampage or take out just one target. Dick felt it was unlikely. He would not budge further.

Dick was defeated by former police commander Jim O'Grady, running as a Republican. O'Grady had been the 21st police district commander when we lived in Hyde Park and were in his district. I had come to know him as a professional, dedicated public servant. I was very pleased when he instituted 24/7 coverage of the courthouse with metal detectors and gradually expanded their use to other court facilities.

I recognize in our modern society that taxpayers are forced to pay huge amounts, due to terrorists and other gun toting criminals intent on doing harm. Years after the shooting in Judge

Gentile's courtroom, a judge I knew from judicial and bar association committees suffered an irate litigant entering his courtroom in Champaign, Illinois. The man threw a Molotov cocktail at him. Judge George Miller was taken to a local hospital for minor head injuries suffered as he ducked. Later, however, we found it was not a divorce or domestic violence case or even a criminal case that prompted this attack. The attempt on Judge Miller's life was due to a ruling he made in a medical malpractice case weeks earlier. The perpetrator, John E. Ewing, age 37, endangered about 25 people who were in the courtroom. Those in attendance were not just court personnel but jurors, litigants, lawyers, witnesses, and spectators.

Who knew when I was trying to become a judge that it could open me up to the possibility of serious injury or death? Years later in Chicago, we learned that the shooting of a federal judge's husband at her home was due to her ruling on a civil case. Not only judges, but their families were in jeopardy. Judicial administrators have raised the level of security, limiting the access to the home addresses of judges and instituting many other procedures.

I thought back to when I had my stints at 11th and State for night bond court and remember seeing a three-month list of assigned judges for each week, with their names, addresses, and telephone numbers. I complained to deaf ears at the time, saying that as police officers brought in informants, who were often drug addicts or criminal perpetrators, they and the officer, as well as clerks, sheriffs, cleaning help, and who knows who else could record a judge's contact information. Administrators and the office of the chief judge and presiding judges then had no sensitivity to the security dangers. Seeing my contact information on the wall sent a shiver up my spine then and even now when I think about the recklessness.

Physical assault was not the only assault I hadn't anticipated. I was at a social event with my wife shortly after becoming an associate judge when a women confronted my wife. We realized she was the wife of the then 8th Ward Alderman, James A. Condon. She told Maureen that unlike her, Maureen did not have to field telephone calls at all hours regarding sewer backups or flooding basements. The Condon family members were deserving, unlike Maureen and her husband, who became a judge at age 31, without paying his dues. Maureen was startled. She remained silent until we were alone.

About five or six years later, the Condon's son became an associate judge while in his mid 30s, but that must have been fine with Mrs. Condon since they were entitled. I did not ever know why she resented us. In the next election he was replaced as alderman by William Cousins, an Ivy league-educated Black lawyer who later also became a judge. Unlike Condon, who was a close ally of Mayor Daley, Cousins was an ally of Alderman Despres and a gadfly pain in the neck to Daley.

When I represented the city and police officers accused of civil rights violations in federal court, Condon, while serving as an alderman, brought suit against the city and an officer. I always questioned his conflict of interest, but was told to defend the city and officer as best I could. I understand his son did a great job.

Now regarding Cousins, before he was an alderman, he was an active practicing attorney. He appeared before me at 51st and Wentworth on a Monday, and found himself before me at 89th and Exchange on a Tuesday, and before me at 61st and Racine on a Wednesday. I think he thought I was stalking him. I had no control over my assignments, filling in for sick or absent judges. He saw there was no escaping Jordan.

I do recall getting a call from the judge assigned to 61st and Racine, Howard Miller, a Black man, who was sworn in with me as an Associate Judge. He told me that since he was running for circuit judge in 1976 and did not want to call attention to his race, he wanted me to take his call the next day. There were racially sensitive cases coming up in his courtroom. He would absent himself and I would probably get a call from the court administrator. We hung up and shortly thereafter I did get that call and then presided the next day at 61th and Racine when not only Cousins was there, but cases stemming out of White racist marches and violence in Marquette Park. Those arrests fed into this courtroom.

A Neo-Nazi named Frank Collins was one of the defendants. A special prosecutor, Raymond Grossman, was assigned that day by the states' attorney's office. He advised the clerk to call Collins's case using the defendant's name given to him at birth—Cohn—since that was his legal name. Yes, this want-to-be Nazi was a self-hating Jew. His father, Max Simon Cohn, was born in Munich. He was Jewish. He came to the United States and married a Catholic woman, Frank's mother. When the case was called, his name, Cohn—also known as Frank Collins—was called. He flew into a rage. Grossman then asked that he be examined by the court psychiatrist. I so ordered and continued the matter until the court had the results of the examination.

Collins's public defender made a jury demand, so his case was transferred to Branch 46 downtown, where misdemeanor jury cases were heard. It was refreshing to know on his next appearance he would be seeing Judge Charles Durham, who happened to be Black. Sometimes justice does prevail. I later had the opportunity to be in the Justice Lodge of B'nai B'rith with Ray Grossman. We became friends. Years later we each experienced training in better getting in touch with one's emotions. At the last courthouse I served during my judicial career, in Skokie, I was hearing some criminal cases. Many times, I had young defendants before me on charges I realized stemmed from their resorting to drugs or excessive alcohol use due to poor self-esteem or immaturity. I connected my own experience in college having too much liquor with their experiences and tried to be understanding.

There were many sentencing possibilities for both felonies and misdemeanors that allowed me to sentence with conditions, when satisfied, that would result in a clean slate for the defendant. Most of these defendants were young men or older immature men, but sometimes they were women. I required an evaluation before sentencing and, where appropriate, provided for their entry into a physically and emotionally challenging program through the Mankind Project or the Women Within. Both not-for-profit entities accepted the defendants that I referred. I always took into consideration my own one-time drunken experience.

Most of those I sent fulfilled all conditions and went on to a productive life. Some instances of recidivism did occur, but less than for the general population. The problem cases were brought before me as violations of their supervision, conditional discharge, or probation; but usually the men and women came back only to successfully terminate their supervision, conditional discharge, or probation. It was much more common for these defendants to thank me and state how they wished they could give me a hug, unlike other defendants who merely walked away. After I retired, I received some feedback from lawyers like Ray Grossman who would tell me how clients I had put through the program had turned their lives around with family, friends, jobs, and community.

Speaking of getting delayed feedback from a lawyer reminds me of a most challenging child custody case I had. A custodial and loving Black mother died and her 9-yearold son, Nick, was claimed by his mother's mother, his biological divorced father, and by his mother's last live-in boyfriend. The biological father lived in Virginia and the grandmother and boyfriend were in Cook County.

The law regarding a custody fight always prefers the biological parent so long it is in the best interests of the child. In this case, I had a concern the grandmother may be too old and a male figure might be best for a young boy. Yet, I was not entirely comfortable with the father. I knew this case would be difficult to decide. I decided to appoint a lawyer for the child so I would get an indirect channel to the boy.

I also interviewed Nick in my chambers in the presence of the court reporter, with the parties' lawyers at a distance so he would feel free to confide in me. The lawyer I appointed was a classmate of mine from law school, Irv Polokow, who I saw interact with his own children. I trusted him and respected his judgment. He was in the banking arena as a trust lawyer and was adept at serving as a fiduciary; I knew he had the right instincts I needed to uncover this boy's best interests. For the time he put in, he got peanuts in compensation. Irv gave me much more than he got. He certainly was not enriched by my appointment.

With the input Irv and Nick gave me, and the evidence I heard, I was uncertain it was in the best interests of the child to yield to the legal preference entitling the biological father to custody. I decided to grant the biological father temporary custody only and set the matter for a status to either enter a permanent order of full custody or, if the future events proved it was not in the best interest to keep the status quo, to explore options.

Within a short time, the arrangements began to reveal themselves as needing change. Nick was being isolated from his family and friends in Chicago. Letters and cards were intercepted by his father. The grandmother's telephone calls were refused. Nick was unhappy and no longer thriving in school. A hearing was set up promptly and I found it was not in Nick's best interest to remain with his biological father. I learned that the boyfriend no longer had any interest in Nick, learning that he would not necessarily be in control of Nick's inheritance. The grandmother and grandfather were still healthy and interested, so I awarded them full permanent custody.

When the grandmother's lawyer appeared before me on other cases, he said Nick was doing well. He would update me regularly, so I learned the young 9-year-old Black boy became a Harvard Law School graduate. I have a great sense of fulfillment knowing that he graduated from grammar school, high school, college, and Harvard Law School. Whenever I think of him and the ultimate success of his placement with his loving grandmother, I feel thankful. I hope, pray, and trust that Nick will live a full and happy life due to the nurturing of his loving grandparents. I only wonder about the many other children whose lives I changed hoping for the good but never knowing if I erred and they suffered as a result.

It was always my belief that two great parents would contest a child for custody and my choice was between good and better, but more often, I found the choices were bad and worse. In many custody cases, one parent would claim the other was a drunk, a drug addict, or a child molester or was guilty of other bad conduct. Sometimes both parents made similar claims. It was difficult to sort out the truth to make the right decision. I always felt that child custody cases were so much more important than anything else I did since it was like imposing a lifetime sentence to be with a parent who could either ruin the child's life or enrich it with love and support. I did not feel the weight on my shoulders as much in serious criminal cases. There, the odds were that if a defendant was found guilty beyond a reasonable doubt, he did it and the real issue was the type and weight of the penalty. If I was off, they personally put themselves in the predicament, unlike a child in a custody case who did nothing.

When I had a child custody case pending before me, I was insufferable at home, wanting to talk about the details to flush out the facts in my own head. My wife and especially my own two children suffered from hearing too much. I needed to contain myself. I had the responsibility; they did not have to endure the stress and strain. I regret that and apologize to my family.

Other Interesting Divorce and Family-Related Case Histories

Sitting in divorce cases provided me with many interesting stories. Some of these stories were unbelievable. One of those cases that stands out in my memory involved a doctor going through a divorce. He had insisted that his wife have surgery on her vagina to better fit him and his needs. He belittled and berated her until she complied, but then he was unhappy with something else. Her self-esteem was destroyed. She should have sought a divorce years before she actually found the courage to act.

Another case led me to learn what may not have been disclosed if I were hearing a medical malpractice case. Again, another doctor, a surgeon, was involved here. He was constantly under the influence of alcohol. After his surgery procedures, calls from the hospital would come into the family house in the evening regarding the care and treatment of recovering patients. Since the wife knew he was too drunk to get to the phone, she claimed he was in the shower and would convey the facts and then relay his orders. She said she knew what he would do from other calls when he was sober, so she acted as though he said what she then put out as his orders.

I had to learn enough about the customs of families coming from different backgrounds and heritages to make decisions as to which custodial parent would have custody and who would made decisions regarding religious, medical, and educational issues. One case I decided involved an Orthodox Jewish family. I heard testimony that a young boy, while in his mother's custody, was brought to the synagogue by her, but since males and females were seated separately, he was not allowed to be with his mother once inside, since he was already nine years of age. He was seated with men he did not know. I felt it would be best to assign custody to the father, since custody with his mother did not really afford him time with her, and time in synagogue was a tremendous part of their lives.

Religion arose as the major issue in another case in Skokie where both of the parties filed a case with briefs attached to the pleadings and did so at the Skokie courthouse on the condition that I would be assigned to hear the case and rule immediately. Clearly there was judge shopping but both parties actively participated! The lawyers had an agreement that they wanted a chancery matter heard by me after their research on the case and on me led their clients to believe that I was the best available judge to consider the issues. I put on my chancellor's hat and acted with dispatch as best I could. An Orthodox Jewish woman had died and the immediate issue was whether she should be buried or cremated. Orthodox Jewish custom and law required burial and not cremation. The woman had written an instruction that she wanted to be cremated. One child wanted to honor her wishes, while the other child wanted to follow Jewish law. Each side called a family member and a rabbi and tendered the briefs. They all wanted my decision immediately since Jewish tradition requires an immediate funeral and her body was waiting.

The facts were clear. I learned that she would not be the only one of her own siblings to have been cremated. She made it clear that this was what she wanted while she was of sound mind. One rabbi explained the Orthodox Jewish law required burial but conceded that Judaism and its teachings—*Halachick Law*—also has the tradition of following the law of the land. The law of the land in Illinois required that I adhere to the expressed intent of the deceased if the intent was clear while the deceased was able to know the facts and make an independent decision. I took only a few minutes to deliberate and made my decision that she be cremated. Both parties cried and then hugged each other and left the courtroom to fulfill her wishes.

The lawyers had two draft orders prepared and the prevailing lawyer handed me his draft order, already approved as to form by the other side. I signed it and my clerk stamped and entered the order. The lawyers shook hands and left. I think the lawyers and perhaps the parties knew what the outcome would be, but preferred to have the decision in a judge's hands rather than their own. I think the family felt comforted to have a judge they must have known was Jewish hear their very sensitive matter and perhaps knew I had some knowledge of the religious law as well as the civil law. While I would not want anyone that I know to have a cremation, I was duty bound to follow the law, which required me to honor the clear wishes of the deceased made when she was competent.

I spoke about this case many times, since it tested my beliefs and their conflict with the civil law. If I had recused myself, the parties would have faced delay that no one wanted. If someone not familiar with basic Jewish law heard the case, the trial might have been extended. It was not quite out of necessity which is a reason to hear a case, but I felt they needed for me to proceed and act promptly. I recognized that they brought this Chancery case to me in Skokie. Many Jewish people might say, "It was *bashert*" (meant to be) for me to hear this case, but they did pick me. They knew I would follow the law and respect the need for immediacy.

I did not feel threatened by that last case or by any case, at least not to the extent I might have been had I not had a year of being a roving judge hearing many different types of cases. This was just another unusual case. I was assigned the second year on the bench to be available to go anywhere and hear anything. Since court watchers had made adverse reports about courtrooms being underutilized and the new chief judge, Harry Comerford, who succeeded Judge John S. Boyle, wanted courtrooms used even when the assigned judge was on vacation, I was assigned cases out of the Presiding Judge's office of the First Municipal District and assigned courtrooms throughout the Daley Center to use whether for a bench trial or a jury trial. I heard cases of all types.

12 GROWTH

My Experience Widens and Deepens

During my rotating assignment, my first products liability case was a challenge, but fortunately I had excellent lawyers on each side. Their briefs were a primer for me. From that case on, I could preside over other product liability cases with some sense of ease. I heard a professional malpractice case and was guided through it again with suburb lawyers. I heard unemployment fraud cases with the attorney general's office involved and learned a new area. I found myself in the post judgment room for collection and satisfaction of judgments learning about citations to discover assets, garnishments, attachments, confirmations on confessions, everything excluded from the subject matter in my procedure courses. I learned the specifics about evictions. I learned about ejection matters. I heard personal and property damage claims. I learned about subrogation matters.

Every day was a new day with a new type of matter for me. It was during this period that I was sent to misdemeanor and preliminary hearing courtrooms. I even did a few days in marriage court and learned many different ceremonies. It was a challenging time. I felt I was back in law school, but nothing was theoretical; everything was real. The lives and fortunes of real people were at stake. Later, when I retired from the bench and people would call me regarding a case for mediation or arbitration, I could honestly say I had tried such a matter. I had experience. I realize that that year was the best opportunity for training and career development I could only have dreamt of having. Later, as I would get permanent assignments for an indefinite period of time, I could become more experienced in a subject and even expert to a degree.

During my year of roving assignments and later in permanent assignments, I got to meet my judicial neighbors on various different floors in the Daley Center. Some judges were quite friendly and helpful when I had problems, while others were quite distant. One of my former supervisors in the Corporation Counsel's Office, Allen Hartman, was assigned for a while to hear the odd numbered non-personal injury jury cases in the First Municipal District. Next door to him was another friend, Daniel Coleman, who heard the even-numbered cases.

I had the privilege to be assigned to their courtrooms when they took vacations. At that point, each judge presided over all motions pertaining to their cases, conducted pretrials for case management and settlement, and conducted the jury trials, or bench trials when a jury was waived at the last moment. Each day in those rooms about 50 cases came up for trial. About 45 of them required more discovery or had some other issue before both sides agreed they were really ready for trial. Therefore, there were about five cases ready for trial and only one judge in the courtroom.

The goal of the sitting judge was to quickly settle at least four of those cases and then try the one remaining case. If more than one case was ready for trial, the ones that could not be handled by the assigned judge had to be farmed out. If the other judge hearing similar cases had settled all of his cases, he could take one. If they both had a surplus of ready cases, the court administrator was contacted and ready cases could be sent to an available judge if he or she had a courtroom available.

When I was a floater that first year, I was assigned many of those cases and heard them in the one of the courtrooms made available when judges were on vacation. It was a juggling act when I was in those rooms and I admired both judges for their even-handed temperaments, moving everything along without people feeling like cattle. It has to be understood that many of those cases took more than a day to try so that on the second day of trial, there were another 50 cases with usually another five cases ready to go. I quickly understood why there was a need for so many unassigned judges.

Sometimes I could not be used to take those overflow cases, especially when I lived on the south side and was needed to cover an open criminal branch court on the south side. I did know that once I started a jury trial that I would not be pulled out to cover a criminal branch. If I had a bench trial, I could be pulled out and the trial would be continued—to the chagrin of the lawyers, litigants, and witnesses. Experienced lawyers knew this was the system and not my fault. The administrators tried to minimize this disruption as much as possible. I saw how necessary I was to the successful flow of court cases.

There was one occasion when I was assigned a jury case and I was told to use an open courtroom. After the jury was selected, I received notice that the judge would be returning the next day and was told of another open room to use the next day. That case found itself in four different courtrooms before it ended. The assigned sheriff's deputy was tasked to remind the jurors where to go the next day. I was amazed that we did not lose even one juror during the course of the trial. I always gave thanks to jurors for their service, but this jury got special thanks for the challenges they faced. I tried to keep Maureen aware of where I was each day in case of any emergency. Friends found it next to impossible to reach me for lunch or to visit, since my location was not well known.

Perspectives

In my first ten years especially, all of the other judges were much older than I; some were old enough to be my grandfather. When I was in traffic court or misdemeanor courts, the officers were usually much older than I. During my last years assigned in Skokie and when I heard traffic or criminal cases, I had somehow gotten to be older than most of the officers. Likewise, in the beginning, most of the lawyers were my age or older, but in the last years I found more and more were younger.

The place where I found the most contemporaries was in the post judgment collection courtroom, where winning plaintiffs came to court for assistance in collecting on their judgment; that is, getting the judgment paid. It was a high-volume courtroom requiring about eight court clerks to process all of the files. Over 90 percent of the matters each day were routine, but the rest had some interesting factual and legal issues taking more than a third of the time.

Even the largest and most prestigious law firms had lawyers assigned to collection. They were usually the youngest lawyers. I, therefore, found that I was older than many and was able to guide many to avoid mistakes. To my surprise, years later my patience and mentoring paid dividends. I found those lawyers who made their first career motions before me or tried their first cases before me remembered my patience and fairness.

When I left the bench and began to mediate and arbitrate cases, these formerly young lawyers were now the partners and managing partners in their firms picked me for their cases. At many bar association events, it was common that someone I did not recognize would come over and mention that his or her first motion or trial was before me, and they appreciated my help and the atmosphere I created. I know my own first jury trial was before Bernard Decker in the United States District Court in Chicago. At the end of the trial after the jury ruled in favor of my client, I thanked Judge Decker for his fairness and for helping to make my first jury trial a great experience. He gave me the best compliment, saying he had no idea that this was my first; he thought I had many under my belt. Just as I had always remembered him, I suspect many lawyers never forgot me when they appeared before me early in their careers.

In Cook Country, unlike smaller counties and circuits, every sort of case I heard had a different group of regular lawyers in the field, whether it was for traffic, misdemeanors, felonies, forcible entry and detainer, collections, divorce, personal injury, business, or commercial. I found for each area of practice there were some very scholarly lawyers and then there were others less skilled. In the divorce practice there were lawyers who appeared to have a large volume of small uncomplicated cases, and then there were some who handled a smaller volume of cases with high value assets to be distributed and much property to be evaluated.

In the divorce arena, the low volume-high value cases were handled by the best skilled trial lawyers who were knowledgeable about tax consequences and other important factors. These lawyers were in a national organization known as the National Academy of Matrimonial Lawyers. They had a peer review program to accept new members who were invited, passed a test, and had a minimum number of prior cases as a threshold for membership. Lawyers in one city would refer cases to Academy lawyers in another city. In Chicago each year the Academy had a formal dinner dance welcoming their new members and celebrating the accomplishments of existing members. They extended an invitation to each judge sitting in the Domestic Relations Division hearing their cases. Their annual event was one to anticipate each year.

I found in every area of law, there were very intellectually challenging cases for me. In collection, the legal assistance foundation and legal aid clinics raised novel legal and constitutional issues for their clients. Those clients were unfortunate enough to be sued and their lives were usually in shambles, but they were lucky to have found the offices and the diligent lawyers assigned to them. When the regulars in collection court who represented retail merchants, doctors, or other creditors came up against these hard driving young idealistic knowledgeable lawyers from the legal assistance foundation or the legal clinics and saw the writing on the wall, they wrote off the loss and settled. The hard-nosed less pragmatic and less knowledgeable lawyers fought and created precedent that hurt not only them but other lawyers who wanted to avoid the adverse precedent.

Most of the collection lawyers knew you could not get blood from a turnip and made agreements with the debtors for a fair amount to avoid a lengthy process with no monetary results. The debtors always had the possible nuclear weapon of bankruptcy at their disposal. Every day, judgment creditors came before me and moved to stay all proceedings, since there was a pending bankruptcy in federal court and they were enjoined to go forward. After I sat in collection court for several months, I had the opportunity to see most of the issues and understand the process. I was asked on several occasions to speak at bar association meetings regarding what a young lawyer should know about collections. I usually titled my speeches in a way to reflect that getting a judgment is not the real goal. The real goal is satisfaction of the judgment—getting payment.

Using My Experience to Help Others

After a few years of service in the high-volume courts in the First Municipal District, I saw some reoccurring problems that I felt needed attention and solutions. I went to my Presiding Judge, Eugene Wachowski, who gave me his blessing to pursue solutions to as many of the problems as possible. One issue I noticed involved those people living at the bottom of the economic ladder. Those living in public housing because of unemployment, family illness, or other catastrophic reasons were being evicted because they could not pay their rent. They would become homeless unless there was an intervention.

I knew from my time with the City of Chicago that when property was condemned for highways, school construction, or other public projects, the city's planning department had a relocation service. I invited the relocation unit to use the conference room of my courtroom where evictions were heard to help the evicted tenants find shelter. That project was very successful for many years. I was proud of the achievement and the safety and emotional comfort it brought to many.

When I was in the collection court, I saw that many people had debt caused by illness, since they owed doctors, hospitals, and funeral parlors for their unexpected expenses. Little could be done since no one plans on illness and death, and when it happens, people at every income level can be pushed to the limits of their means. However, for those living beyond their financial capacity and buying on credit, education and counseling were necessary to understand which purchases were necessary and which were indulgent.

I convened a meeting of several social welfare agencies—federal, state, local, and private—that provided public service and legal aid for the underprivileged. My intent was to create a program on financial and legal counseling. I worked with future mayor Jayne Byrne who was in charge of the Chicago Department of Consumer Weights and Measures; Chris Cohen, who was then the regional head of the U.S. Department of Health Education, and Welfare; a representative from the Illinois Department of Agriculture and its extension center; and Catherine Ryan, a lovely lady from Legal Aid at the Mandel Legal Aid Clinic affiliated with the University of Chicago.

A program was developed that caught the attention of many thousands of people. The program was known as the Consumer Counseling Service. It received publicity with television and radio public service announcements inviting people to avail themselves of the free service. I was overwhelmed by the cooperation of all of the agencies I enlisted, of their representatives, of the media, and of the public who trusted us in using the services. I will never know the number of people saved from more severe financial hardship, including bankruptcy, that they may have otherwise incurred without this program.

The Illinois Supreme Court's Judicial Conference created a committee to study high volume courts. I was one of about nine judges statewide asked to study the functioning of those courtrooms and to make recommendations. First, we had to identify which courts were to be included in our study and then make recommendations. Over a period of a few years, we issued a report with hundreds of recommendations for the court system and individual judges to implement. We included the courts where many people have their only contact with the system. We included the traffic courts, small claims courts, criminal misdemeanor courts, post judgment courts having citations and garnishments, and eviction courts with forcible entry and detainer cases.

Some of the recommendations were very simple and cost nothing; others were more complex. I think the most important recommendation for the public was to have every judge make an opening statement so that those in attendance would understand what was going to happen and what their rights were. The judge should tell the people the process and the persons they would interact with besides the judge, such as the clerk and the sheriff's deputy.

Those summoned to the courtroom could be advised of the available legal resources and could be given a list to take away when they left. A most important recommendation was a reminder to each judge that each was the administrator of her or his own courtroom, and unless he or she acted as an efficient, capable, and understanding administrator, the flow of cases and people would be inefficient and the administration of justice would be inhibited. A judge who did not monitor the performance of the court personnel assigned to his or her courtroom may allow corruption, favoritism, or inefficiency.

The many recommendations we made were approved by the committee that had appointed us as well as the Illinois Supreme Court and were distributed to every judge in the state. The members of the committee discussed everything in the book and each of us had responsibility for a particular chapter. There was great consensus among all of us, whether we were from Chicago or a rural downstate area.

In those days, 1974 to 1980, all downstate judges were regularly assigned to Chicago for several weeks each year. What assigned rural judges may not practice at home, they would practice in Chicago. The first visit of a rural downstate judge would not be as daunting with their Court-created bible in hand—the handbook report with its recommendations.

I had developed a strong professional relationship with all of the members on the committee plus our two liaisons from the coordinating committee and our research assistant. I had worked for our chair, Judge Irwin Cohen, when I started as a prosecutor in Chicago's Traffic Division in the Law Department. I met Judge Roland J. DeMarco, the vice chair, and would see him year to year at judicial conference meetings or when he came to Chicago to serve.

Judge Francis Barth and I got to be friends and I felt at ease calling him from time to time, particularly in the years when Governor Dan Walker was governor and the state was in dire financial straits and our paychecks were not always timely. Frank and I both needed the checks to live on, unlike the many judges convicted of corruption during the Operation Greylord investigation and prosecutions by the FBI, who considered the state pay as petty cash. When the two of us failed to get our checks in a timely manner, it was stressful. If one got the paycheck, the other's check could be lost.

Also on the study committee was Edward W. Kowal, who later as a circuit judge became the chief judge of DuPage County. We would stay in touch for many years. Judge Emanuel A. Rissman, from Cook County, was an older experienced man who was like a kindly grandfather who shared his wisdom always. Judge David Costello was not usually able to attend our meetings in Chicago for lunch at the Covenant Club, so I have little recollection of his participation or where downstate he served. Judge Milton S. Warton, from Belleville near St. Louis, always brought a perspective of the poor, undereducated, and scared litigant based on his empathy and kindness. The two judges serving in the role as liaison, Judge Charles L. Quindry from downstate and Judge Everette A. Braden from Chicago, participated fully in all of our proceedings and were a great source of information and inspiration. I later served with Judge Braden in Domestic Relations.

His brother used to appear before me in the southside criminal branch courts.

The committee's research assistant, Professor Edward J. Schoenbaum, from Springfield, kept a record of our actions in his minutes. In later years, Ed and I served many years together on both the Bench Bar Section Council and the Alternative Dispute Resolution Section Council. We made presentations together dealing with mediation and arbitration at many seminars, and he helped me with a power point presentation that made it appear that I was quite professional. My assignment to that committee was very illuminating and allowed me to develop great relationships throughout the state that lasted for many years. I believe our service on the committee helped create a closer connection to our court system for many citizens around the state.

My father Ben Jordan, my father-in-law Harry Pearlman, Alderman Claude W. B. Holman, and my brother-in-law Jerry Landy's maternal uncle, Barney Ernstein, at my stag party the week before my marriage to Maureen

13 11:00 AM

My Installation as a Judge

I recall it was about 11:00 AM, April 1, 1974, the time for my installation as a judge. I had arrived with my wife, Maureen; and our parents were all there. Since our daughter was just an infant of 16 months, we decided she would have to miss this historic day. She stayed with a neighbor friend who had a little boy in her play group. My son was not yet born. I noticed in the crowd many former office mates, a few relatives, and countless strangers who must have been there for others being sworn into office.

There was one special guest I had invited. I had appreciated any help he may have given me. I did not know but I suspected that he may have made a few well-placed calls of support for me. Ultimately, all of the opportunities I had in his administration where I met his appointees who helped me so much, I attribute to him. I had called "the mayor" and invited him to come to the installation, speaking to his secretary. I gave the date, the time, the room, and place, saying with the short notice I would understand his having other commitments, but would love for him to be able to come.

To my great surprise, Mayor Richard J. Daley showed up. Seeing him, I knew I had been his candidate—or at least one of his candidates. My good friend Dan was there too. Mike was in Springfield working with Wolfe, yet I thought of him with gratitude. My great friend, Claude W. B. Holman, had died the year before. I knew he was with me that day as well, welcoming his friend, Richard J. Daley. True friendships are important and can sometimes last beyond death.

I was so grateful that my parents were both able to attend and experience the great joy of seeing their son achieve this position. My sister was in Miami, Florida, where she lived, and was unable to get to Chicago in time. I thought back then as I sat with the other soon to be judges and reflected on my life to this point, asking myself how Michael Stephen Jordan got to be in this seat. I thought back to the motivations of my ancestors to come to this country to avoid religious persecution, to find economic security, and to help raise their children in a better environment than they had in Europe. They wanted better for their future generations. They wanted the American dream. I was the descendent living out their dream.

I thought of my Grandpa Hymie Kritzer, who came to this country and then brought his father, stepmother, brothers and sisters, and the woman who would be his wife—my Grandma Celia Lisagor. I thought of his uncle who had sponsored his arrival in New York to pave the way for the others. As a teenager, I met my grandfather's uncle in New York, then in his 90's, shortly before his death. I never knew how he got here, but I was very grateful. I met Uncle Meravankin's daughters and granddaughter.

All of my ancestors who immigrated to America struggled with English and worked to become citizens. They all found their way, helping each other, and made their children feel comfortable finding economic security so that my generation could more easily become professionals rather than store keepers and factory workers. My success came on the backs of my ancestors on my mother's side and on my father's side. While my father became a lawyer, he had worked in a grocery store to bring home food. His father was a tailor working long hours to support his large family as best he could.

My father had said to me that he knew I did not have the money to buy the position, so I had to have made some really great friendships and earned the respect of many. My father rarely expressed his emotions, but I knew that besides loving me, he was very proud of me. My mother could not find enough people to tell, and thereafter, I was always her son, the judge.

Years later in December 1990, after my father died, my mother was at a beauty parlor when a horrendous snow storm overcame the area and traffic was interrupted. Nita was a lady who drove her to the shop and waited with her. While they were waiting, my mother met another lady her age who began telling my mother about her family. The woman said she had a son who had become a lawyer and my mother said likewise. The other women said her son had become a judge and my mother said her son also became a judge at 31 years of age. The other women said her son only became a judge when he was about 36 years of age. My mother, I surmise, felt she won the competition.

When I heard the story and learned who it was, that judge and I said our two mothers had much in common although one was Italian Catholic and the other Jewish. They each shared the same pride and enjoyed the experience, forgetting they were stuck for several hours in this small beauty shop. They focused on the chance to tell of their pride in their sons. They bonded in a way and gave me and the other judge a connection. Daniel Locallo and I shared the story more than once after both of our mothers had died.

I sat in my assigned chair in front of the bench where Judge Wachowski would preside. I was in one of two rows with my fellow inductees. My thoughts drifted away with thoughts of my life to this date. I could only imagine the events that would transpire in my future; but really, I could not even come close to imagining the highs and lows and challenges of the future.

Rather than trying to think ahead, I reflected back on my life in the few moments I had, as a drowning person in seconds has their entire life go before them. I had thoughts of so much of my life flash before me in this happiest of occasions.

Who am I?

My grandfather Hyman Kiritzer's "Uncle Mervankin" who sponsored his entry into the USA shown with his four daughters: Rose Levy, Doris, Sylvia, and Leah Mervankin, and granddaughter Marsha Levy Lazurus O'Toole

I was born on a Tuesday in the Spring of 1942 during World War II while Hitler and his fellow thugs were killing Jews as fast as they could. They were happy to also kill communists, gypsies, gays, artists, writers, democratic leaders, and all those standing in their way to conquer and control the world to allow their kind—Aryans—whatever that was—to reign on this globe. I was born at Henrotin Hospital on North LaSalle Street in Chicago to Benjamin and Sally Jordan. Ben was born in Philadelphia and Sally was born in Princeton, West Virginia. I add West Virginia since no one would assume a Jewish person came from West Virginia. Philadelphia, everyone knows, is in Pennsylvania.

My father, the oldest child of seven, and his younger brothers and sisters were brought to Chicago by his parents, Max and Ida. Max was a tailor who was tall and pleasant and well groomed. Ida was the homemaker who showed no emotion and would only allow her daughters to place a little touch of lipstick on her for rare occasions, like a child's wedding. She was quite superstitious and would never tell the names or ages of her children to anyone. There had been an older son who died in infancy. Infant mortality was common at the turn of the 20th century. My first name, Michael, was selected since I was given Max's Hebrew name, Mendel. He died in 1939, a few years before I was born. I was given the second name, Stephen, in memory of Ida's mother Sula, so my second Hebrew name was Sholom.

Eight days after I was born, when my family brought to the house a mohel who completed the Jewish covenant with the Almighty by having a briss, I was given my Hebrew names. Fortunately, I do not remember a thing that day, including even the good food that must have been served to all my family in attendance. When I was old enough to take care of my important documents, my father gave me the certificate signed by the mohel. That was my second certificate in recognition of a major accomplishment after my birth certificate and the only times I got a certificate or diploma without a lot of study. One might say, it was a breeze with beginner's luck. While I have preserved my briss certificate, I realize that no one has ever asked to see it.

I know a couple of my uncles were not present at my bris. My mother's younger brother Abe was in the navy with his duty station in Panama. He later told me he would have been going on after more training to land in Japan if we had a land war in Japan, and that he and at least 250,000 American troops were probably saved by President Harry S. Truman dropping the atomic bombs on Japan. The United States had to do it twice since the Japanese emperor, Hirohito, did not surrender when just one of his cities was destroyed. He fought on until the second city was hit. Hirohito was the 124th emperor of Japan. My uncle was always convinced that Truman saved his life. Thank you, Harry Truman! Uncle Abe Kritzer lived until he was over 100 and was always a guest in our house for holidays after my mother died. He would regale us with stories of his war experiences.

One of the many stories he told us that stands out in my mind was when he was in the Panama Canal Zone serving temporarily as a Navy military policeman, doing shore patrol duty. He saw some young sailors acting up after having too much liquor. He stopped them and admonished them for their foolish conduct. They apologized and he did not pursue the matter further. His supervisor learned of the event and felt my uncle committed a crime by not arresting these boys in uniform. He put my uncle in the stockades for dereliction of duty, making some remark that you Jews are all alike. Fortunately, an officer higher up countermanded the arrest and my uncle was released. My uncle learned that while we were fighting the Nazis, we had a few like-minded knuckleheads in our own ranks. He resumed his normal responsibility of being a supply officer after that brief duty assignment.

I learned that my father had something to do with the development of the atomic bomb. My sister has had a plaque on her walls since our parents died attesting to the fact that our father, Benjamin Jordan, was honored by the Secretary of War for his efforts and actions in support of the Manhattan Project. When I was born, my father was about 36 years old and he was assigned by the War Department to serve undercover in intelligence and monitor the scientists working at the University of Chicago at Stagg Field under an Italian born scientist, Enrico Fermi, and his team of physicists trying to develop atomic energy and a weapon to stop Hitler and his allies as well as Japan and Italy.

My father and his higher-ups were charged with insuring that no spy, saboteur, fifth columnist, or loyalist to the enemy succeeded in infiltrating our labs and getting any of our secrets. After successfully developing the weapons' grade materials, tested in New Mexico at Los Alamos, the military delivered the bombs and devastated their targets. Later, in the 1950s, we learned that some Russian spies had succeeded and had uncovered our secrets in spite of my father's best efforts. My father was only one man and had to take breaks. It must have been on one of my father's breaks that the secrets were stolen.

Speaking of breaks, my father found it always convenient to have lunch at home. It was rare not to see him when I came home for lunch. My father, of course, was at my briss. My mother said he never had a job where he couldn't come home for lunch. She did make a great lunch. I would even bet that they served lunch after the briss was over. How many men serving in the armed forces during World War II could serve full time, but come home for lunch and be at their son's briss? We were very lucky. My mother sometimes complained that it could be a nuisance.

During the depression, after my father was licensed as a lawyer and his clients could pay only in barter, such as art work or furniture, he had to take a detour to support his wife. He took a job at my grandfather's grocery store at 28th and Cottage Grove. My grandfather had opened a store close to where his family lived, in the Armor Apartments that are now part of IIT. The grocery store was not so far away. Besides my father, my mother and a cousin worked there. One day they were the victims of an armed robbery. All of them were forced into the meat cooler. After the robbers left, they could not get out since the handle on the door was only on the outside. There was a small window and my family could see customers come and look around and leave. One customer saw one of the family in the small window and opened the door and asked if they would be out soon. They all escaped freezing from the cold. No customers looted the store while they were locked in the cooler. It was generally a great neighborhood. Once the economy picked up and they all took out some of the profits, they could give up the store and make investments with their shares.

My Uncle Reuban also missed my briss, since he was stationed in Asia. He caught tropical diseases, had malaria, and the effects lasted for many years and affected his hearing. Wherever he was stationed, he found decorative spoons and sent them to my parents. His father had died and his mother lived with her sons and daughters on a rotating basis. My father was the oldest of seven children—five boys and two girls.

After the war, my mother mounted the spoons on two boards and had them framed with a glass cover. They have been in my house since my mother died in 1999. My father died in 1990. I offered the mounted spoons to one of Uncle Reuban's sons, but he never followed up on my offer. Maybe he felt his older sister or brother should have them, but I offered them to him since he was still local while his sister Susan had moved to Arizona, where she was the executive director of a nursing home, and his middle brother had moved to Minnesota. In any event, I still have the spoons that are beautiful to see, and they remind me of our family's contribution to the war effort. Our family was typical of American families making great sacrifices to support the war effort.

I was taken home from Henrotin Hospital on North LaSalle Street to 5210 South Drexel Boulevard, where my parents and sister Gayle had been living for a few years, after moving from 5005 South Drexel living with my mother's parents, Celia and Hyman Kritzer, and my mother's sister Esther and her husband Milton Epstein. Gayle was the first grandchild on either side of the family and she was adored by all. My parents lived with the family for a few years while Gayle was very small, but then moved to 5210 S. Drexel. Gayle was the flower girl for at least one of my uncles when he got married. Gayle was deservedly the constant favorite niece and grandchild on both sides of the family not just because she was first but because she was so loving.

Eventually our small apartment at 5210 South Drexel became too crowded with my basinet, crib, high chair, buggy, and other paraphernalia. Among my pieces of equipment was also a buggy. I heard stories how people pushed me in the buggy at Drexel Square near the fountain at Hyde Park Boulevard and Drexel Boulevard. I thought the fountain was placed there so the local pigeons had a place to drink. My mother pushed me with another mother, Mrs. Ruth London, the daughter of a woman my grandmother Celia knew, Mrs. Edwards, who pushed her son, William. Years later in 4th grade, I met Billy London and he was one of my friends in grammar school, Hebrew school, and high school.

In any event, due to the need to move and the opportunity to have a larger apartment in the same building my extended family lived in, around the corner, we moved to 917 East. 50th Street on the first floor. My mother would lament that our apartment was over the coal bin, since she felt she could never clean enough. The building had 24 apartments on three floors with two entrances on Drexel and two entrances on 50th Street. The basement in our apartment building connected all the way around. My grandparents, aunt and uncle and later cousins lived on the Drexel side on the third floor. Our entrance was one of the two on 50th Street facing K.A.M Temple, now occupied by Operation PUSH.

My First Companions

By the time we moved to our new apartment on the first floor with two bedrooms and one bathroom, my Aunt Esther and Uncle Milton had a son, David. He was a year and a few days younger than me. The family all got together for every holiday, religious and secular, and by the time we were two and three, David and I played together in our apartments. When we were a little older, we played in the back yard with other boys and girls our age. One neighbor in the entrance next to mine, Warren Weisberg, was David's age. Later, they were in the same grade in school. I was a year ahead. We all went to Charles Kozminski Elementary School at 52nd and Ingleside.

Our apartment was larger, but it only had one bathroom. When the four of us were coming home we had to negotiate who needed the washroom quickly and who could wait. If someone was going to be really quick, they could go first but for anything longer they had to wait for the urgent ones. I learned in our negotiations that full and honest disclosure was necessary and consideration to the needs of others was very important. The difference between interests and needs was useful later in mediations. My father taught me early in life to use the washroom whenever it was available, since one never knew when the next opportunity would present itself. He had experience as one of nine in his household. As I got much older, that lesson came to mind very, very, very often.

When I started kindergarten, my mother took me the first day, but after that my sister Gayle took me by the hand until I had to enter through the boys' entrance and she through the girls' entrance. Since she is almost seven years older than I am, when I was in kindergarten, she was in eighth grade. The next year when she went to Hyde Park High School, I led David and Warren to school. I felt like a bigshot their first day. After that first day, they knew the way as well as I did.

When we came to Drexel Boulevard and Hyde Park Boulevard, a very busy intersection, there was a police lady who served as a crossing guard. I asked her why she had to wear her heavy jacket when it was hot out in early September and she told me she had no choice unless her Captain allowed her to wear a lighter uniform. I thought that was quite unfair and that whoever her Captain was, he had to be quite mean.

I saw that there were a lot of people passing through that intersection, so when David, Warren, and I decided to make some money by having a lemonade stand, I knew the perfect location. We did not even have to cross the street. Between the three of us, we could carry a pitcher of lemonade made by one of our mothers, a sign showing the price, paper cups, and a crate to hold everything. We were in business and even sold a few drinks. What we didn't sell, we drank, so there were never any wasted drinks.

As a small kid, I never felt I had to develop friendships in school or elsewhere, since there were plenty of neighbor friends in my back yard. Someone always suggested something to do. It might be a baseball game in the adjoining back yard, steal the flag in the front yard of a Korean church next door, Simon says, or just riding our tricycles around the block.

Halloween was always a treat. The mothers in the building had us all gather in the part of the basement in the middle of the building, where washer tubs were used by us for bobbing for apples. We walked into the darker part of the basement to hear strange noises from a monster, who we learned was a neighbor boy about four years older than us. His name was Billy.

All of the children went trick or treating around the block of our apartment building. Around the corner, once we passed the "haunted house" at 50th and Ellis, there were many homes and most had their lights on, welcoming us as we came. Each house had treats better than the one before. Laid out in front of us on trays were every type of candy, cookie, and brownie. Without much effort, we could all get awful stomach aches for several days with the amount of candy we took in our bags. In those days there was no talk of razor blades in candy—or of being careful and staying away from strangers. Anyway, there were seven or eight of us going together. No one mentioned that the house at the corner of Ellis and Hyde Park Boulevard was the home of Bobby Franks, who had been murdered by Leopold and Loeb not too many years before. We were innocent. We only heard stories about the haunted house and believed the neighborhood gossip of other older children.

In the summer, we went to South Haven, Michigan, where my grandparents had a small resort with stand-alone cottages. No food was supplied, so people prepared their own food except when they went to a large resort or to a downtown restaurant. We ate my grandmother's delicious cooking in the big house. My mother rented out the cottages, calling repeat customers in the winter to assign weeks for each cottage. I went to the beach most days and loved playing in the sand and swimming in beautiful Lake Michigan. In the evening, we could see the sun setting over the beach. My grandparents' place was called Kritzer's Sunset Beach.

On rainy days, kids like my cousin David and I would play board games or cards. We played a lot of war. When cousins stayed in the cabins, I played with those cousins as well. David's grandmother on his father's side had another small resort several blocks closer to town, where he stayed with his mother and sister. We could walk to see each other without crossing any streets. Our fathers would come and see us on weekends. The traffic in the 1940's was slow, with no superhighways. The two-lane roads were usually backed up with slow moving trucks and horse-drawn wagons or tractors. We all had our share of sunburns, but I got used to wearing shirts and having a towel over my legs. Once you have a bad sunburn, you don't want another. Generally, we loved the time spent there. My grandfather sold the place in about 1949.

Thereafter in the summer, David, Warren, and I were sent to Playmore Day Camp. A station wagon picked us up and took us to Avalon Park at 1215 East 83rd Street in Chicago. It seemed to be quite far away, but we did not care, since we sang many songs along the way. At Avalon Park we were in groups of nine to ten kids with a counselor for each group. We played games and had great experiences. Usually, we brought lunch from home, but sometimes we were taken to a restaurant as a treat. One of the owners of the camp, Chris, sometimes hid watermelons around the park, and the winning groups could share a watermelon. It did not take long to realize that Chris hid one watermelon per group so everyone was a winner and there were no losers.

Each day at camp we were taken by car for swimming. On rainy days we went to George Williams College, a school for gym teachers, that was located across the street from my grammar school, Kozminski. We sometimes used their gym as well. On nice days we went to Green Lake or Wicker Park to swim and had a fun time. Those summers passed by quickly since we had so much fun.

When we got older, David, Warren, and I went to a YMCA overnight camp sponsored by the Hyde Park Y. It was Martin Johnson in Irons, Michigan, a very long ride by bus. The first year we went, they had just opened new cabins that were beautiful. There were three camper villages for the youngest, the next older, and the oldest campers. The first year I was signed up for just one month but when my parents came up on visitors' day, they asked if I wanted to stay longer and I said yes if I could have a few more pair of underpants, since I was running low. My mother said she would send more as soon as they got home and put my name labels on them. The nice part of staying for the second session was that with a smaller number of kids, we had special activities. We were taken to the town to a roller rink and treated to ice cream. It was special and my tastes were very simple.

At camp, we could take classes. I took boating, canoeing, sailing, swimming, rifle range, archery, and crafts. I also became a junior life guard. We went on overnight trips with our cabin mates, either hiking or by canoe. On rainy days or during rest breaks, we played games like submarine. The campers in the cabin could decide upon activities for certain periods of time. Sometimes we decided to make a campfire and tell ghost stories while we ate snacks, or agreed on doing our laundry, or taking a slow leisurely group shower. Somebody suggested and everyone usually agreed.

The second year I was at Martin Johnson they opened the camp to girls, so the village for the youngest was now the girls' village and the other two had the younger and older boys, respectively. During my third and last year that I was at Martin Johnson, I moved up to the Pine cabin for the oldest boys. The year before, my cousin Spencer Jordan, who is about ten months older than me was in Pine. We saw each other and several other cousins and friends. It seems like all of our parent's friends told each other so that friends' children were all at the camp together with my cousins.

My cousin David's younger sister, Andrea, came to the camp the second year they had girls. She was about three years younger than David. With my first and second cousins on both sides, there was no chance of being home sick. Basically, my friends and family were with me at camp. If I were home, I might be lonely. The second year, my father came up to see me. He brought another cousin who stayed with him in a cabin on an island for the night. My father said my cousin Howard should enjoy even a few hours of the lovely experience.

Moving from Hyde Park to South Shore

In late summer of 1951, my family moved again. I found out later that our apartment building in Hyde Park was being converted into smaller apartments by the real estate manager, Baird and Warner, for the owners. I would always wonder how they could make the apartment into smaller livable units. There was only one kitchen and one bathroom. The front room could be divided but it would become two narrow rooms if each had a window. The back bedroom was next to the kitchen but separated from the bathroom by the dining room. Maybe our apartment would be merged with the neighboring apartment so the fronts and the rears could be realigned, but I could not see that working either, since none would have more than one entryway and that didn't seem safe. In any event, we were out and I never returned to see how they did it. I did return years later with my wife and children to show them where I grew up and the back yard that we played in. To my amazement, the back yard had shrunk. I could not figure how we did anything back there. While I showed them the windows to my apartment, we did not venture to ring the front door bell or knock on the back door. I did learn about perspectives useful in mediations.

We moved to South Shore into a first-floor apartment at 7524 South Essex Avenue, in a six-flat with three floors. In a few weeks after moving, I would be enrolled in Myra Bradwell Elementary School at 7710 South Burnham. Gayle would be going into her third year of high school at South Shore High School at 7627 South Constance. We finally had separate bedrooms. Later I wondered how my teenage sister could endure having her nine-year old brother with her when she was turning sixteen. My bedroom was much smaller but a few years later when she went to college, I kept my bedroom and also could use hers, especially when I had a friend sleep over.

Mr. Abe Ring was the owner of the building we moved into and was the neighbor next door to us on the first floor. On the second floor was Rabbi Fox from South Shore Temple, followed by the Terwiliger family. I still remember when Rabbi Fox's body was taken away in a hearse. For weeks I felt an eerie feeling walking down the steps from our front door to the outside exit, where I knew they had taken his body. The adult male in the Terwiliger family was a doctor working at Michael Reese Hospital. I think they were from the South, since his wife, a very friendly women, had a strong southern accent. In the other second floor apartment was the Sax family. They had a daughter a year behind me in school. She grew up to be a director at the Jewish Federation for Chicago.

On the third floor were the Goodmans. The mother had died, but the father had a daughter, Rachel, a semester ahead of me and her two older brothers Eddie, a Chicago policeman, and an even older brother who had already moved out. The other third floor apartment was occupied by the Pritikin family. The father was a foot doctor. The mother had been a Rockette dancer in New York City. Their oldest son, Jimmy, was about a year ahead of me. He went on to be a divorce lawyer and appeared before me on many cases many years later. Their middle daughter, Carol, was a year behind me in school. She was a lovely singer. All of the bathrooms in the building faced an inner court for ventilation. When she sang in her bathroom and our window was open, we could hear her lovely voice. Their youngest daughter was Beverly, five or six years younger than me.

A few years after moving to South Shore, when several of my close friends skipped from the February class to the June graduating class before eighth grade, a couple of my other friends went with me to summer school, the summer before eighth grade, to keep up with the others and also be able to graduate in June of the next year. We found that the only summer school we could attend was Phil Sheridan Elementary School in South Chicago. It was quite a distance requiring a train and a bus or three buses or a car ride.

I learned that my upstairs neighbor, Carol Pritikin, was going there to get ahead and take the last semester of sixth grade and she would be going with a classmate of hers, Jackie Spitzer, who lived on the block next to ours at 75th and Kingston. Jackie's father was driving and there were only three seats taken. I asked if I could be included together with my good friend Lawrence Weprin, who was a few blocks away. Mr. Spitzer agreed and we traveled together in his car each morning with every seat taken. At the end of the summer, to show our gratitude, Carol, Lawrence, and I gave Mr. Spitzer a dress shirt. Lawrence Weprin became Larry in later years and that's what I call him when we speak. He became a head and neck cancer surgeon in Dallas, Texas, where he lives with his wife, Brenda Kaplan, who also lived on Essex, although they did not have the time of day for each other in those days when we were all living on Essex Avenue.

On our return trip from summer school, we took the three buses or the IC train since we did not have a time schedule to worry about. We felt we had safety in numbers being together, although in those days we were young and did not see ourselves as vulnerable kids riding with many potentially dangerous adult strangers. Guns were not a concern in those days. On our first day of classes I saw another classmate from Bradwell in our class, Lee Chalmers. I felt bad that there was no room for him in the car. We went back with him for sure. I don't know if he wondered how we got to school or if he knew, but did not want to say anything. Years later Lee and I remained friends.

The first time our seventh grade summer school teacher at Phil Sheridan, Miss O'Toole, gave a test, a boy behind me who I believe was several years older than me and was over a foot taller, told me to make my paper visible so he could copy it. I felt threatened and did not want to antagonize him, nor did I want to get caught cheating. I got through the test and made it home, where I told my parents, who found a way to call the school and reach Miss O'Toole. She told my mother that she would take care of everything and the boy would not know I told her what was happening.

The next day in school, Miss O'Toole announced that now that she knew who everyone was, we no longer had to sit in alphabetical order. We would sit according to height so everyone could hear her and see what was going on in the front of the classroom. There were 48 seats in the classroom, typical of most all Chicago classrooms, with six rows of eight seats. There were 49 students, so the tallest boy would be at the table at the front where he could stretch his legs.

Miss O'Toole was so discreet, so caring, so protective, and so creative. She gave me security and I was grateful to this day. The boy never realized why there was a change in seating and he had to study and survive on his own merits. I learned that working through the "system" was usually the best and that my parents could be very helpful and proactive on my behalf. I learned a lot by that experience. I had a meaningful encounter with a bully and found a peaceful way of dealing with the bully. On the last day of summer school with the eighth graders having graduated that day, Miss O'Toole asked me to go to the principal's office five minutes before the end of the school day to push the bell for adjournment. I was proud to go down to the office, and at the signal of the secretary, I pushed the bell and heard it ring throughout the school. I then met my class as they descended the stairs and I became an eighth grader.

I found my way back to South Chicago in high school when Schmegglers, my high school fraternity, had teamed up with a sorority to give a dance and raise money for a charity. The charity picked by consensus of the members in both groups was Muscular Dystrophy Association. The spokesman for the charity was one of my childhood favorite comedians, Jerry Lewis. He called the beneficiaries of the charity his kids. Others said they were Jerry's kids. All members of both groups did what they could to raise as much money as possible. I drove to 91st and

Commercial in South Chicago several times and stood on the corner with my hand out holding a can marked for the charity. The people there were very kind and generous. I felt so good that I was getting my can filled so easily and seeing so many nice people in such a short period of time.

The boy in my seventh-grade class at Phil Sheridan was not the only boy who tried to bully me. I was walking south on Essex Avenue from my house towards my friends to see if anyone was available to play. I think it was a Saturday afternoon. As I reached 76th Street, I heard footsteps behind me sounding closer and closer and then heard the breathing of someone. I glanced over my shoulder as a boy was approaching me. I saw a slightly older unknown boy as he caught up with me and said he needed some money from me. I told him I did not have any money, but was going to a friend who owed me money. I was going now to see if he was in. He stayed very close to me as we continued to walk south and passed 77th Street. Fortunately, I saw a friend, Ed Kallish, approach me after we passed 77th Street. We were about 12 buildings away from my friend's building. Since this boy was so close to me, he could not see me move my lips to mouth "HELP!" as we approached Eddie.

Ed was a year ahead of me in school. He often played hearts with Lawrence Weprin, Larry Lichtenstein, Ronnie Opper, Billy London, and me at Mickey Pinchuk's apartment now just a few doors south of where I was walking with this boy at my side. I did not see what Eddie did or where he went, but within a very short time, I saw him follow Mickey and his older brother, Jerry, who was carrying a baseball bat while holding the leash of their German Shepard dog. They were racing towards us from the entrance of their apartment building.

The boy fled, being greatly outnumbered and not wanting to be mauled by a dog or hit by a bat. If only he knew their dog, King, would most likely lick his face and wait to be petted. Ed was totally winded. He had run into a gangway to the alley in back and over to Mickey's building, and up the steps to Mickey's apartment two flights up, yelling for help; and they were fortunately available to respond immediately. In less than a minute they came to my rescue. Ed was clearly bright, understanding, resourceful, and fast-thinking, and he cared for me and my safety. We could all laugh about it afterwards. I felt very grateful to Ed. Mickey, as an adult, changed his name to Parke, as his older brother had done years before. To new acquaintances, he was now Michael Parke. I still call him Mickey, which he said is fine with him.

After Ed graduated from high school, I did not see him again for over 30 years until he appeared before me as a lawyer on several different felony cases in the Skokie Courthouse. The first time I saw him I knew I would have recognized him had he not identified himself for the court reporter and even if I had not seen his written appearance. His head was shaved, he had an earring in one ear, and seemed different. Eddie told me that he was gay and had been in different circles for many years. I learned years later that he died, and I felt like a part of my past had died with him. Eddie was probably the first gay friend I knew who came out to me.

At a pre-hearing conference with him and the assigned assistant states' attorney meeting to find an agreeable disposition on his client's cases, I disclosed our previous friendship in grade school and high school as well as my continued gratitude to him. The prosecutor said he felt I could and would be fair and there was no need to put our childhood experience on the record or to recuse myself. He said I will let the two of you talk a few more minutes about your earlier times. I asked Ed who he saw and he asked me who I saw. I don't believe I ever saw him again. While Ed saved me from one bully, there would be others to encounter.

Another Bully

Another bully was someone in the class ahead of me in high school. We had many mutual friends, but I choose to keep my distance after an incident when I was about 16. My friend Lawrence Weprin asked if I wanted to go with him to Riverview, a large amusement park in Chicago at Western and Belmont.

The place closed in the 60's and was replaced by a police station and courthouse, where I served for a few days. We had all gone there for many years as children. Since Lawrence had his driver's license, he could drive. He had his family's car that day and could pick me up at a certain time. I said yes.

When Lawrence picked me up, I jumped into the front seat, and he said he had a couple of other stops, telling me who was also joining us. The next stop we picked up someone I also knew, who jumped into the rear seat behind Lawrence. We went to the last pickup and I saw Howard come over to my car door and tell me to open it and get out. I asked why and he said so I could sit in the back and he could take the seat in the front that he wanted. I quickly said I would be happy to have him trade with me on the ride back and he made clear that he would have the front seat both ways or else. He was much bigger than me and I was no fighter. Lawrence whispered to me to let him have his way. I listened to my friend and opened the door and moved to the rear. I realized it was best for me to maintain a distance from him in the future. Sometimes with bullies, flight is better than fight, especially if they are older, bigger, and stronger.

Lawrence, Billy London, Jim Andrews, another high school classmate, and I were to share a room together on the junior year trip to Washington D.C. sponsored by the high school. I learned that Howard would be on the trip when I saw the list of those going. I figured I could keep my distance. The day before the trip, I got a call from Lawrence telling me he got the chicken pox and could not go. He had already called the class sponsor, Mrs. Betty Feldman. There would only be three of us in the hotel room. I would miss Lawrence. I wished him well and told him I would tell him about the trip afterwards.

We took a train to D.C. in a coach car. The train traveled through the night and after a while everyone tried to sleep. It was difficult sleeping while sitting, but we all tried. Howard, however, gave up quickly and began walking up and down the aisle. He made every effort to knock into everyone's elbows and shoulders to keep as many people awake as possible. It just couldn't be an accident and he laughed and joked about it when people complained how tired they were the next day.

I rarely saw him after that trip, which was great in spite of him. Years later, when I organized lunches for our classmates at Max and Bennie's Delicatessen in Northbrook, one of the classmates, Lyle Felsenthal, who would play golf with Howard in Scottsdale, Arizona, saw him in the restaurant and brought him over to say hello. Other times when I spoke by telephone to Lyle while he was golfing with Howard in Scottsdale, he would put Howard on the phone to say hello to me. Likewise, another friend, retired judge Michael Zissman, when he was in Scottsdale playing golf with Lyle and Howard, he would put Howard on the phone. I don't know why they thought Howard or I would want to speak to each other. I was sorry to hear their friend died. I just did not want to socialize with him or be in his company. Those were not the only bullies who challenged me in my life. I will discuss another when I discuss Operation Greylord later.

When we completed our eighth grade at Bradwell, Larry, Lawrence, Billy, Ronnie, and I wanted to learn what to expect in high school. We thought we were coming of age. We all had our Bar Mitzvahs the previous year and each of us attended the others' services and parties. We went to Ronnie's apartment on Yates Avenue and his cousin, who had just completed his freshman year, was there to tell us everything. We were fascinated. We learned that we were all expected to take gym and that swimming was included as part of gym, which was great to me, since I was good at swimming, unlike my poor performance in other sports. His cousin said we did not need a swim-suit, since we swam in the nude. He said the first day is uncomfortable but after that everyone seems not to care. He warned that after showering before going to the pool, we would walk through a narrow corridor and the metal rods on each side would squirt us with cold water. We figured better forewarned than surprised. In those days all gym activities were separate for boys and girls, including health class.

We learned that we had only four minutes between classes, so planning our path to classes was important and we needed to have the necessary books with us to avoid too many trips to our lockers. We would share a locker for our coats and books with probably two other boys and it could get pretty crowded, especially in winter with either a musical instrument, art supplies, gym shoes and shorts, and other things. The girls in our home room division had separate lockers.

Ronnie's cousin spoke about some of the teachers he had his first year and told us about activities and groups he knew about that we might be interested in. It was a useful afternoon and made us all much more comfortable. We knew there was an early lunch at 10:30 AM and a late lunch at 1:15 PM with two other lunch periods in between. Sometimes there was no choice, but sometimes we could have a choice. The freshmen were usually the last, sophomores next to last, which was great, and juniors before, a little early, but the seniors were too early at 10:30 AM. Some seniors had job opportunities their last year and with earlier classes and early lunch, it worked out for many who wanted a few hours in the afternoon for work.

We learned we could volunteer to be registrars after our freshman year. Registrars are allowed to register first before anyone else, and all desired classes with desired teachers as well as lunch are open. We could all arrange our classes together and get lunch when we wanted with gym before and not after. Starting our third semester we were able to be registrars. We all picked other activities and some were assigned to us.

I became the Tide yearbook salesman for my home room division each of the four years. Every group or activity at South Shore had a nautical theme so it was not unusual for the yearbook to be named Tide. I was in band for a year to satisfy my music requirement, but I stayed in band another semester. We played at assemblies. I dropped band after that third semester, since I knew I did not know what I was doing. I was assigned to play the baritone horn that makes a sound like a trombone, but is bigger and bulkier and was a pain to carry home on occasions when I needed to practice.

I was assigned the baritone horn after I placed poorly on a music tone test that Mr. Gorbach, the band teacher, gave the first day of class. Those with a high score picked their instruments first and those with the lower grades were afforded a choice of the leftovers. If you had your own instrument, you were allowed to play that instrument. I neither had an instrument nor a good score. I did not get stuck with a tuba, but the baritone horn was almost as bad. Phil Reed, a classmate in my home room, was the other baritone horn player. Boy, I envied the flute players!

My friend Larry Lichtenstein played the trumpet and my close friend in later years, Michael Grossman, also played the trumpet. Sitting near me in band class was the trombone section and I got to know and like a trombone player, Joel Zemans, who became one of the star athletes for the school. I met Joel the first day of school and saw him in my band class, gym, and Spanish classes as well. We both noticed that we would be seeing a lot of each other that semester. I learned of the good character that Joel possessed even at that time. When he saw me come up to the gymnasium from the locker room before the teacher called the class to order, he invited me to shoot baskets with him. I did not know he would be the best player in our school and one of the best in the city when he called over to me. He certainly did not know of my lack of skills.

Joel and I shot baskets for about five minutes before class started. The next day events repeated themselves. Joel could have been quiet, pretend he didn't see me, or invite others, but as soon as he saw me, he called over for me to again join him, now knowing I was terrible. I came to learn he was a really nice person who did not know of any way to be mean. I always had pride in his accomplishments. He went on to play varsity basketball in college when he attended the University of Chicago. When Maureen and I were looking to move from our small apartment in Hyde Park, he urged us to move into the building where he lived in Hyde Park. He had studied finance and was working for a bank.

When we moved, Maureen and I decided to relocate to Glenview instead of staying in Hyde Park. I knew his company would have been great. Joel had been the treasurer of our high school class reunion committee for many years because he was liked, was trusted, and was generous with his time. At a certain point, other issues took his attention. I suggested Stan Leon, who I knew from grammar school and who was an accountant and a nice and decent person as well to take the job of treasurer. Stan, like Joel, was also a banker. I am hoping COVID-19 will end someday soon so the remaining funds in our treasury can be spent with a lunch or dinner for the survivors in our class.

I was thinking more about being placed into band. I think the South Shore High School registrar who came to Bradwell when I was in the last months of eighth grade had to find enough people to fill the beginning band class and when she heard I was interested in music because I liked to sing, she clung onto the music part and moved me to band. I did enjoy the classmates I found sharing the same experience; and the teacher, Mr. Gorbach, was nice and reassuring. I would have preferred chorus with no instrument to carry around.

During the four years of high school, Larry, Lawrence, Billy and I would walk together to school as we had done while in grammar school. Ronnie Opper moved to Pill Hill at around 93rd and Jeffrey Boulevard during our second year of high school, so he no longer walked with us. Somehow the school learned he moved out of the district and had him transfer to Bowen High School during the second year. It seemed unjust.

On some cold school days, as we were walking to school, one of our nicest teachers, Mrs. Audrey Watson, a math teacher, would stop her car and offer us a ride. We took her up on her offer several times. She said she had to drop us off a block before the school came into sight since it might look like she had favorites if someone else saw us getting out of her car in the teacher's lot. She was one of many very kind and decent teachers. She was a great math teacher as well.

One of my other teachers, Mr. Ralph Becker, was an inspiration to me. He was a history and civics teacher. He took our questions and then fired back a question to the questioner to hone in on the point. He encouraged discussion and debate between classmates on an issue, better reinforcing the pros and cons of issues. As a result of his teaching methods, he instilled in me an interest in the institutions of our government and a need to serve the community. Years after his retirement, I found a way to thank him and contacted him with an invitation for lunch. I took him to the restaurant across from the Metra Station at the Glen in north Glenview and expressed my appreciation for his service as a teacher and a motivator for me. I hope I made him feel good; I knew it made me feel great to share my gratitude and thanks. I let him know that his teaching was not only educational but was inspirational and motivating for me.

I didn't know that several years later our democracy would be placed in jeopardy by Donald Trump and his insurrectionist testing and challenging of every facet of our constitution, attempting a coup. Trump showed us the weaknesses in our governmental institutions. Unfortunately, his enablers have made things worse and have not acted to protect the guardrails of our democracy. In history I learned how a democracy in Germany had yielded to the brute force of Hitler's henchmen moving quickly from a democracy to an autocratic dictatorship. In the beginning, every judge, lawyer, and citizen could have stood up and spoken against tyranny, but spines disappeared. Lawyers and judges acquiesced when Jews were removed from the bench and bar based solely on their religion. Edicts of the Third Reich were not challenged. Everyone was afraid to say the emperor was naked. I see now how easily our democracy could be destroyed and a despot put into office. Time will tell if spines will develop in the backs of certain Republican party leaders. A few Republicans have risked their careers and their personal safety to stand up against the lies being fed to the public that election results cannot be trusted and that Trump had not been defeated by huge numbers.

Since the time when I went to high school, most school districts around the country have sadly eliminated civics from their curriculum. I wish sounder minds would put that course back so all students can see the importance of our institutions and how fragile they really are. Already there are some successful demagogues advocating that many controversial books be banned in schools and libraries. Others are urging that history be distorted to only show how great we have been to each other rather than expose the truth regarding hatred and discrimination in our past as well as in the present. I hope our American experiment in democracy will prevail.

Unlike Mrs. Watson and Mr. Becker, some teachers were awful. They were not awful due to their politics but due to their inability to teach and their inability to be fair and make proper character assessments. One such teacher was the only physics teacher in the school, Mr. Oscar Mongerson. He would face the blackboard and mumble. No one heard or understood a word he said. I told my parents I needed help since the teacher was not teaching. Somehow my resourceful parents found Mrs. Benedict, who lived near the public library and within walking distance of our house. I realized she was the mother of a classmate in my physics class. She would help from time to time with classes or chapters I couldn't understand. Somehow, with her help, I got through the class and passed.

Her son was clearly very bright, but he was very quiet—perhaps shy. I do not know if I ever had any conversation with him in high school. At our 50th reunion, we encountered each other and spoke. We probably said more to each other then than ever before. I told him how helpful his mother had been to me in physics. He seemed to appreciate my compliments. I learned that after college, he returned to teach at South Shore. I hope he found his voice.

When I needed to take physics in college, I was afraid of the poor foundation I had from high school. I decided to take physics in summer school at Roosevelt University. The teacher, Mr. Shelton, was a great teacher, and while I did not shine in the class, I seemed to understand what was going on. In my class was my friend Lawrence Weprin, who was with classmates of his from the University of Illinois, who were all in pre-med. Also, I saw someone I knew from my high school fraternity, Schmegglers. George Shuster was a year ahead of me in school. After he was absent from class a couple of days, I received a call from his mother saying he had mono and would like to come over to borrow my notes of the classes he missed. I agreed, but warned that my notes probably were not as good as his had been and definitely would not be as legible. She came and returned them the next day. He came back to class a week later and struggled to catch up. I lost touch with George and always hoped he became successful in life. He was always very conscientious and kind.

I had no animosity for Mr. Mongerson. He was a bad teacher, but I did not know what sort of a person he was. There was a teacher who was a bad person. Miss Roach taught second year English class, when we studied Silas Marner, written in 1861 by English author George Eliot. The book was rich with many themes and various symbols referring to the claimed theft of gold involving a weaver. Miss Roach gave me a D for my best efforts since I did not see or appreciate enough of the symbolism. I accepted my grade as being fair after I learned from classmates of the many points I missed.

When I received my course book at the end of the semester and saw the anonymous cumulative character evaluations made for me by my teachers that semester, I was astonished, disappointed, and bewildered. I asked my home room division teacher, Mrs. Loraine Harris Patinkin, who told me she was not allowed to tell me who gave me a check for being deficient in dependability and in reliability. I have always been both dependable and reliable. Mrs. Patinkin suggested I politely ask each of my teachers. She said I would be revealing to them that someone else saw me as lacking those character traits so I would be putting myself at risk in a way.

I had enough confidence that my character was clear and obvious, so I decided to probe and take the risk by asking my teachers one by one. I found almost all of my teachers saying they never would give anyone such a mark and certainly not to me. When I got to Roach, she was defensive, saying it was not my right to know. I decided to be direct and forthright and told her every other teacher not only denied doing so, but told me I did not deserve such a mark. I told her she was the only one who could have done it. She admitted it was her and she did it because I got a bad grade. I told her politely how unfair that was for her to not only give me a bad grade which I may have deserved, but to also attack my character in a way that I could not defend.

I said my grade has nothing to do with my character. I am dependable and I am reliable. There is no meaningful correlation between my poor grade and those traits. I studied as best I could regularly and consistently, but did miss the mark. I asked her to reconsider, but she refused, not really appreciating my arguments. I left with disgust in my heart and have held her in contempt in my mind ever since. I had done everything I could and yet failed to convince her, since she had her own agenda. I realize that I am far from perfect in my character since I cannot and probably will not ever forgive her for putting this mark on a 14-year old's permanent record.

To prove to myself ever after that I was reliable and dependable, I have gone out of my way to do more than has been expected of me. If that has been for the good, then, maybe I should thank her for motivating me to do more. If that is true, then even from bad or evil can come good results. I surprised myself that I was able to speak up to power and express my truth yet being respectful and firm. I did not feel a need to involve my parents as I had in seventh grade. I advocated for myself. There are many ways a boy comes of age and perhaps this was my way.

During my senior year, I asked my chemistry teacher, Mr. McClellan, to reconsider a grade he gave to me. We had a give and take as to why the grade should be raised. I gave him an accounting of my grades on quizzes, exams, and papers, and he said he was convinced and changed the grade. I thanked him and saw that with reasonable decent people, honest discussion can prove useful and result in change. I left high school with a high regard for Mr. McClellan's character.

Miss Roach was not to be the last person who I considered evil that I would have to interact with as I moved through life. I faced evil and greedy persons later in my career after becoming a judge. They did damage to the judicial system and to me personally. Throughout the time I worked in the Law Department of the City of Chicago, I had found only people who helped me in my work or in my career. That was also true in my part-time and summer jobs as well. When I came on to the bench, I had wrongly assumed the same would be true. I learned afterwards when it became public that an investigation by the feds had been ongoing for three and a half years that would prove beyond a reasonable doubt that many judges, lawyers, clerks, sheriff's deputies, police, and others found ways to monetize the judicial system, with some using me as a pawn. The federal government had initiated an investigation into corruption known by the code name Operation Greylord.

14 TRIAL BY ORDEAL

Operation Greylord

The Supervising Judge of the Traffic Division, in the First Municipal District, Richard F. LeFevour, built a network of corruption that earned him 12 years in the federal penitentiary. As the supervising judge at traffic court, he was the first supervisor for almost all new associate judges. LeFevour was put into that position by Chief Judge John S. Boyle. Boyle had been the Oak Park Township Democrat Committeeman years earlier, where LeFevour lived before either became judges.

LeFevour gave the public appearance of being a good government public official. He had been an Assistant U. S. Attorney in Chicago for the Northern District of Illinois, and he won several annual awards from the American Bar Association for the efficiencies in the Chicago traffic courts after he became the supervising judge.

LeFevour only installed in the courtrooms that heard drunk driving and reckless driving charges—the major rooms—judges he could trust, who were on the take and who would share the bribe proceeds with him. One of these judges, Allen F. Rosen, when discovered, committed suicide to protect his pension for his wife—the wife he had been cheating on with his affair with another horse lover who later became a judge herself.

I met Rosen years earlier when I was first hired by the city and placed in the traffic division as a clerk and then as a city prosecutor. I was going to John Marshall Law School's post graduate program for about a year after my admission to the bar of Illinois. In night school, another student heard I worked at traffic court and asked me about the strength of a drunk driving case. He wanted to discover if the case was worth taking. He was just starting his career and wasn't sure if the case was a loser or one that could be won. I said I only handled minor municipal violations in the minor rooms, but I would inquire.

The next morning in the corporation counsel's traffic court office where many of the judges stopped in for coffee or donuts that were always present before and after the court calls, I was asking someone who might know about a drunk driving case. Judge Rosin overheard the conversation and took me aside, telling me it could be a winner. Everything was possible if my friend took the case. I realized then that Rosin was in the major rooms for a purpose, but I had no real proof he was on the take or involved in fixing cases. I saw he was one of five or six judges regularly rotated through the three major rooms and he wanted to talk.

Later as a judge, I was never assigned to any of those three major rooms The judges, besides Rosin, who seemed to be assigned there by LeFevour, were Judges John H. McCollom and Paul O'Malley (the number one and two in charge, if LeFevour was off for a day), J. J. McDonald, David Shields, John Murphy, Michael E. McNulty, and Martin F. Hogan. After a three and a half years investigation, over 90 convictions were entered involving about 17 judges, 48 lawyers, and 10 sheriff's deputies, clerks, and police officers.

These were the same lawyers who appeared before me daily on minor cases and who I had to list as references for my upcoming associate judge retention in 1975. I saw LeFevour walking on the street one day with John Connelly, the President of the Chicago Bar Association, immediately before Connelly announced that the Chicago Bar Association was finding 12 associate judges up for retention unfit. That announcement was made the day before my interview with the judicial evaluations committee that found me unqualified. How could Connelly know there were to be 12 before at least one of the 12 had been interviewed and voted upon? There was clearly an agreement between LeFevour and Connelly. I realized LeFevour had directed the lawyers in his web to bad mouth me since I was not on his team. In fact, information given to me later disclosed that LeFevour told lawyers they should do business with him and his people or they would find themselves and their clients before Jordan, where there would be justice and he knew they did not want actual justice. They wanted to win.

One day before the annual judicial conference for all judges except associate judges and which the judges were required to attend, LeFevour told me, as an associate judge, to cover the three major rooms, but only give continuance dates and not to try any case under any circumstances. The day after the three-day conference, LeFevour summoned me to his office and was outraged. He said I had not followed his orders. I disposed of a case in a major room. I said I continued everything but there was one case where the lawyer, Andrew Raucci, working for Stanley Kusper, who had been the County Clerk before, and who I knew, wanted to dispose of the case since he knew it was clearly a loser. I took his plea and accepted the agreed disposition between him and the prosecutor.

I told LeFevour that I did not try anything as he directed. I merely accepted a plea agreement and gave all of the necessary admonitions. What I did not know was that every case, even a plea, was a money maker. The lawyer, Andy Raucci, had saved about $150. I had not known this until years later. Andy did not know he was saving money by entering a plea before me and not before a member of the LeFevour crew. I also learned that the only way their statistics would look realistic was if all the public defender clients and those of uncooperating private lawyers were to lose and get more severe sentences. There was no justice, but a lot of profit. There was gross injustice!

While writing this book, I had the chance to speak to Andy. I knew he gave great service to the people of our state, having served for several years on the Illinois Court of Claims working with my cousin David Epstein. I saw he was still licensed as a lawyer since being admitted a couple of years after me in 1968. I asked if he was still practicing law. He said he was not practicing law but he needed his license since he was asked by the Illinois Supreme Court a few years before to take charge of the bar admission process. He was in charge of the bar examinations. He said he was appointed shortly before COVID-19 showed itself and it has been a nightmare. Plans for bar examinations have to be made at least six months in advance of the actual testing to arrange for the site, the test, the proctors, and other matters. They moved to virtual testing and wish to have in-person testing again, but cannot tell what the latest variant will require. He has made a great sacrifice to administer the process and receive no pay, yet maintain his law license that requires the payment of an annual fee and taking the necessary courses to satisfy the required continuing education training hours.

Andy was a man of character and a dedicated public servant, but he was subject to the whims and bullying of people like LeFevour and Rosin. Andy told me that a few weeks after he had appeared before me and helped his client enter the plea on a drunk driving case, he had another client on the same charge appearing before Rosin. After a trial, Rosin found the man not guilty. About a month later, Andy had another case before Rosin. All other cases were completed for the session and the assistant states' attorney stepped out to use the washroom and the clerk walked away. Rosin then said to Andy that the case a month before could have gone the other way. He knew Andy was with Kusper so he let it go, but on second thought now he would probably find him guilty since nothing else happened. He then asked what Andy wanted to do on this case. Andy recognized a shakedown so he said he was filing for a change of judges.

Overcoming Corruption

With the help of many friends, I was retained in 1975 in spite of the illicit agreement between LeFevour and Connelly. I learned later how I was set up then by the man I saw every day. It was a gift every day Gene Nesgota had me assigned somewhere else. LeFevour used me many times over. Other judges, not in the crew, were rotated out of traffic court, but the first 4 years I was in 11 months the first stint, then 9 months, then 7 months, and then 5 months. I went repeatedly to Judge Wachowski for a transfer, and he kept saying how much LeFevour wanted and needed me since I was able to handle large volumes of cases better than the many judges much older than me.

I told him it was not fair. I deserved other opportunities. After the first 11-month tour, he did put me on my year of having the rotating assignment, which gave me more experience than ever and showed how valuable I could be out of traffic court. Once out of traffic for any period of time, I could list honest lawyers who would be contacted by investigators from the bar association and hear about the great things I was doing. My ratings for the 1979 retention were all good and my retention was recommended. In 1983 I was given highly recommended and recommended ratings, prompting me to seek slating as a full circuit judge in the 1984 election. I had tried in 1982 and had circulated nominating petitions on my own. After I withdrew my nominations, I was transferred at my request from the First Municipal District to Domestic Relations.

My personal conduct in circulating nominating positions for every upcoming countywide judicial position in 1982 led to legislative changes to the process. To be listed as a candidate, I needed 500 signatures of registered voters for each position I sought. It took months to get good legitimate signatures. To minimize the opportunities in the future to do what I did for anyone not endorsed by the party, the new law set dates before which and after which no petitions could be circulated. They also further restricted the process so one may not file for multiple vacancies and withdraw from all but the most likely winner. I realized that those in power were aware of my maneuverers. My friend, then the Speaker of the House, may have been the one to tighten up the processes. I knew he did not mean to hurt me and my future chances; he only wanted to maintain control of the access process for all and tighten the guardrails.

While I was transferred to Domestic Relations by the new Chief Judge Harry G. Comerford, I was given a courtroom outside of the Daley Center at 54 West. Randolph Street, in an office building with only my courtroom. It had been used for collection of nonsupport for women who were mostly on public aid, but eventually I heard all post judgment matters and later any assigned trials. I was assigned to this outpost courtroom during each stage of the transition.

When I began hearing post decree domestic relations cases, I could see all the mistakes and errors by judges signing ambiguous decrees drafted by the lawyers, later requiring clarification or modification. I learned what not to allow in decrees I would later enter. It was a good educational experience. When Presiding Judge Charles J. Fleck told me he would start sending me cases for hearing post decree issues, he said he would first send me the best lawyers so I could learn from them. At a certain point, he said he was no longer sending me the best. I had hopefully learned enough to have no need to blindly follow a lawyer who would try to mislead me. He did the same with the first trials.

While I was alone, I had the telephone and a great clerk, Wally Machos, and a great sheriff's deputy who had been a Chicago Police Lieutenant, William McQuire, until he retired and was replaced with Deputy Sheriff Bledsoe, another great public servant. The courtroom was larger than those in the Daley Center. Besides having private chambers, I had a nice conference room and there were more distant rooms on the floor the lawyers could use to confer or to interview their clients or witnesses. Although there were no windows allowing a view, it was great for trials, especially when I had multiple parties. I did have multiple contestants for custody as in Nick's case or when I had appointed lawyers for children.

After a year, I was transferred into the Daley Center, but given a jury deliberations room as my chambers and courtroom on the 18th floor. It was very uncomfortable. I had no washroom, closet, or any other amenities. My office supplies were all on the table. I kept the lawyers and litigants a few feet away on each side of the table. I did have a working telephone. The day of the shooting of Judge Gentile, I was in this jury room with two lawyers hearing their arguments on a case. We were told by the deputy sheriff that there had been trouble on another floor so we should stay put. We finished the arguments and I gave my ruling. We then learned what had happened. Judge Henry Gentile had been shot dead in his 16th floor courtroom—1610. I got a call later that afternoon from the Presiding Judge that I was being assigned to the room, 1610, where the incident occurred starting the next day. The police were conducting their forensic investigation in the room that day and evening.

When I came in the next day, I saw the wood chips on the floor from the wall, bullet holes or marks on the wood and blood stains on the carpeting. Learning that Judge Gentile was merely implementing my order in the Moore case and that it could have been me made me feel sick. My mind drifted many times that day and the days following as I heard other post decree matters. I moved into his chambers, finding everything as he left it before taking the bench the day before. I was working in a crime scene. I felt like I was intruding into his space and using his books, files, papers, pens, telephone, and close space and washroom. Why me? Yes, I had asked for a real courtroom and chambers, but not at the expense of another person. The presiding judge never told me how he selected me for this room at this time.

At a certain point a few weeks later, I received an order directing me and two other judges, Howard Kaufman and Bob Cusack, to report to 13th and Michigan for us to hear domestic relations cases there in that remote building. We replaced three judges who were being transferred to the Daley Center. I took the chambers and courtroom of Judge Julia Nowicki. She had as many shoes as Imelda Marcos of the Philippines. Julia apologized, but said with short notice of the transfer, she had no chance to move all of her things and she would drop by with her car over the weekend to take her things, which she did. The other judges to leave were an older man named Wayne Olson, and Barbara Disco, a very close friend of Judge Allen Rosen, who was now also assigned to the Domestic Relations Division. She was an officer in the Women's Bar Association and must have used her connections to get to the Daley Center to be closer to Rosin.

About another year later, I was again assigned a courtroom in the Daley Center and found that there were several questionable people in the Domestic Relations Division besides Rosin, like John Reynolds from traffic and misdemeanor courts, Judge Dan Ryan from criminal, and a few others. Some of those judges would take matters under advisement for a long time and the gossip was they were waiting for an incentive to rule a certain way. I decided to rule immediately in all of my cases, and I did so for a couple of reasons.

One, I did not want to give any impression I was fishing for and waiting for a bribe. Two, I wanted to dispose of the cases quickly while I had the facts in hand and as soon after I heard the evidence and arguments—usually after a ten-minute break or a lunch break. I knew if I waited longer, I would mix the facts of one case with another. It would not be any easier to make a decision later than sooner.

I heard that a man I believed to be honest was taking cases under advisement. I made it my business to visit Judge Willard Lassers, and told him my candid feelings and beliefs regarding a prompt decision. I told him I believed he was honest, and that he had to put daylight between him and some of the other judges. He thanked me. I do not know if he changed his habits.

One day, I received a call from Monica Reynolds, a lady I met years before who had worked in another division of the Corporation Counsel's Office. She was a judge and also worked in the Domestic Relations Division. She wanted to give me a head's up notice that I would be in the Chicago Tribune the next morning. They did a lengthy investigation of the goings on in the division. I was concerned. She reassured me. She said six of us were cited as being the best in the division. The two of us and Willard Lassers, Ben Kantor, Susan Snow, and the new presiding judge, Richard Jorzak.

A few months after that beautiful newspaper article that sainted the six of us, certain events began to unfold. Several of Rosin's cases were transferred to me after petitions were filed in front of Rosin for a change of judges. Those cases were all highly contested. I gave my rulings in them as the facts required. I then learned that while all of the bar associations issuing ratings on my judicial performance in my run for the Circuit Court gave me highly qualified or qualified ratings, the Women's Bar Association rated me as unqualified. That was the bar association where Rosin's close friend Barbara Disco had great influence. The judicial evaluations committee was chaired by a close ally of Barbara Disco. I learned later that Rosin believed, as the feds were closing in on him, I had given them information on his cases transferred to me. That was never the case. Those lawyers or parties would have no right or even opportunity to confide in me. Yet, Rosin must have believed I was out to hurt him and may have enlisted the help of his friend Barbara Disco. He may have feared I would remember and reveal the conversation we had years ago when I was a city prosecutor in traffic court.

It did look silly. The Chicago Bar Association rated me qualified. The Chicago Council of Lawyers rated me Highly Qualified and other similar ratings came from the Cook County Bar Association, the coalition of regional bar associations, the Arab American Bar Association, and the Asian American Bar Association. I also received the strong endorsements of the Chicago Sun Times and the Chicago Tribune besides local and neighborhood papers. The Women's Bar Association was an outlier due, in my opinion, to Disco and Rosin.

I was not only nominated in the Democrat primary uncontested, but to my relief, won a countywide race in spite of the huge 1984 Republican victory of Ronald Reagan as President of the United States. At the time of my installation, I again had a real courtroom in the Daley Center. My campaign treasurer was my friend Dan Pascale. My friend Mike Madigan allowed one of his secretaries to process all my checks for deposit and worked with Dan very closely, providing a mailing address. I had been running with a large group of judicial candidates. At the time the positions to fill were either countywide, which I sought, or Chicago citywide only—sure winners for Democrats, or suburban only—sure winners for Republicans. In the Democratic primary everyone running countywide initially had a challenger or two. While two candidates filed for the same vacancy I filed for, they both withdrew, so I was one of the few unopposed in the primary.

Several of those running countywide who were opposed lost their battles, including the other two Jewish candidates, but also the co-chair with me on our team, Mike Getty. Those running in the city wide and suburban only races were unchallenged and prevailed. The candidates running only in the city were unopposed in the general election so they easily won with just their own votes. Those on our team running in the suburbs all lost and since all were associate judges retained their existing positions. The countywide candidates all won. One of those who had defeated our candidate in the primary approached me the day after he was declared the primary winner and asked if I would introduce him to Mike Madigan, the state party chairman. He wanted to join the team and help the ticket win. I made the introduction. Thomas E. Flanigan served for many years in the Law Division with honor until he retired. He always asked me for my recommendations for voting on associate judges who might also be preferred by Mike. I learned that allies can be found where you don't expect them to be.

When I was a candidate for Judge of the Circuit Court in 1984, the leadership of the Democrat Party in Cook County was in disarray, split along mostly racial lines with a split between Harold Washington's Black and independent faction of 21 versus the White ethnic old guard faction of 29 led by then Cook County Democrat County Chairman Edward Vrdolyak and Demo-

Elect on Merit   Highly Qualified
MICHAEL S. JORDAN
Judge
of the
Circuit Court of Cook County —
Countywide

Vote Democratic
Tuesday November 6, 1984
Punch #138
Integrity ★ Experience ★ Courage ★ Independence ★ Ability

Handout Card used in the November 1984 campaign for election as a Circuit Judge in a countywide election.

In my courtroom following 1984 installation as a Circuit Judge with Dan Pascale and me preparing remarks as my clerk Wally Makos looks on as the guests are assembling coming from the ceremonial courtroom where I was sworn into office with all of the judges elected in the November election by the Chief Judge Harry Commerford. Rabbi Carl Walkin of Congregation Beth Sholom of Northbrook is sitting under the American flag.

The standup crowd in the entranceway to my courtroom following my installation in the ceremonial courtroom as a circuit judge in December 1984 with judges, lawyers, and friends including my friend Michael J. Madigan, Speaker of the Illinois House of Representatives

crat Committeeman Edward Burke. Their faction was known in the press as the Vrdolyak 29.

As co-chair of the Democrats slated by the regular wing of the party, I made every effort to unite both wings of the party in supporting our group. Those of us running had allies in both camps. We were successful getting Washington's endorsement for our entire group, bringing unity for the judicial slate. I was fortunate to be elected in the 1984 general election.

Becoming a Judge

The judges sworn in as new circuit judges in Cook County at the ceremonial courtroom in the Daley Center in December 1984, including me in the center of the second row, presided over by Chief Judge Harry Commerford

December 1984 installation showing Association Judge Michael S. Jordan about to become a Circuit Judge with others elected all about to take their seats for the ceremony

15 TRANSFER

Skokie, Illinois

In 1987, I was transferred to the Skokie courthouse as a swap with a judge in Skokie going to Domestic Relations. We took each other's court calls and chambers. The first day I was in Skokie, a man came into my chambers and announced he was my probation officer. I did not know I was in trouble. He said about once a month any person I place on probation on any criminal case I hear will be assigned to him and he will come before me monthly to terminate, extend, or violate probations depending on the conduct of the probationer. I received a visit from two others announcing they were the court officers who would alternate and appear on my motion termination call regarding all cases where I placed someone on supervision or conditional discharge reporting through social service. All of these people and their successors—or replacements when sick or on vacation or leave—were highly professional and had the court system's interest at heart in all of their actions. They would seek my guidance when there were issues to decide, but handled most things on their own. Several pre-trial service representatives also came to see me. They would review the backgrounds of defendants to provide useful information when I set a bond. I was impressed with these civil servants. I did not know if the system had improved or if the services that I observed were unique to District 2 for the northern suburbs.

Each month my assignment varied, so I would hear traffic and misdemeanor cases some days, child support cases at times, preliminary hearings, civil motions and trials, prove ups on divorces, and felony trials. One day I felt like a downstate judge hearing some traffic cases, a motion on a murder case, some preliminary hearings, some civil motions, and trials of cases that were filed in both the Law Division of the Court and the Municipal Department of the Court. It was great! The most interesting case was the one posing the question of whether to cremate or bury the deceased women I mentioned earlier. That case came from the Chancery Division of the Court.

I had the opportunity to try major criminal cases, including a capital murder case, as well as civil cases that were both personal injury tort as well as commercial. It was a dream come true and I was much closer to home, cutting my commute time. I was able to take my bicycle, which I kept in my chambers, to the forest preserve bike path and go south to Chicago or north to the county border, passing through the beautiful Botanical Gardens in Glencoe. I could easily access the health club during lunch or after work. I motivated a couple of other judges to put their bikes in their chambers and when schedules were compatible, we rode together. Sometimes, when I was alone, I visualized plots for murder mysteries revolving around the bike path. Nothing came of any of my contrived fantasies for novels.

The capital murder case I heard involved a defendant named Montero, who was accused of brutally killing a disabled man with his own cane, which he broke while hitting the man. The killer used sharp pieces to stab the victim. Unfortunately, there were no eye witnesses. There was plenty of circumstantial evidence. No fingerprints were found at the scene or on the weapon except the victim's own prints. Strangely, the defendant had no fingerprints. They had been burned off when he used a grill as a short order cook. He was, however, seen in the area before and after the probable time of death. The prosecutors put on every available witness, including forensic experts. The defense never called the defendant but put on witnesses to raise reasonable doubt. Many motions were made to suppress evidence or for limited use of other evidence. I took a strict view to protect the rights of the accused. I was more protective than usual for me, but with the death penalty on the table here, I wanted no mistaken finding of guilty by the jury that might take the life of an innocent man. At the time the death penalty was in force in Illinois.

At the end of the trial, I personally believed Montero committed the murder, but the proof did not meet the standard required of proof beyond a reasonable doubt. The jury properly found the defendant not guilty based on the evidence I allowed to be presented. If the State had not sought the death penalty and I had allowed more of the suppressed evidence to be heard by the jury, there might have been a guilty finding.

I have continued to ponder the question of what is justice generally and was it employed in this case for the victim and for the accused. I have no answer. I do believe that every participant involved did their job according to the rules—prosecutors, public defenders, witnesses, jurors, and hopefully me—and the result was an acquittal with a probable killer released to the streets and an unfortunate victim gone to his family after suffering during his last minutes of life. True justice is not perfect. The final judge may correct man's errors. If another judge had not suppressed certain evidence, opinions, or statements, conviction was possible, but then might an innocent man have been executed rather than a guilty man be released?

I will never know what I might have done regarding imposition of the death penalty. It would have been my responsibility to consider imposing death if the jury found Montero guilty and eligible for the death penalty, but would my personal question about the ethical and moral right for me to take another man's life prevent me from doing so?

Another criminal felony case I heard while in Skokie involved a defendant who had immigrated to the United States from Laos. He was one of about 130,000 Hmong tribesman who fought in Laos for the United States under the leadership of the Central Intelligence Agency. He came here in 1975 after the United States military withdrew from Laos during our fight in Vietnam. This fierce Hmong fighter, who had supported our national interests, was being charged with a serious felony and his case appeared on my docket. I realized that while I sat in a courtroom in Cook County, Illinois, USA, I had to quickly become aware of the culture in a part of the world on the opposite side of the planet.

The public defender made a motion on behalf of the Hmong defendant asking me to participate in a Hmong custom of saying prayers over a chicken's blood at a ritual slaughter. This event was to take place immediately before the commencement of a jury trial. I heard the motion and the state's objection and I denied the request giving several reasons. I am sworn to uphold the law of Illinois and the United States. That does not include the law, mores, customs, or traditions of the Hmong people or of the places in Asia they come from. A judge here does not participate in any way with a party to a pending case except to fairly and promptly administer the rules under the law in the courtroom during the trial. What may have been allowed in China, Laos, Burma, and Cambodia under tribal control was not allowed here under our jurisprudence. My denial of the motion to participate in a tribal ritual was immediately covered by the Chicago Tribune and other media outlets. Some comments were accepting of the denial and the reasons given, but one comment was harshly critical and suggested the court had disregarded the defendant's heritage to his constitutional detriment. Even had all of the media supported my participation in the Hmong tradition, I would have refused. My adherence to the rule of law did not adjust itself to conform with popular demands.

All of the public defenders and assistant state's attorneys were professional, bright, and hard working and they worked well together. One prosecutor told me in passing that her husband was recently out in the public again after a secret undercover assignment. He had been an FBI agent in the investigation of corruption in our court system and was part of the Operation Greylord investigation team. His testimony had already put in jail many judges, lawyers, police, clerks, and others. I learned from his wife what was disclosed to the defense and what was revealed in open court. I learned how I had been used to threaten hesitant lawyers who were given the choice of paying a bribe or taking their guilty clients before me and getting justice; that is, a guilty finding. They were being pushed to pay bribes to judges to win their cases. I was learning so much by reading the newspapers, and getting commentary years after events was most revealing. I could tell the strain that this young state's attorney and her husband must have faced. They were both quite brave and truly fought for the integrity of the rule of law.

I read about one of the downstate judges I had worked with in traffic court in 1974 and 1975 who had a microphone hidden in the heel of his cowboy boots to record incriminating admissions by corrupt individuals. He had been mingling with the corrupt judges at the behest of the federal prosecutors. The public may never know the courage that was required to detect the cancer in our judicial system and the need to root it out. Every such act of courage was essential. If one sits back and does nothing, evil flourishes. When we all step forward and take action, evil fails.

Since the last days of the Trump presidency and for years after, we will see the need for heroes and there have been many. Unfortunately, there are too many spineless sycophants in leadership positions in the Republican party, enabling those like Trump who perpetuate the great lie that President Joseph R. Biden was not duly elected in 2020. The rule of law must be uniformly followed in the courts and in Congress if our democracy is to flourish, with people having faith in the institutions of justice and the rule of law.

16 LOOKING BACK

Reflections

Looking back on my judicial career, I realize my youth was a problem for many, especially me. I was seen by many as undeserving and was resented. I was a useful tool for assigning heavy caseloads since I was so much younger than my peers. Most of the other judges could be my parents or grandparents. It was hard for them to relate to me and for me to relate to them. Once I was seen as that young wonder boy on the bench, I don't think the perception ever changed. That's why I was routinely given high volume assignments and sent to the outpost courtrooms at 54 West Randolph Street and 13th and Michigan and given a jury room as chambers and courtroom.

I was an easy foil for men like LeFevour, since he predicted I would follow the rules and that I could be used to induce bribes from defendants to avoid me and the few like me. None of his crew trusted me. When I entered the washroom, they left. I must have interfered with their deal making. I saw how one of the judges would sometimes fail to put the top of his tie in the loop, and learned later that was his signal that he would fix the case before him, that the bribe paid was sufficient. Clearly, his bagman—court police officer, deputy sheriff, or deputy clerk— had given him the bribe. Some of the crooked judges had little to do with me and did not give me the time of day to even say hello or good bye. Others like McCollum, Shields, and McDonald were always friendly to me.

One of those who did not have time for me was John Reynolds. Years after I left the bench, I received a call from him telling me he understood that I performed marriage ceremonies. He said he had one for me at the facility for boys at Maryville Academy in Des Plaines. He knew I charged and that would be no problem. He expected nothing in return. I performed the wedding and was paid—all to my amazement. I never heard from him again.

Shortly, thereafter, I received a telephone call from Charles LeVerde. His father was a traffic court judge with LeFevour. The son later became a judge and was assigned to Skokie when I was there. He said he called me to apologize for all of the slanderous things he said about me and all of the bad things he had done to me. I just listened, since I had no idea what he was talking about. He asked for my forgiveness. When we hung up, I began to think what harmful things he could have said, to whom he had said them, and what he had done. Did he give damaging information to bar association investigators for my last retentions in 1990 or 1996? Could he have done something earlier in 1975 for his father? I will never know what he did and who motivated him. I was only beginning to appreciate the number of unknown people who had been actively working to damage my career and reputation.

Maybe some priest or parole officer had told the former judges who called me that it was in their legal and spiritual best interest to make amends, apologize, or give some token of repentance or restitution to me and perhaps others who directly suffered from their malevolent conduct. If they gave me anything, it was some degree of understanding how far some of the evil men involved in the corruption had gone to harm people like me.

Other judges who proved to be corrupt had used me as well. I realized they did so after I learned of their corruption, as they were indicted. Alan Lane was an associate judge who came on the bench after me but was about my age. He called me at home and asked for some advice on a case. He wanted to know reasons to give if he wanted to rule one way or the other. I told him to listen to the opposite side's arguments and use those arguments as his reasons, but he could also give a few other reasons either way depending on how the facts guided him. He apparently was fixing cases for money and wanted to have some logical reasons and legal justification and basis to rule as he wanted to in order to support the position of the party paying him. He was clearly nowhere as smart as Allen Rosin, who had a good legal reason for everything he did. Lane must have respected my level of intelligence and wanted to take advantage of my reasoning.

Another judge, Daniel Glecier, got into trouble as well. He was assigned to the collection court after me and had questions. I gave a tutorial, thinking he just wanted to do a good job and was not just trying to find a legal reason to justify misconduct. Later, I learned in the news that he too was in trouble with the Feds. Glecier, like Lane, was using me; but they were not the only ones or the last ones.

The last example I relate here was a very personable man, David Shields. He became President of the Illinois Judges Association for a year. Years before, when he was assigned to gun court at 11th and State, he regularly stopped by traffic court and whispered into LeFevour's ear and then took off for his 9:30 AM court call about two miles south. There was talk about cases in gun court being dismissed on technical grounds. I wondered what all of Dave's secrets with LeFevour were about. Were they about traffic cases or gun cases? Each of them whispered to each other on a regular basis. Perhaps if LeFevour did not insist on my presence at traffic court so often and for so long, I wouldn't have been in a position to observe as much as I did—never enough to know but enough to suspect.

In any event, when David was transferred to a calendar in the Chancery Division of the Court, he called me and said he knew that I had done a lot of work in Chancery. He said on his administrative review cases, he was presented with huge books of transcripts. He wanted to know how he could avoid reading such a lengthy record. I told him he was bound to read the entire record to determine if the totality of the evidence supported the outcome below or whether the order under review was against the manifest weight of the evidence, but a legal way to avoid the reading occurred when a motion to dismiss was filed based on timeliness. Only the dates had to be read. I told him of a few more bases to avoid reading the entire record. He was grateful. I concluded that he was lazy and trying to find shortcuts and that could be dangerous. His later criminal conviction came as no surprise to me, although I had no evidence of his wrongdoing. He was always gracious and friendly to me and in social gatherings, and always welcomed me to his circle of conversation.

On the Positive Side

Cook County's Circuit Court is the largest unified court system in the country, yet while there are many judges, I found I had rubbed shoulders with a lot of characters who should never have been given the power bestowed upon them. For every bad actor, however, there were many more who worked hard and did their best to be fair. A man I have is mind is Martin S. Agran, a former assistant attorney general who shifted into private practice before being elected a judge from a northwest suburban Republican subcircuit.

Marty was assigned to the Chancery Division for a number of years and then asked to be transferred to Municipal District 3 in Rolling Meadows to hear civil cases. It might seem like a demotion, but he wanted to cut his commute time, have less pressure, and enjoy the continued company of the new presiding judge who he had worked with in Chancery, Judge William Maki. Marty told me how he had been spending long hours reading lengthy records and briefs in Chancery, and he wanted a break. I believe he read every word, unlike Dave Shields who had sought shortcuts. Marty was working himself into a burnout. He closed his career as he began it, with great public service.

When I was in the Skokie courthouse from 1987 until I retired in December 1999, many judges came and went. A few went on to the Appellate Court or the federal district court while others retired. I had served in the Second Municipal District during the summer months in 1978 after my son was born and before there was a dedicated courthouse building. I asked for the temporary assignment so I would be able to stop home lunch time to give my wife a break, since our son slept little and required a lot of attention. My wife needed a nap for even a half hour. I thought of my father coming home for lunch. Now I was doing the same thing.

The temporary assignment was great, with me going from one village in the morning to another in the afternoon and stopping home in the middle. The three months of respite were just what my wife needed. Some days I came home and found they were both napping. I got a sense of a circuit rider like it must have been with Abraham Lincoln and others years ago, with greater distances and awful roads. The town of Evanston usually had enough activity to keep me all day, so I stayed in Evanston and ate lunch there. If Maureen had errands for me, I could go to stores near the city hall where the courtroom was in the council chambers. In each village, I would take the seat of the village president. Each place was unique and it made for an interesting summer. The presiding judge of the Second Municipal District, Harold Sullivan, was stationed in the second-floor offices of the Skokie police station. Harold had his office next to the courtroom. When the Skokie court house was built years later, before I came again in 1987, his office and quarters and staff had increased tremendously.

Judge Sullivan was an interesting character. He rarely, if ever, heard any cases. He was an administrator and was active in a lot of activities, like the formation of the Illinois Judges Association. He volunteered his administrative secretary as the executive director of the Judges Association. He was active in several bar associations. He liked to meet with the police chiefs in the district and other groups as well. When there was a shortage of judges for any reason and Judge Sullivan was filling in, his administrative assistant would continually check in with each judge in each room to see who was finishing up and could relieve Judge Sullivan. On one occasion, when I was the one to take him out of his misery, I saw him foundering as to a disposition on the matter he heard. He quickly said he had to attend to other matters and that Judge Jordan would take over.

Harold Sullivan had been one of the first assistant public defenders in Cook County when only a handful started and the office was formed and growing. He kept his pro defense attitude all of his career. He was a perennial social worker and wanted each judge in his district to mirror his habits, acts, and beliefs. He would tell every judge separately that everyone else was doing something a certain way—which was always the way he wanted it done. When a new judge was assigned to his district, he would tell them what everyone assessed as penalties for each offense to insure consistency. He had never had much experience with civil matters so he interfered only in the criminal and traffic matters.

Most of the judges assigned to him were associate judges he requested, who I believed he felt he could manipulate. His goals were usually good and never corrupt. When there was public criticism about a lack of diversity in some courthouses, he began to recruit minority members, usually black, but sometimes Hispanic. He tried to get a double minority so he favored Black women. One Black woman assigned to Skokie was Joy Cunningham, a phenomenal person. She had been a nurse and a lawyer and legal counsel for Northwestern Memorial Hospital before becoming an Associate Judge.

Harold thought he could push her around, but found otherwise. He told her that she must have advanced to the positions she held due to her being a Black woman rather than because she was accomplished, bright, and capable. His comments were very insulting. She came back to her chambers adjoining my own and was clearly distraught. Joan Corboy, another judge assigned to Skokie but not answering to Sullivan, told Joy she should report this slur to the Chief Judge, Donald O'Connell. Joy decided to follow Joan's advice. Joan was one of four judges in the Criminal Division who heard Chicago-based cases in the Skokie courthouse and reported to the Presiding Judge of the Criminal Division, not to Sullivan. Sullivan was the Presiding Judge of Municipal District 2.

Joan and I collaborated in many ways. Since we were both circuit judges and could vote on candidates for associate judge, we discussed the merits of each candidate and helped each other come to the same consensus. Most of the candidates we decided to support made it. After we conferred, we each called different friends and somehow, we usually succeeded. I don't recall that any of our supported candidates lost.

Joan died in a tragic accident while away on vacation in Florida with her family. Her husband, Jim Epstein was a criminal defense lawyer who had cases in front of me from time to time. I knew his grandfather who was honored for his service years before at Rodfei Zedek, when Rabbi Ralph Simon put me in charge of the committee to honor Judge Epstein's service to the community. Jim had two small children to raise, one with special needs. He married again after a period of time and was appointed a judge. He even became president of the Jewish Judges Association. Joan was a strong, powerful, and colorful lady who told me life can be a "bitch" when she gave me a hug after my father died.

The chief judge, Donald O'Connell, had been a staff aide to the Chief Judge John Boyle after becoming a lawyer. Sullivan was a locally elected judge in Skokie who was appointed by his friend and, I believe, cousin, John S. Boyle, as Presiding Judge of the north suburban courts when the court system was organized after the 1964 judicial reform. Harold Sullivan continued on as Presiding Judge, based on his connections to Boyle ever after, until he went too far in the wrong direction without Judge Boyle to protect him.

O'Connell had moved up to court administrator under Boyle when Ben Mackoff left that post to become a judge. O'Connell later ran for judge himself as a circuit judge. He was elected and quickly became a supervising and then presiding judge equal in rank to Sullivan. He had taken over the Law Division, one of the most prestigious assignments in the system. Sullivan still saw Donald as the young boy and not his equal. Sullivan consistently treated O'Connell in a disparaging manner. Even when Donald became the chief judge, Harold could not appreciate that he now must answer to Donald as the chief judge. Donald always kept his temper in check and took actions, as needed, without rancor.

When O'Connell received Joy's complaint, he convened the executive committee of the court to investigate and decide what to do. After a thorough investigation and hearing, Harold was told he must ask to be relieved as a presiding judge or just leave the bench for acting in a racist and sexist manner. If he acted quickly, no formal charges would be brought and his reputation would not be publicly exposed. He quickly left the bench and was replaced by a series of other judges serving where he had served for decades.

Joy had been easy to befriend; she was smart, kind, open, and caring. As a former nurse, she could advise me on any minor medical issues. She gave sound advice on legal issues I had to resolve. Joy had been legal counsel for Northwestern Medical Center. Joy moved on to other meaningful assignments in the Circuit Court until she resigned as an associate judge and was elected to the Appellate Court. After a great record of accomplishment, on September 21, 2022, she was appointed to sit on the Illinois Supreme Court beginning December 1, 2022, taking the seat of Chief Justice Anne Burke. Joy follows Supreme Court Justice Scott Neville as a former law clerk to my friend Appellate Court Justice Glenn T. Johnson, who made it to the Illinois Supreme Court.

Joy was a stark contrast to the kind older man who had occupied the chambers before her. He was a former state representative in Evanston elected as a Republican. He found it hard to find anyone guilty of anything. If someone violated an order he had entered, he would rarely make them fulfill their obligation and do the community service or pay the fine or make the restitution. He would merely end their supervision. They suffered no consequence. His violation call was short and only took minutes. Mine on the other hand, took hours. I would extend the supervision, conditional discharge, or probation until the conditions were meet or if someone was flagrant in disregarding my orders, I added additional conditions for them to fulfill. I found that some clerks and sheriffs wanting overtime asked to be assigned to my room on the afternoon each month I had a violation call. Their bosses were not as happy with the long calls. I was given a second call to make each violation call shorter. I believed with criminal cases, a fitting and fair penalty was more important sometimes than determining the guilt or innocence. Not many, but a few defendants, wrote to me later or came by the courtroom to thank me for helping them to get their acts together since most others in their lives had let them ignore obligations without any consequences.

Harold wanted to have diversity in his ranks since it gave him merit, but if a Jewish judge took off for too many Jewish holidays, he was provoked. He made politically incorrect comments about most of the racial, religious, and ethnic judges and other employees without even understanding that his conduct and comments were not appropriate. A few years after he left, I learned from his lovely daughter, Sharon, who served as a judge, that he had memory problems.

I wondered when he had first developed those issues. He and I were the only full circuit judges in Skokie in December 1996, assigned to District 2 when we were both to be sworn in for another term of six years. The chief judge said there was a shortage of judges and that we should swear each other into office rather than coming downtown for him to swear us in. I understand we missed a beautiful ceremony, but we administered the judicial oaths to each other in the privacy of Sullivan's office.

I swore him into office and then he swore me into my office for what would be the last term for each of us.

I was greatly relieved that we were not going downtown since the last time we did so he insisted we go together and he was the driver. His erratic driving almost gave me an immediate ulcer. I vowed never to get into a car with him again unless he was the passenger. At least no tragedy would occur before or after our last installation.

Fear of Depression

Many friends and family heard I was thinking of quitting the bench in 1999, and some, like my dear friend who I had met early in 4th grade, Stuart B. Dubin, were quite worried about me. Stuart thought I would become depressed with nothing to do and without people showing me deference and saying yes, your honor and laughing at all of my bad jokes.

I had recently moved to South Shore in 1951 and was riding my two-wheel bike to Hebrew School for class. My fender was bent and was interfering with the movement of the wheel. I could have just walked the bike the short distance and fixed it later, but Stuart came along. He said he could help fix the bike.

I did not know him or know who he was then, but I quickly learned Stuart would be a close friend until he died. I hadn't asked for his help, but as I would learn every day I knew Stuart, he wanted to help always and sometimes before you even knew there was a problem. He had a heart of gold. After a while, I concluded he was not the best mechanic I could have found. I said I would be late to Hebrew school. He asked who my teacher was. I said it was Mr. Bender. He said I shouldn't worry since he knew Mr. Bender and could talk to him. Everything would be all right.

Here this "pisher" who was only a year and a half older than me, who was not only going to fix my bike (which he couldn't) but was going to fix up everything with my teacher. I thanked Stuart and said I could still get to class on time if I left now and I really appreciated his help. I looked forward to seeing him soon.

I didn't see Stuart often or regularly, but I did see him from time to time and he was consistently optimistic and friendly.

Years later when I was at DePaul Law School, I saw Stuart in the halls between classes. He graduated and became a lawyer ahead of me. We saw each other again when I prosecuted in traffic court, but wherever it was, he was always upbeat and friendly. We kept each other abreast of our activities. He told me he had gotten involved in the 10th Ward Democratic party and I told him I was in the 4th Ward party. When he learned that I was trying to become a judge, he first offered to help and then told me I was too young and did not know the hardships of private practice. He repeated his theme throughout his life that private practice was always a struggle. He had to work to get clients, get them to listen to him and take his advice. It was hard to get paid. Often, since his clients were working people, he had to stay downtown in his office into the evening. He convinced himself of all of his assumptions.

When I we moved to Glenview where Stuart was living, he often offered to drive me downtown to court. The traffic was always heavy and he was always later than the time we agreed upon. He would constantly switch lanes, go off down-ramps, and go up on-ramps to save a few seconds. I usually arrived on time but agitated.

His conversation was interesting. He lobbied me to go easier on defendants with lawyers. I tended to go down a rung from whatever I would have done by way of penalty, knowing the person took the ticket seriously enough to have hired a lawyer and was paying money to that lawyer. He was already fined for his minor infraction before I said anything. I always listened to Stuart. Stuart might have a case or two in traffic court and then would go to the Daley Center to represent tenants being evicted or landlords trying to evict a nonpaying tenant. Stuart also represented merchants and others involved in contracts where one side or the other defaulted. There were also some divorce cases he handled. He often complained that there were so many bad, stupid, or uncaring judges and he seemed to get assigned to each of the bad ones. Whichever side he represented was always the deserving side and, for him, a must win or there was no justice.

Stuart lived just about six blocks from me in Glenview, but his son, Jonathan, and my daughter, Elizabeth, went to different grade schools and junior high schools. They would both be going to the same high school, Glenbrook South. His son and my daughter knew each other since they were the same age. When we moved to Glenview, Stuart would bring Jonathan over to the house and he would always have Jonathan shake my hand and say, "Hello, Mr. Jordan."

Jonathan became a very handsome, athletic, and bright young man as the years moved on. He and Elizabeth were in the same grade and had many of the same friends. He had gone to B'nai Joshua Beth Eloheim, a Reform temple in Glenview, and Elizabeth went to a Conservative synagogue in Northbrook, Congregation Beth Shalom, but they were always in touch as friends. We learned that if anyone tried to bully another kid in school, Jonathan was there to intervene and stop it. There was only one Black kid in the school, and he was Jonathan's friend. Jonathan played on the baseball team and basketball team in high school. Elizabeth was a cheerleader and Maureen and I went to see Elizabeth, and Stuart and his lovely wife Bernice went to see Jonathan. It was always great.

The best thing happened—Stuart acquired an interest in a boat with a divorce lawyer, David Grund. Several times Maureen and I were invited to join Stuart and Bernice with and without our kids, when Stuart used the boat at the Abbey Resort in southern Wisconsin. We always enjoyed the time together. I learned that the best thing in the world is not having a boat—it is having a friend who has a boat. There is much upkeep of a boat and winter storage. The obligations are endless. Stuart complained of them all. After only a couple of seasons, he dumped his interest in the boat.

Stuart had been in a study group in law school with people I came to know— Chuck Bernstein, Leon Wool, Wayne Rhine,

Warren Marx, and Wally Dunne. They were all a year ahead of me at DePaul Law School. I knew Chuck from the south side. When Maureen and I were members of Rodfei Zedek Congregation, Chuck and his wife Roberta belonged as well. Chuck opened a law firm of his own, which supported him and his family of three sons.

Leon was the son of my parent's friends and he became a precinct captain in the 4th Ward until he moved to Skokie. He got a job in the law department of the Chicago Transit Authority (CTA). I knew Leon for many years. Both he and his wife, Bunny, were kind and sweet. Leon became an associate judge and served well until shortly before his death. When I was at traffic court, I would see him and his great friend, Marv Luckman. They were inseparable. Marv also worked for the CTA. His son went on to follow in his footsteps when Marv became a judge. Marv retired after a beautiful career and died not long after, leaving a lovely wife Gail, who socialized with my sister Gayle. It is a small world.

Wayne Rhine, who also became a judge, had moved to Glenview and had two sons close in age to Elizabeth. Chuck's oldest son, Eddie, was Elizabeth's age, but only saw Elizabeth on occasion when the Bernstein family visited our house. Eddie and his brothers Louie and Henry brought their baseball bat, ball, and mitts when they came to our house, since they enjoyed our back yard and the space we had. They came a few times when we had put up our sukkah.

While Warren had been in my high school class, I did not see him apart from the bigger group get-togethers that all the couples had from time to time in various restaurants.

Wally Dunne and I found a lot in common in every move we made. He and his wife, Joannie, would be at annual meetings of the Illinois State Bar Association and we could socialize without the pressures of the city. He became an associate judge in Lake County. When we were both retired from the bench, we were engaged for arbitrations and mediations, and still continue those assignments. We have served on panels together or run into each other when we were each assigned on the same day to different cases. We also visited at meetings of the Jewish Judges Association. He was the only member of Stuart's group who was not a Southsider.

When my daughter was getting married and I was to be in New York and possibly join her new husband for morning minyan (religious services), I needed to relearn how to put on tefillin. Knowing that Wally put them on regularly, I asked him to teach me. He was kind and patient. That marriage failed quickly, but the wedding was beautiful. On another occasion, I had to put on tefillin and I had again forgotten how to do so. I went to Wally again and this very patient man taught me again. His kindness has earned him credit for only good things now and forever. Stuart left me a legacy of friendship lasting beyond his own years. There are many other people I see today who were close to Stuart. Stuart cemented many relationships.

Another man I still see today is Steve Margolin. I graduated with him from grade school and high school. When I went to summer school at Roosevelt University, I saw Steve and he asked me what my class schedule was and then told me he would pick me up each morning in front of my apartment building. Both of us were prompt and the ride was with ease, unlike the later rides with Stuart and Judge Sullivan.

Steve said he was on a different schedule going home, so we could not car pool both ways. The next day he came by, finding me waiting outside. He parked at a meter. I offered to feed the meter between classes, but he said his schedule was fine to take care of it. I offered to pay for gas and the meters but he refused, saying he was spending the amount anyway and he was not taken out of his way by even an inch. He appreciated my company. We lived on the same one-way street going northbound; and he was a few blocks south and had to pass my house.

Steve has always been the same giving person he was then. He had been going to Florida to spend some time but later decided to live in south Florida except for time that he and his wife would spend in the north Chicago suburbs to be with their children. When he started going to Florida, he and later his family stayed with his parents, and he was also in the company of Al Lipton, staying with his mother and her new husband, and Barry Grossman, another friend I met at South Shore, staying with his parents and later bringing his family. I found Barry in my law school class when I transferred to DePaul my second year. We have been friends ever since.

Steve and Stuart and one or two others would, when possible, play tennis at night and then have a late dinner. More often they had a late dinner and still later tennis game. After Stuart died, Steve and I would tell each other stories about Stuart. Another friend I had worked with prosecuting cases at the liquor commission when I was in the law department was Barry Greenburg. He was a few years older than I was and had gone to O'Keefe grammar school and Hyde Park High School. He belonged to Rodfei Zedek. When we left work before a Jewish holiday, we always wished each other a good holiday. When Barry was in his private practice, he handled mostly divorce matters, but did other things earlier in his career. He ran into Stuart a lot and unsurprisingly with so much in common, as south siders who became lawyers, they became close friends. Barry and I would share stories about Stuart as well. Barry had some heart issues but was still able to practice law into his 80s. We served on a couple of bar association committees together and would see each other at various events. Maureen and I socialized with him and his wife, since Maureen met him when she visited the Corporation Counsel's office. I had shared an office cubicle with him.

Another lawyer who would occasionally be in traffic court downtown, I saw even more when I was assigned to Skokie and heard over-weight truck cases. He had a niche practice confined to overweight truck companies, trucks exceeding the tonnage limits for certain roads and bridges. Richard Adler found a simple practice where the bond posted always guaranteed that his fee was paid. He learned the applicable law in a flash and found a way to negotiate a win-win for his client's company and the city or village seeking revenue.

I admired Dick, who had developed interesting hobbies. I had met him in Madison. He was a year ahead of me in school but we had a couple of classes together. He had joined ZBT fraternity. He loved to lecture about the ethical points to be learned by lawyers in movies, plays, or books. He would study the work and then give an interactive lecture for bar associations. While his law practice was not particularly challenging to his brain, his presentations were challenging and entertaining to others. Whenever we would encounter each other at the health club, he would expose me to literature, culture, and the arts, and he showed the ethical lessons to be derived. When our daughters were in high school together, we would see each other at parent-teacher conference nights and when dropping off or picking up our daughters at parties. It was great he lived nearby. He too knew Stuart and would keep me abreast of Stuart's son Jonathan. If I heard something from Barry or Steve, I would share the news of Jonathan with Dick. Dick and I had found a few opportunities to go bike riding together in the neighborhood.

Jonathan Dubin was a very handsome man. He modeled for a short time. One day Bernice, his loving mother, was shopping in a store and saw picture frames on sale. She noticed quickly and lovingly that the frames contained the image of her son Jonathan. She bought up all the frames she could. When she got them home and Stuart and Jonathan saw what she did, they said she could take Jon's picture any time and make a million copies but she didn't have to do that; she had Jon in the flesh. Now, what were they to do with all the frames? It should be understood that Bernice found it hard not to buy things that she saw and fancied, but if there was anything possible to get for Jon or because of Jon there was no stopping her.

Stuart and Bernice were so delighted when Jon came into their lives, since they were unable to have any biological children of their own. They protected him, nurtured him, and showed him great love all of their days. Jon felt they were over protective when he wanted to be on the football team at high school and they refused his pleas. Years later, after Jonathan became an assistant state's attorney in Cook County, he told them it was getting boring and he had applied to be a federal employee. While Stuart thought he meant an assistant U.S. Attorney, Jonathan told him he was going to be an FBI agent. When they learned he was undercover in counter-terrorism and narcotics, they were horrified with the dangers he faced.

Fortunately, after noble service with the FBI, Jonathan went on to start a security company and seemed happy in California near an "uncle" and famous south-sider, Larry Ellison, founder of Oracle. Larry took Oracle from a company having just a couple of employees to a company with over a hundred thousand employees and a wealth of over a billion dollars, making Ellison the richest man in California. I am not going to worry about Jonathan's financial security, since Larry cares for Jonathan like a son, having been a friend of Stuarts.

Although Stuart and others entreated me not to quit, I did quit on Sunday December 12, 1999, by sending in my letter of resignation to the Chief Justice of the Illinois Supreme Court, the Chief Judge of the Circuit Court of Cook County, and the Pension Board. I quit because a new pension law took effect on Friday December 9, 1999, upon the signing by the governor—George Ryan. The law provided that I could resign before reaching age 60 due to credits I earned by working months beyond 20 years, and not suffer any penalty in my pension. According to the formula, my months of service over 20 years eliminated the entire penalty I would have faced before the bill was signed for months shy of age 60. In fact, I could have quit a few months before. I was happy as it was and not bitter over a few months. I had a few weeks left that year to get some social security credits, since most of my work history, working for government, was not covered by social security credits. I wanted to provide for my golden years and thought that social security checks in the future would provide security.

17 LOOKING AHEAD

I Had Plans for a New Career

What prompted my move besides the pension was my belief that at age 57 I could begin a new career and arbitrate, mediate, teach, and write. I had a plan, so Maurice Handelsman's experience of death did not scare me. I had a wife and children and many interests. I loved reading and I exercised several times a week. I would do well. I was too busy to even think I was depressed getting myself on panels to arbitrate and sending out applications, getting malpractice insurance, and setting up an identify for my business. I began working a 16-hour day calling people to find out the possibilities. I also sent out thank you notes to people like Mike Madigan for his help getting me to this place in life.

Another person I called was a judge in Lake County, Charles Scott. He was close to me in age and came on the bench just a little after me. Charlie and I had both been appointed to several judicial education committees. We taught as a team at judicial seminars and became close friends. We learned to collaborate and share ideas. He had grown up in South Chicago, where I had gone to summer school, had gone canning for charity, and had sat as a judge.

Charlie's family moved to Lake County as Democrats. He became an associate judge and it was then that our paths crossed on judicial committees. When he ran for circuit judge as a Democrat, he saw his path to success was limited, since Lake County then was overwhelmingly Republican. The next time around, Charlie became a Republican and won. He went on to become the chief judge of the circuit. His retention elections were, of course, non-partisan as the county slowly emerged as more Democratic than Republican.

In 1998 we both attended the National Judicial College in Reno, Nevada, to take the fantastic course in mediation given by John Paul Jones of Florida and Nancy Yend of California. We met judges from around the country, although there was a healthy contingent from Illinois. I recall at least 12 of us, including Dick Elrod, the former Cook County Sheriff who was now a judge. He was in his mechanical wheel chair and aided by another Cook County judge, Edward Burr, whom I will mention later. While we were there learning how to be mediators, we would get news from home. We learned that a bill was up for consideration that might alter the pension plan of Illinois, affecting judges. There was a possibility that judges like Charlie and me could take an early retirement based on years of judicial service. It could mitigate or eliminate a penalty for early retirement. Each day we asked each other if our sources provided any new information.

So, a year later, when the governor signed pending bills, I called Charlie and told him I was writing my letter of resignation. I asked if he was doing the same. I thought there was advantage to do so before the end of the year. He said he needed time to ponder the idea. It took him several months into the next year, but he did retire and pursued a path, as I was intending to do, to mediate and arbitrate. Our mediation course was very timely, as it must have been to all of those attending. I believe that sooner or later, most of those in our class from Illinois became mediators. Each year the competition was expanding.

One of the other people I contacted was Dennis Dohm, since he had recently joined ADR Systems to arbitrate. Dennis took me to see Marc Becker, who had recently started a company with the contacts he had made as an insurance adjuster who could settle cases with plaintiff's lawyers. He had hired some other people like himself to administer cases and was recruiting retired judges to be the mediators for the lawyers and insurance adjustors he could attract. He started with a handful of retired judges and was expanding as much as he could, as competitors were starting and expanding as well. I met Marc and told him of my interest. At that time, no mention was made of having an exclusive with him and his company. I figured I would take what he gave me, but I did not want to be dependent on any one source for my future success. I spoke also to the manager of Resolute Systems, based in Milwaukee. I found other companies, and during the next year or so, I was on multiple panels. I was beginning to get assignments and was developing my skills.

To my surprise, I received some phone calls from lawyers who learned I was open to direct referrals, and I received my first mediation in Lake County. Since I was already serving on the Lake County mandatory arbitration panel, I got permission to use their facilities to conduct a mediation out of Lake County, using several of their rooms for joint meetings and individual parties. While I met once with the lawyers at one of their offices, we completed several more meetings in the Waukegan offices of the Lake County arbitration center.

Before starting on the assigned case, I contacted Nancy Send of California, my teacher from the National Judicial College who taught me mediation skills. She always gave me helpful hints and invited my updates for more tricks of the trade. I relied on her for many of my first cases. Years later, when she was hired by Cook County to train local judges, she asked me to assist, and it was my pleasure to do so on several occasions. I relied on her for questions, although I took an advance mediation course through NASD (now FINRA). I found that getting skills from different teachers in mediation was like getting trial techniques from different teachers. You see different methods of doing the same thing and get a feeling of what is best for you, especially in a particular circumstance.

When I taught mediation with others, I learned their tricks and adapted some for my use. I had taken trial technique in law school from Harry Aaron, a fantastic and patient teacher, who later became an associate judge in Cook County. After law school, I took another course from Ken Kutsky, another great teacher, at John Marshall Law School, now known as the University of Illinois Law School at Chicago. I took still another course from Irving Goldstein, a former judge who sat in Skokie and was in his last year teaching the course. He brought with him Fred Lane, a former state's attorney and now plaintiff's trial lawyer.

The following year, Fred took over the course, bringing it under the auspices of the Illinois State Bar Association. I had the benefit of having both Judge Goldstein and Fred Lane during the only year they taught together. I was truly fortunate to have learned from so many masters. I learned the basics, but developed my own style and technique. I felt comfortable in the courts, trying cases according to the rules in a way that was comfortable for me. Fred went on to become the President of the Illinois State Bar Association. When Maureen was rear-ended a few years later in 1970, I made the wise decision to take her case to Fred's office for representation. I felt comfortable in the courts trying cases according to the rules.

What brought me to John Marshall after law school was the Vietnam War—referred to there as the American War. We had a draft of all able-bodied men from the age of 18 to the age of 26. All able men were classified as 1-A and could be taken at any time. Those in regular attendance at an accredited high school, college, professional, or graduate school were exempt and classified as SS—student deferment. Those with medical disabilities were listed as 4-F. There were a few other classifications. In those days, women were not subject to the draft and those women who enlisted were not allowed to assume combat roles. Years later, our society concluded this disparate treatment made no sense. Back in the 60's, if you told the parents of a nurse near the front lines that their daughter was not really at risk, you would see the disbelief in their eyes.

Most of my law school classmates, although patriotic, did not believe this war was needed and with young men coming back in body bags in greater numbers every month, the war was viewed as tragic and disastrous. After law school, those who weren't married got married and had children as soon as they could, since Uncle Sam was raising the requirements for a deferment every year and exempted for a while those married and then those with a child and later with two children. Some became teachers, a job that resulted in a deferment. Others, like me, went on to graduate school. Many of my contemporaries were becoming the most educated in the community. As soon as these men turned 26, they dropped out and lost all interest in education. I was younger than most in my classes so I lasted until the end of the year. I still had about 10 months to go before I would turn 26. As a kid, I wanted to be 16 so I could drive. I wanted to be 21 so I could vote. Now, I wanted to be 26 and free of the draft.

My draft board did have many enlistments to fill their quota. I registered at age 18 when we lived in South Shore, and my board covered neighborhoods in South Chicago, where there was a high enlistment rate of very patriotic Hispanics. Still, the board was drafting some in South Shore each month. I was referred to our U.S. Congressman, Barrett O'Hara, the oldest congressman in the entire Congress at the time. He had a Chicago office at the 5th Army Headquarters near our apartment in Hyde Park. His office manager told me I could enroll in the Judge Advocates Corps of the Army, but I would have to agree to at least three and maybe four years of committed service. I was only willing to volunteer for two years so it didn't work out. I went to several National Guard units to sign up and hoped I would come up on at least one waiting list before I got a draft notice. The months went by with great trepidation and anxiety and, to my satisfaction, I turned 26 without being drafted and before my name rose to the top for any unit of the National Guard. Someone was on my side. Maybe, it was Uncle Sam.

Years later I learned of all the hardship suffered by friends and family who served and illnesses and death due to being in proximity to agent orange, a defoliation agent. Some had joined the National Guard and were called to active duty to respond to riots and civil disorder in the late 60's. Disorder followed the Martin Luther King assassination and the police crackdown during the 1968 Democratic National Convention in Chicago.

I remember the police sergeant assigned to the liquor and license commission was required to get into his uniform and go onto the street in four-men cars. In August 1968, all hearings were suspended to allow as many police as possible to be on the street instead of in hearings. Many people found their cases in traffic court dismissed in the absence of a police officer. Manpower was allocated where it was needed most.

It was clear that the city then was politically divided between those favoring law and order and supporting the police versus those supporting the demonstrators protesting the war and our involvement in Vietnam. This divide was not limited to Chicago; it was a national divide.

I learned years later that the co-valedictorian of my high school class became a rabbi and decided to enlist in the army to serve in the chaplain corps in Vietnam. He served in spite of his moral objections to the war. He felt that men like him, exempt from the draft as clergy, had a duty to serve, to bring comfort to the young Jewish men who, like him, were opposed to the war, but who had been drafted into service. Rabbi Sheldon Lewis could not ignore those men and have them serve without the moral and spiritual support they deserved. He felt that too few Jewish chaplains were available to these deserving men. Shelly risked his life many times and had to take cover with the onslaught of enemy fire. The incoming fire gave a clergyman or a medic no immunity. Thankfully, he returned home to northern California and his twin brother, Sherwin, a doctor, physically intact to give spiritual guidance and pastoral care to thousands for many years after the war. However, Shelly suffered a great emotional toll.

Shelly wrote a book about his experiences that had to be an emotional release for many veterans to read and for Shelly to write. He based his recollections on the letters he wrote to his new wife who he married shortly before going off to service. His book *Letters Home: A Jewish Chaplain's Vietnam Memoir* was published on September 4, 2021 by Hakodesh Press.

Mediation & Arbitration Services

After my service on the bench in Cook County, I decided it would be useful to develop contacts to help cultivate my arbitration and mediation practice. In pursuance of my goal, I contacted another friend, Barry Simon, who I knew causally through other friends. Barry became one of my greatest resources, strengths, and supporters, sometimes at his own expense. He is selfless and kind as well as very bright. He in turn introduced me to others, including a man who became a dear friend, Jack Fletcher. A new dawn had arrived and I was beginning a new independent life without court watchers and public scrunty. I would still be adhering to my judicial code and lawyers' code of professional conduct, regarding ethics, and the code of other entities I affiliated with such as NASD (which became FINRA), the American Arbitration Association, the Federal Mediation and Conciliation Service, National Mediation Board, court mandatory arbitration panels, and mediation panels for different courts.

Barry Simon suggested I speak to Leo Parcels, the Midwest Director of the American Postal Workers Union, after he and Jack put in a good word for me. Leo told me he would speak to his management counterparts to see if they were willing to have me placed first on an expedited panel, and he suggested I would start at $600 per case, which would entail the hearing of up to six hours and the writing of the award due within 48 hours after the hearing. Any expenses would be reimbursed. If I had to travel out of town, I would be paid a-half-day's pay for the travel time.

At the next contract period when arbitrators were selected for regular panels, I would be considered if the parties approved of my work. I received many assignments and within two years I was placed on a regular panel with a higher fee for the hearing and pay for writing up to one day per award with the travel fee being the same one half day and expenses. Management was clearly happy with my work and they recommended me to the Mail Handlers Union, where I would be paid for two days of writing. I received assignments in Illinois, Missouri, and Michigan. I was getting quite busy. I was recommended to the National Association of Letter Carriers, and I did some of their cases in nearby places like southern Wisconsin and Illinois. Later, I had panels in Michigan, Indiana, and Illinois.

I had to decide when to drive and when to fly. I had to decide at which hotels I would stay. I made sure I joined all of the airlines' and hotels' frequent flier and club groups. I tried to use the same companies repeatedly to earn the most points. I usually stayed at a Hilton franchise, most often a Hampton, where I could have a breakfast and they gave me a goodie bag for lunch. When a Hilton hotel was not available, I had secondary hotels, usually a Holiday Inn. I checked for pools and gyms, but often I arrived too late and just went to bed, checked out in the morning to go to the hearing, and left for the airport or the drive home. I kept a list so I knew which hotel to avoid and which to book again when assigned to the same city. I visualized traveling salesmen and their lives a century before.

In addition to my postal cases that were becoming a reliable source of income, I had been placed on the NASD panel (later, after merging with the New York Stock Exchange, becoming FINRA), where I would hear arbitration cases involving securities issues. I also heard employment matters between the brokerage houses and their employees. Issues were sometimes complex and quite diverse. I had to learn a new set of concepts, such as a put, diversity, suitability, and other industry concepts. I found everything within my ability to master and was quite happy, usually serving with two other arbitrators. The largest case I heard in my career was through FINRA, dealing with a regulated bank where unsavory securities traders used day trading to steal huge sums of money, using deception and fraud. We heard about three weeks of testimony in the matter, and our interim rulings made it clear that if the respondent bank was found guilty, what the damage amount would be, disregarding any possible punitive damages. On the last day, the parties told us they reached a settlement and we would not have to deliberate. I understand the settlement was slightly under a billion dollars, based solely on the compensatory damages.

The case was the best lawyered case I had ever been involved in, as either an advocate, judge, or arbitrator. Each side had at least six lawyers in the room at all times. As a witness was called, sometimes another lawyer would appear to examine or cross examine that witness or to assist the lead lawyer on their side. With certain witnesses under indictment or under investigation, their personal lawyer would also appear to advise them and interact with the panel when self-incrimination issues were at stake.

The Sunday night before the case was scheduled to start, I received a call at home and heard an unfamiliar voice say he was the U.S. Attorney for the Eastern District of New York, which I believe is based in Brooklyn. He did not say he was an assistant. He said he was the U.S. Attorney. He said he was calling to have me adjourn the case so that the examination of his witnesses, who he would be using to convict several indicted bankers, would not be compromised by the respondents and their lawyers learning of their testimony.

I told the caller several things. One, I had no idea who he was. I could not believe a United States Attorney from any district would make an *ex parte* call to me as a hearing officer presiding over a case of any sort without lawyers from both sides being present. Two, I said first thing in the morning, on the record, I would disclose this call to the parties and the other arbitrators. Three, I would ask the parties to notify the appropriate authorities in New York of this call to learn if it was fictious or real and what ethical rules were being broken.

I then told him I was ending the call and that he should not contact me again. The next morning, I did as I said I would. The respondent Bank said they were joining in the motion of the government for an indefinite continuance. The claimants' lawyers acting on behalf of thousands of people in pension plans whose funds had been greatly diminished by fake trading strongly objected. They asked the panel to look around the room and consider the hundreds of banker boxes full of exhibits. There were more in adjoining conference rooms. They said numerous witnesses and lawyers had firmed up their schedules for this hearing and many had come from New York and other parts of the country. They said they believe it was the U.S. Attorney who improperly contacted me and that he could have sought judicial relief from the federal courts in New York but failed to do so. Claimants asked to proceed immediately.

On this important issue and on all of the important issues that arose in this matter, I consulted in private with the two other arbitrators. One was an industry arbitrator who I found to be knowledgeable, fair, and attentive. He was outraged by the shenanigans we determined were committed by the respondent's agents. The other was himself a chair qualified arbitrator with extensive experience in commercial matters, including securities and banking. The three of us never once differed in the actions I took. We denied the motion and ordered that the case proceed as scheduled.

The lawyers on both sides were superb. We learned as the case progressed that the respondent's lawyers were relatively new to the case. Another firm was present at most of the depositions used to impeach witnesses. We learned that there was a smaller test case before that was lost by the respondents. The bank dropped the original law firm and hired the current law firm. I assume both firms were top notch but just could not win a losing case. The claimants had the services of Jenner and Block with the lead lawyers coming from their New York office, but with some lawyers from the Chicago headquarters responsible for the logistical issues. The lead lawyer for the claimants was a New Yorker, Andrew Weissmann. He was perhaps the most talented, prepared, logical, and concise lawyer I had ever experienced. He showed calm, perseverance, a clever approach, and great preparation. He had mastered every detail of the case and he had a big picture goal in mind at all times.

It was years later, when a special prosecutor and impeachment proceedings became necessary due to the actions of Donald Trump, that the name Andrew Weissmann became known to the general public, being special prosecutor Mueller's number two man. When I heard the disappointing arguments and statements made by Mueller, I had only wished he had been under and not over Weissmann. When I more recently saw Weissmann as a frequent commentator on cable news, I observed how he cites facts and gives only opinions based on facts. He is not prone to hyperbole in any way. My career was enhanced by having him appear before me.

The case provided an opportunity to see what can be done with an unlimited budget. There was a court reporter hired by the parties with electronic equipment, so I could see in real time what she wrote as others spoke. I normally take good notes, but my spelling is far from perfect. As I paused to write a word on my yellow legal pad, I saw the correct spelling. The testimony from the morning was given to me and the other panel members and lawyers before the afternoon session. The transcripts for the afternoon session were given to us before the next morning's session.

FINRA supplied lunch to the arbitrators, so the three of us ate together and discussed the previous session. We discussed the important points made and what we should be looking for to clarify issues raised. We developed a collaborative process. We formed no real opinions on the merits but raised each other's consciousness regarding the importance of small pieces of evidence. I thought that there would never be a collaborative process like this again. I knew this was one of the best lawyered cases I had ever heard and probably would ever hear. For that reason, I was sad it ended, but knew a settlement is always best, allowing the parties to determine their own resolution and find a way to minimize further costs and expenses. They did not know what punitive damages, if any, might be forthcoming. Business decisions are made often to avoid the unknown if the unknown includes the possibility of a difficult and expensive outcome.

Some Plans Actualize and Other Plans Dissolve

I mentioned earlier that I had intended to arbitrate and mediate following my exit from the judiciary, and those intentions were actualized. I also planned on teaching and writing. My schedule was getting too complicated. I realized that I could not commit to teaching since I was out of town a lot and committed to my case load. I had taught several courses in the past while I was a judge. I served as an adjunct faculty member for Roosevelt University in the Public Administration Department. I taught my favorite course, Judicial Administration, regarding court systems, Administrative Law, and Criminal Law. Usually, I taught at the main building on South Michigan Avenue in Chicago, where I had attended classes as a summer school student. Sometimes, I was asked to teach at Roosevelt's satellites in Arlington Heights or Wheeling before they moved to a beautiful building in Schaumburg.

I particularly enjoyed the Judicial Administration course I taught since it involved all aspects of the court system and how it fit into the governmental system as a co-equal branch of government. We discussed the system of laws and court rules and the application of case precedents. I had a topic on selection of judges at all levels—Trial, Appellate, and Supreme Court— by either appointment or election, giving consideration to the advantages and disadvantages of each method. We covered the independence and dependance of the courts and other offices such as the clerks and sheriffs and the numerous other court officers needed to administer the courts and its programs. In about sixteen weeks we covered almost every related subject and still had time for a mid-term and a final. I felt essay answers were most appropriate and spent a lot of time reading and determining in the test answers what everyone learned and what a few missed. It became easy to see who deserved an A and who deserved something else. I found that most students are very attentive and have the ability to answer whatever question is presented with a slightly different angle, based on their own perspective. Fortunately, I never found that all students missed the same thing. If they all missed, the fault would have been mine and I would have flunked the test. When almost everyone understood the subject and merely expressed themselves differently, I had succeeded.

I found that my classes were well attended. After the first semester, the enrollment in my classes increased. It was a pleasure connecting with young college students with an interest in law enforcement, the courts, and other public service. I was happy and learned from the head of the department of the need for more adjunct teachers. I recruited my friend Judge Francis Barth, who taught a few classes, as well as our mutual friend Judge Dan Coleman. Frank later recruited his brother. The pay was not great but the work was enriching.

Frank was always busy but found time to do more. He had told me that when you need to find someone to do something, ask a busy person. They can usually find a way to do the task in a better than satisfactory manner since they are well qualified and well organized. I remembered that piece of advice and used it whenever I was in charge of a project that needed people to assist.

I realized that each new course required a familiarity with the text book. When a new book came out, I had to spend a lot of time learning the contents. I had to prepare a syllabus and lesson plans. There were papers and tests to grade. When all the hours were counted, I was paid less than *bupkes*—peanuts or more accurately, buttons. I did it for a few years while working days as a judge, since the classes were in the evening, but I realized that I could not afford to do this regularly with my arbitration and mediation practice and the travel that was required.

While I was assigned to hear cases in Skokie, I was recruited to teach paralegals the fundamentals regarding the law so they would understand how the tasks they would be asked to perform fit into a bigger picture. I taught about litigation with summons and complaints being filed and motions to dismiss, forms of discovery, summary judgments, and other terminology. Nothing in the course was taught in depth, but I provided a general survey of matters. Likewise, some students would not be employed by a litigator; some might be involved with real estate closings or commercial transactions, and they had to be generally aware of the forms used. It was always interesting for me to interact with the students. I suspected that some might want to go on to law school after getting a tangential exposure to the law. After a year of teaching at Harper College, the junior college in Palatine, I decided not to pursue my teaching career except for an occasional lecture for a bar association.

Likewise, I did not have time to write the perfect novel that would attract a lot of attention, make me famous, and make me rich. I did know that a few Cook County judges did write some great novels, but I could not find the time or inspiration. I would have to settle on writing book reviews and legal articles to satisfy my lust for writing. Once I was off the bench, I was writing reasoned awards for my arbitration cases, which kept me busy. As a result of my activities, I was unable to follow through on my original intention to do all the things I dreamt of doing, now that I had retired from the bench.

Writing Can be Fun

From the first article of mine that I saw published, I got a thrill seeing my words in print. When Alderman Claude Holman told me his newspaper, the News Clarion, could benefit from a political writer, I jumped at the chance. I hoped I would display some of the talents of my esteemed cousin, Peter Lisagor. I found that writing was a great hobby. I wrote about things I observed or heard in the news that prompted an opinion on my part. I regularly gave my copy to Alderman Holman or his law partner Evelyn Johnson, who also worked on his newspaper. After submitting a particular article one week, I got a call from Alderman Holman and heard him say that while my last article was great and accurate in its criticism of someone, he felt I should be shielded by having an alter ego; that is, a pseudonym. He was going to put as the by line, Keen Eyed Pete. I concurred. I realized he was trying to protect me but publish my comments, where he would take any resulting heat. The more interactions I had with him, the more admiration I had for him, and I realized he took me under his wing and provided protection and an opportunity to gain experience.

While I was writing for the News Clarion while at DePaul in my second year of law school, I was also working on my own law review article. The article was on the need for greater oversite and more stringent requirements for the insurance industry, including increased reserves for each insurance company operating in Illinois. In the previous year there were 23 insurance companies that were deemed insolvent. I came to believe that the Director of the Department of Insurance, John F. Bolton, lacked sufficient power and authority to improve the system and keep the past events from repeating themselves. I interviewed State Representative Cecil Partee, who served in the legislature then, and had a deep interest in improving the insurance system.

The topic I choose for my research and writing efforts seemed very timely. I made a great friend in Partee and enjoyed the knowledge that I was now published in a recognized legal journal—the DePaul Law Review. For a while I memorized the citation to my article: Insurance—Insurance Company Insolvencies: Relief for Victims in Illinois, Volume XV, Number 1, Autumn—Winter 1965, Page 170. As I stated in my realistic conclusion, the need for reform was great, but the likelihood of enacting any proposed changes was slight in light of the powerful insurance industry lobbyists.

About ten years later I became involved in the monthly newsletter of the Judicial Administration Section of the Illinois State Bar Association (ISBA), later to be known as the Bench Bar Section. That newsletter was distributed to every state judge in Illinois with my name affixed as assistant editor or co-editor. I was quite proud to be involved. A few years later the report of the Study Committee on High Volume Courts was released by the Administrative Office of the Illinois Courts with copies distributed to all state court judges in Illinois, and the credits showed my participation on the committee and my role as a co-author.

A few years later, when I was assigned to the Domestic Relations Division of the Court, I was invited to join the American Bar Association and the Family Law Section, where I was placed on the Editorial Board of their quarterly journal. In addition to serving as a screener for submitted articles, I wrote an article on child custody issues. That subject was dear to my heart.

Shortly thereafter, I was invited to join Maryjane Placek—a public defender who worked on murder cases in Chicago and a clinical psychologist who had expertise with abused women who assaulted or killed their husbands or former lovers—in writing an article for the Illinois Bar Journal on the Battered Victim Syndrome. It was an interesting collaborative effort with three points of view, the neutral hearing these cases, the defender of the victims, and the expert for the defense. We argued the validity of such a defense. It was very educational for me. Since I sat on the editorial board of the Illinois Bar Journal at that time, the article was published without any objection.

I served on the editorial board of the Illinois Bar Journal for several years, first being appointed as secretary on the recommendation of my law school classmate Donald C. Schiller, who had been elected president of the ISBA to serve in two years. He would first be the second vice president for a year and then the first vice president for a year, and then president. He placed me as secretary on the Editorial Board and as Secretary of the Publications Committee so I would advance to be Editor-in-Chief and Chair of the Board and Committee when he was president. Everything worked as planned. I moved up each year, acquired the needed experience and understanding of the operations, and then was placed in charge.

The editorial board distributed every article submitted to a panel of three of the ten members. I had to read a lot of articles. When I became Editor-in-Chief, the workload increased three-fold, since the Editor had to read every article. I took my responsibility seriously. Some submissions were easy to read and well prepared and quite interesting. Some articles might be hard to read, not so well prepared, and quite boring or esoteric. I knew that the readership was diverse and, therefore, we needed not only bread and butter articles on practice and procedure, criminal law, domestic relations law, tort law, and real estate, but also an occasional article on less practiced areas like mineral law, admiralty law, and other areas with a smaller audience.

I scheduled the articles so that only one less popular area was covered in an issue and we rotated the popular subjects. We screened out the undesirable articles unless we saw they could be edited to an acceptable level. We were fortunate to have a fulltime staff person, Isolde Davidson, who was the managing editor. As my year as Editor-in-Chief was coming to an end, she advised me that she would soon be retiring and we needed a successor for her position.

I asked her to initiate a nationwide search for candidates. I also notified the incoming President Leonard Amari, Don Schiller's scheduled successor, that there might be some problems in continuity since we had to hire a new managing editor, and while I would be ex officio on the Board and available to help, there might be some problems. He said the best way to avoid any problems was for me to serve an additional year. He had trust in me and felt the position should be for two years in any event. We interviewed and hired Mark Mathewson, who served for over 20 years before he retired. I was proud of my role in approving his selection.

The same board also served as the committee for all bar publications. We published the Bar News in a newspaper format, much less scholarly but full of news. It came out every couple of weeks. We had to make some broad editorial decisions, but the managing editor, Steve Anderson, needed little supervision. We also had to approve all brochures, pamphlets, and other materials put out by the Bar Association. We had many hats to wear. I was so pleased that the Bar News received a professional journalism group's recognition as best publication one of the years while I served as Publications Committee chair.

Leonard was instrumental in rewarding my service on the editorial board and the publications committee by having the Board of Governors— the governing board of the entire bar association—present me with the Board's award for my work in the area of legal publications. Board member Lionel Brazen, a very studious and highly ethical lawyer I knew from service on several bar associations and from having seen him practice before me, was the one who drafted the resolution, presented it to the Board, and argued in support of granting the award to me. I have cherished and appreciated that recognition for my efforts ever since the day I received it. The following year, having read every article coming down the pipeline, I decided not to read the Bar Journal and did not read it for almost two years.

In my time in charge of the ISBA's publications, I was able to publish articles by esteemed veterans of the practice as well as young lawyers. On occasion, I wrote an editor's article or column. We decided to mark the bicentennial of the US Constitution with a series of articles on the protections provided by the constitution. We invited scholars to write articles during the year. We also had a writing contest each year named for Abraham Lincoln, where the winner is guaranteed to see his or her article printed in the February issue. The second and third place winners might be published as well but were not guaranteed. We also had a series on mental health issues, with experts demonstrating how those issues affected practitioners in several fields. Readers might find the articles useful if their practices included any voluntary or involuntary commitments, criminal cases involving insanity or mental capacity defenses, juvenile delinquency petitions, or domestic violence cases.

I also contributed articles to the Northwest Suburban Bar Association Journal, the Chicago Bar Record of the Chicago Bar Association, the Decalogue Society of Lawyers journal, the Tablet, and the Chicago Daily Law Bulletin. Articles I wrote on various subjects appeared in the Bench Bar Newsletter, the newsletter of the Labor and Employment Law section, and the Alternative Dispute Resolution Section Council Newsletter.

An Arbitration Experiment

Quite a few years after working as an arbitrator, I was invited to serve on an American Arbitration Association (AAA) panel consisting of three arbitrators. My panel consisted of two other retired judges, one from Michigan and one from Missouri. We learned that a class action case had been dismissed in federal court based on an employment agreement mandating arbitration and prohibiting class actions. As a result of the court ruling, each of the over 350 class action members had to proceed in separate arbitrations through AAA. The lawyers on both sides agreed the cost would be astronomical unless they could come up with a plan.

The lawyers agreed to pursue discovery relating to liability jointly for all pending cases, since those issues were identical in all the cases. Damages were easily calculated in each case with only a page or two of documents. COVID-19 emerged as they were beginning the arbitration hearings for the first cases. In an effort to avoid needless repetition with many of the same witnesses and to avoid endangering all to the ravages of COVID-19, they decided to record the testimony taken before the first scheduled cases each week so the best presentations could be used in subsequent weeks, where the arbitrators would see and hear the testimony taken before other arbitrators.

Six or seven cases would be heard simultaneously each week by video using the Zoom platform. The only difference in the presentation for each case was one document dealing with damages. Thousands of other exhibits were identical for all the cases dealing with the issue of liability. The parties decided to try several cases together. At a Zoom prehearing conference with the lawyers and panel arbitrators, we were told of the process. One arbitrator serving each week would be selected by the parties from those agreeing to serve as the presiding arbitrator. That arbitrator would determine when a break was in order for lunch or dinner based on the taped schedule for each recorded witness. The arbitrators hearing the cases the week my case proceeded were in time zones from Hawaii to the east coast. Therefore, we could not start too early for our companion in Hawaii, nor could we go too late for those on the east coast.

We reached a consensus on starting and ending times and when short or long breaks should occur. We also insisted that if the consensus among the arbitrators requested a live witness for our questions, that witness should be provided. The lawyers advised us that some witnesses were no longer available due to illness or retirement. We compromised with the lawyers and insisted on certain of the witnesses.

We found that when the taped testimony started, our decision was even more important and essential than we first believed. Two of the arbitrators presiding in the first weeks' arbitrations used for the tapes made rulings on objections that we all deemed overly restrictive, precluding much evidence from being presented. When certain witnesses were presented live to us, we were able to elicit the excluded testimony. The arbitrators acted in a very collaborative manner, agreeing in advance of the witness's appearance what questions we all deemed appropriate. Each of the 11 arbitrators took one subject for questioning. We also limited the time allowed. I had the responsibility of asking the witnesses questions dealing with their interest, bias, or prejudice.

Since the panel I chaired consisted of a member who was also hearing a case other than the one assigned to all three of us, we had a unique situation. One-person panels were used for the smaller cases and three-person panels were used for those cases with greater potential damages. Ours was the only three-person panel that week. We told the lawyers that the three of us would, of course, be conferring and, therefore, our conversations for the claimant we were assigned to hear would also affect the other case of our panel member. Since the parties and their lawyers created this situation, we wanted everyone to know this. The lawyers understood and said of necessity there could be no other way to proceed.

When the other arbitrators heard the three of us going into breaks with conversation or marking documents to highlight certain exhibits and evidence, the other arbitrators asked to join us for efficiency and economy, since we were trying to decide what questions to ask of the witnesses. The lawyers had asked that any live witness be presented serially after all of the recorded testimony was presented. The result was a collaborative discussion with all of the arbitrators during the several breaks. It was sometimes difficult to get a lunch or dinner or to use the washroom and confer but it all worked. Our entire group of arbitrators was a cohesive group. From total strangers, we became trusted partners in finding justice on each of the cases assigned. The ultimate deliberations were separate and the findings and conclusions could be divergent, but farness was achieved.

The Zoom video process, therefore, was fair and economical. Travel expenses were saved. The shipping of huge binders of exhibits was the only major expense. I had 9 boxes containing about 15 folders delivered to my home office. They took a huge amount of space in my office for about two months. I received the materials weeks before the hearing week and then needed them afterwards to be available during our deliberations and exchange of draft awards.

I have been sold on the use of Zoom for all types of litigation. I could easily watch a witness and lawyer in different locations and see my fellow arbitrators by pinning any particular image on the screen to enlarge it. With shared screen features, exhibits could be shown to the witness and to the arbitrators with everyone being remote. It was better than having everyone live in one room. After this experience, I participated with postal arbitrators in training union and management advocates on using Zoom video for their postal arbitrations. I gave training in several sessions and help immediately before a hearing. It worked well for the many advocates who wanted to protect themselves from the COVID-19 virus. I signed up for a Zoom account, allowing me to host up to 99 participants for an unlimited time. I began using the platform for many cases thereafter when I served as mediator or arbitrator.

Planning Ahead

When I started my business, Mediation & Arbitration Services, I anticipated that I might need to provide space to the parties for private mediations and arbitrations independent of any entity that had its own locations. While I did use the facilities at the Lake County, Illinois, arbitration center for my first mediation and the facilities of the Cook County arbitration center for another mediation, I knew I had to make alternative arrangements when those facilities were not available, since I did not want litigants in my office in my home.

With direct referrals by lawyers, I would often use the law offices of one of the lawyers involved in the case. When the issue involved the construction or work on a business or residential unit, I could use the subject location and have the benefit of seeing the problem or contested work areas with every participant viewing the same thing at the same time.

Sometimes, however, I needed private space. I contacted several friends to use their office space. I did not want to impose on any one lawyer or find their space was not available when needed. I used a site in DuPage but more often I used sites in the northern suburbs of Chicago. My friend Ray Grossman offered his law office space on many occasions for use in cases taking only a few hours. His office was off the Edens Expressway at Touhy. I also used the office space of Marv Kaminski, also off the Edens at Peterson. My friend Richard Kaplan offered his space, but I found the need never arose. With a few possible locations available, everything worked out well.

18 GIVING BACK MEANS LIFE RENEWED

Peer Review

Thinking back again to the process of getting to April 1, 1974, and my installation, I thought more about the process. When I was first applying to become an associate judge, I was required to be found qualified by the Judicial Evaluations Committee of the Chicago Bar Association before the Nominating Committee of the Court would consider me. In late 1973 and early 1974, the CBA had an investigators section where one or two lawyers would be assigned to check the background of the applicant, using his or her application as a source to interview lawyers who had cases against the applicant as well as character references, employers, and others. There was a hearing section where member lawyers would randomly appear for hearing and be assigned to one of two hearing rooms.

A candidate and the investigators were all assigned to one of the two rooms. The member lawyers had a few minutes between candidates to review the upcoming candidate's application and the report of the investigator. The investigator would answer questions from the panel members before the candidate was admitted to the hearing room. At the time, the committee had a staff person, Nora Weiss, assigned to coordinate dates, times, and personnel.

After the candidate made a presentation, members of the panel asked the candidate questions touching on his or her background and experience. After the question-and-answer period, the candidate could make a closing statement and was then excused. The members debated the candidates' credentials and the merits of giving a recommended or not recommended evaluation. The rating was given by Nora Weiss to the candidate the following business day. A candidate not recommended could appeal to the CBA Board of Managers. I went through that process in 1974, earning a qualified recommended evaluation from the committee.

Back Story on Process

Although the Illinois Constitution provides for a four-year term for associate judges, by virtue of Supreme Court Rule 39, all associate judges in office were to be subject to a vote of retention by the circuit judges in 1975 and every four years thereafter. The Supreme Court issued the rule after getting a legal opinion from the Deputy Director of the Administrative Office of the Courts, William Madden, who was based in Chicago. Madden knew if judges were sworn in at different times around the state, the office would be involved in elections and retention balloting all the time. Even in each circuit, there could be numerous balloting events, which would be time consuming and expensive. He wanted uniformity and consistency and based his opinion on the best interest of the Court. It is surprising that no judge failing to be retained ever made the claim that their term ran longer than that artificial date in 1975 and every four years thereafter. That part of the rule is believed by some to be clearly unconstitutional and I believe the justices on the Supreme Court have been so advised.

The rule required that every associate judge receive sixty percent of the votes in favor of their retention, just like the Illinois Constitution required for elected judges who were seeking retention by a vote of the citizens before their terms expired. Circuit Judges had a six-year term, Appellate Judges had a ten year-term, and Supreme Court Judges had a ten-year term. All required sixty percent favorable vote in the November elections every two years when voters were asked if Judge X should be retained in office. The two possible answers were yes and no.

Since the process started, the overwhelming number of judges at all levels have been retained, but on occasion, special interest groups like the Fraternal Order of Police (FOP) or a political party has tried to curtail the career of a judge so that they might be replaced by a person perceived to be favorable to the special interest group. Just recently, Thomas Kilbride, a well-respected justice of the Supreme Court, received less that the required 60 percent of the votes, since the Republican party and insurance companies perceived him as too supportive of injured people and laborers rather than employers and insurance interests. He was the first member of the Supreme Court to suffer removal. Some people, mostly Republicans or conservatives, believed he was philosophically too close to the long time speaker of the house, Michael J. Madigan. The fact the decision was based on his view of the law is very disturbing, since that diminishes the independence of the judiciary.

A few years earlier in Cook County, the FOP failed in its efforts to unseat a judge who ruled contrary to their wishes after bar associations and the candidate spent a lot of money in ads to let the public know of the desire of the FOP to corrupt the system. There was a fear by many judges that a ruling on some controversial case could end their career if the ruling was close in time to their next vote of retention. Years before, my friend Judge Howard Miller was wise to duck racially charged cases and pass them on to me, an associate judge not facing the voters but facing the elected judges who understood the law.

I went through the process for retention as an associate judge in 1975, 1979, and 1983. I applied to be an elected judge in 1984 and was elected, so I again went through the retention process as a circuit judge in 1990 and 1996 after being evaluated as recommended for retention in 1984. I retired from the bench in December 1999, during my last term, so I did not go through the process again.

Over the years, the Chicago Bar Association (CBA) was moved out of the position of being the only bar association to evaluate lawyers and judges for fitness to serve. For many minorities, the CBA had its own baggage. It had a policy that restricted membership to men only and refused to accept Jews, Blacks, Hispanics, and other nonwhite persons who were not Anglo-Saxon Protestants.

The Decalogue Society was formed in the 1930's for the protection of Jewish lawyers who were discriminated against by antisemitic judges who required them to attend court on even the most sacred of Jewish holidays. Blacks formed the Cook County Bar Association. Other groups formed similar ethnic or religious based associations due to discrimination against their people. The practicing women had sufficient numbers eventually to form their own bar association as well. It was interesting to me to learn that the grammar school I attended was named in honor of Myra Bradwell, who had been discriminated against in her quest to be licensed as a lawyer because she was a woman. Later, when she was admitted, she did everything in her power to restrict admissions. Her targets were Jewish lawyers. Whenever the Women's Bar Association honored her, I only wished they would realize they were honoring a self-serving bigot.

Some bar associations formed on a geographic basis, since many lawyers found it difficult to travel downtown for CBA meetings. The North Suburban Bar Association, the Northwest Suburban Bar Association, The West Suburban Bar association, the Southwest Bar Association, and the South Suburban Bar Association were formed and became especially useful when their geographic area acquired a courthouse and local issues and needs became evident. There was always the state-wide ISBA. More progressive lawyers had formed the Chicago Council of Lawyers in 1969. The gays and lesbians also had formed their own bar association as did Hispanics, Asians, and others. Most of these bar associations began involving themselves in judicial evaluations, diminishing the importance of the ratings by the CBA.

The CBA's history of restrictive admissions, their conservative slant in favor of old-line large law firms, and the focus on the lawyer rather than the client led to the weakening of the CBA and its exclusive hold on evaluations. With sometimes inconsistent voices issuing opinions on lawyers and judges, the public found it difficult to vote as the lawyers expected them to since the lawyers had no unified voice anymore.

When it came to the evaluation of judges or candidates for judge, each bar association wanted to participate. The suburban bars associations in Cook County formed a coalition to make their recommendations more meaningful. Some of the ethnic bar associations formed an alliance with each other and the ISBA to jointly investigate and evaluate candidates. They invited the CBA to join and the CBA attempted for a few months, but the CBA choose again to go it alone and withdrew. The alliance usually used two investigators for a judicial candidate from two different alliance bar associations. The hearings were conducted with representatives of all of the alliance members. After the hearings, the representatives caucused separately, although each group could hear and give input. Each group issued its own rating and each had its own appeal system.

Giveback Time is Due

After I left the bench, I was approached by the ISBA through the then president and asked if I would be willing to serve on the Judicial Evaluation Committee (JEC), since the perspective of a former judge would be helpful. I found when I joined that a couple of other judges were involved as well. Unlike the CBA, there was one large group. For any candidate, one of our number would be assigned as an investigator. Investigators were trained on obtaining information beyond what the application provided by doing credit checks, checks with the Attorney Registration and Disciplinary Commission for disciplinary actions, and interviews with persons not listed by the candidate—office mates, secretaries in law offices, former spouses, and other sources. Joyce Williams was the staff member assigned to the committee and she ran a fair and efficient process for many years, giving great respect to all candidates and to the members.

I was responsible for numerous investigations during my tenure and was paired with different people each time so we could divide up the work. After a few years, I was asked to serve on the executive committee, helping to make policy, and to serve on the appeal board.

The work of the JEC was important. It took up a lot of time. When I was no longer working in downtown Chicago, it required a special trip downtown for hearings or meetings. After a year or two of service, I decided I could no longer donate so much time and energy to the task, as important as it may be. I resigned after bringing my perspective to the process. I was active in my questioning of candidates, since I had no fear of appearing before the candidate in the future as some of the litigators might have been. Sometimes, I would ask their question for them.

One candidate who did not fare well contended that I had taken control of the room and turned it against her. Her complaint to our staff liaison was investigated and determined to be unfounded. The other committee members all attested to making their own decisions. They might respect me and my opinions, but that did not mean they would go along if they disagreed. In most circumstances, the question I posed to the candidate was their question put to the candidate through me. In any event, I left after believing I had paid back my own debt for all of the time committee members had spent in reviewing my credentials over the almost 26 years I had served.

Surprise Consequences

I find that in addition to my serving the community by being on the JEC, I was benefiting as well on several levels. I began to understand what bothered others and what made them feel comfortable with the service of a neutral that they might have to appear in front of. I learned of their concerns by hearing the comments they made about the candidates. I realized that the point of view of Blacks, Hispanics, Asians, Gays, anti-establishment types, and others might be different from mine. I was open to all of these comments. On another level, I was developing a two-way trust between these other committee members and me. I found that I received requests to mediate or arbitrate matters for their clients.

During a break in hearings one day, a lawyer sitting next to me said he was involved in a case where their client and another couple of partners had developed a serious dispute. They had agreed to have the matter resolved by arbitration. The parties were each to have a partisan arbitrator jointly select a third neutral arbitrator. The other side had already disclosed that their partisan arbitrator was a retired judge I knew who I thought was working exclusively at ADR Systems. The lawyer said he was definitely taking this matter outside of ADR Systems since the lawyer speaking to me believed the lawyer on the other side and this retired judge were close friends and played golf with each other regularly. They had no fear about this relationship since he was not to be the true neutral in the dispute to decide the case, but was involved only as a partisan neutral.

I agreed to serve as the lawyer's partisan neutral, and we decided upon my hourly rate for my services. We discussed what he and his law firm and his client would want in the neutral third arbitrator. This neutral arbitrator would be key to the terms of any resolution. We discussed the disadvantage of selecting someone else from ADR Systems since the other partisan neutral would have too close of a working relationship with that person.

I listed quite a few people who I thought were honest, knowledgeable, and capable. All but two or three were eliminated to include only those the lawyer and his law firm had experience with as a sitting judge or as an arbitrator or mediator. I was then asked who I knew the best and would be best able to work with. I said of the remaining names, retired Judge Edward Burr was the one I felt I knew best. He was at least ten years older than me. When I saw him a few months before, he seemed to be healthy and mentally capable.

After the lawyer heard my comments, he checked with his firm and his client. I was given the go ahead to discuss the last few names with the other partisan arbitrator. He seemed to oppose one of the names and did not oppose or care which of the other two were selected. I suggested we go ahead with Burr, subject to the approval of both parties.

I volunteered to contact Burr about his willingness to serve and told the other partisan arbitrator that he could contact Burr as well. I spoke to Burr, who asked about the case and his responsibilities in it and whether the two arbitrators would be involved in the hearings. I told him that he would rule on any motions and deal with discovery issues, but at the hearing all three of us would be present and hear all evidence. After the lawyers' arguments, the three of us would confer and then he would issue an award with a reasoned opinion.

I told him what I was charging and that it was on an hourly basis. He would probably earn more with any additional hours spent to rule on preliminary matters. I suggested he submit an engagement agreement to both parties since they were sharing his fee. My own fee was payable by the party that hired me and the fee of the other partisan arbitrator would be paid by the party hiring him.

Burr said he was not familiar with an engagement agreement. That did raise concern in my mind. I offered to send him a copy of my standard agreement for him to adapt to the case here. He thanked me. After several months, I learned that the parties had several issues before Burr and he was very slow to respond and did not always seem to appreciate the issues. About a year after being retained, the lawyer hiring me, having reservations with Burr, suggested that we suspend the arbitration and attempt mediation using me and my counterpart as co-mediators.

We would each seek to move the parties closer together, with me primarily working on the party hiring me and the other arbitrator trying to push the party that hired him. I asked that we each get to speak briefly with the opposite party. I concluded that while I had pushed my lawyer's client closer, it did not seem that the other partisan arbitrator had done the same. I thought without him really pushing like I was, nothing was going to happen unless my lawyer's client merely capitulated. I reported my conclusions to the lawyer who had hired me. We never terminated the mediation but merely proceeded to arrange for dates for the arbitration.

This matter was unique since we were empaneled to arbitrate but we took a detour for mediation, allowing the partisan arbitrators to have *ex-parte* communications with both parties and serve as co-mediators before moving back to arbitration. As mediators, I tried to move both parties. My counterpart had no such intention and in fact we were not co-mediating. His tight relationship with the other party's lawyer prevented him from speaking truth to power. The mediation was doomed to fail.

As a practical matter, with the mediation technically ongoing, the other partisan arbitrator could still communicate privately with the party that hired him as I could do as well. Burr, as the neutral, was not part of the mediation process and was not permitted to have direct communication with either of the parties without the other party being present as well.

When it came to the hearing, Burr made many rulings I believed were illogical and inconsistent with rules of procedure and evidence. I asked him to reconsider on many, but he said we'll see down the road. The lawyer who hired me wanted to introduce a document outlining his opening statement for us to better understand the path he would be taking. I thought this demonstrative exhibit would be quite useful to ensure that we later covered all of the material points in our award. The other side objected and Burr sustained the objection. When we next took a break and the three arbitrators were in a room eating, I told Burr by precluding the use of that document, we will only be making things harder for ourselves at the end of the case. He said we will see and everything will be alright.

When the case was coming to a close after days of testimony, both parties said they would want an award by July 5, only a few months away. Burr quickly agreed. The parties then asked for time to have a briefing schedule for post-hearing briefs, but the other side said that because of other commitments, they needed a few extra weeks. As I began to whisper in Burr's ear that he must extend our deadline for issuing our award if he is extending the time for briefs. He ignored me and agreed to the request, which would give us only a very short time to confer, write an award, and get it signed or dissented to by the three of us.

After the first brief was in, Burr told me that his wife appeared to be fine, but, in reality, she had been suffering from memory issues, and much of his time was spent caring for her. He asked if I would take the responsibility of writing the award. I said there would be little time to do so after the briefs were received since, due to his orders, we would lose jurisdiction after July 5. He apologized and said he should have listened to me earlier, but he knew I could handle it. After the last brief was received, I tried to reach both arbitrators, and Burr would say how busy he was with his wife and that he would agree with my position as I stated it. He said, "Write the award you outlined and I will read it and sign it."

The other partisan was not only more difficult to reach, but was unwilling to compromise. I told him he could dissent since Burr had agreed with my position. I told him that I preferred to have a unanimous award and that I would compromise. He told me what he thought was most important and would then consider signing, but he said he was not giving any guarantees. I began drafting an award, cutting some of what I had planned to include by way of damages. I circulated the draft. Burr said it was fine. The other arbitrator did not respond until the day before the deadline. I reached him at his son's house on the 4th of July.

I set up a call where all three of us could hear each other and hammered out what I thought were the final compromise elements of the award. I said I would send them over in a couple of hours, and if either side had an objection, to get back to me, but the deadline was only hours away. I sent out the final version and heard nothing except from Burr, who asked that I affix his signature and name.

I sent the award to the parties in a timely manner and submitted my invoice to the party that hired me. Within a few weeks, I heard that litigation was being prepared by the other side contesting the award since the other arbitrators never actually agreed. They obtained an affidavit from Burr that he did not allow his name or signature to be affixed and that he never read the award before, and, if he had, he would not have agreed to the award as written.

I was astounded on many levels. First, how did the other party approach Burr, *ex parte*, and get his affidavit. How could Burr backtrack on all the things he now denied, such as having read my draft, agreeing to it, having discussions with me and a final conference with all three of us. Had I picked a conning fixer or was he just incompetent or distracted by his wife. Perhaps he had his own memory issues as well. The other arbitrator had said to Burr in my presence that he would be happy to get Burr business with ADR Systems. Was that Burr's incentive?

In any event, after receiving a copy of the motion to set aside the award and receiving a subpoena to appear before Rita Novak, an Associate Judge, sitting in Chancery, I notified my professional insurance carrier and had counsel represent me. In addition, I consulted with my cousin, practicing attorney David Epstein, who appeared in court with me. I conceded on cross examination that I had made a mathematical error in the damage calculations, but that should not interfere with the bottom-line conclusion that there was no fraud by me or the other arbitrators and the award was appropriate to stand.

Judge Novak, after saying she was in a difficult position with three distinguished former members of the court being in disagreement, she remanded the case for further proceedings before other arbitrators. I have no idea what happened thereafter. I acknowledge that I made a mistake in that case. I don't mean my mathematical error that she could have corrected, but my error in recommending Burr.

Not long afterwards, the Attorney Registration and Disciplinary Commission (ARDC) web site showed Burr was no longer authorized to practice law. His health issues, if any, are no longer my business. His health and mental ability were my business when he was under consideration. I experience lingering feelings of disappointment that the system failed the lawyer's client in getting a fair and efficient hearing with a just result without needless expenses and costs.

I have come to the conclusion that the means of resolving a conflict by litigation, arbitration, or mediation does not insure fairness. I had already concluded that the method of selection of a judge, whether by appointment or by election, does not guarantee getting a good judge. Sometimes I wonder what is the best way and who is truly fair and just. What is justice?

Some Conclusions from Working on Judicial Evaluations

Now, getting back to my time involved with judicial evaluations, I had realized something going through the process as a candidate and a judge and it was affirmed when I sat on the other end as an evaluator. There should be a program to improve the performance of judges, enhance the system, and benefit the public in addition to judicial education programs. Even before my service on the JEC, I learned of the need to help judges improve their conduct with proper feedback. I knew from my service on the ISBA Judicial Administration Section Council and as it became known as the Bench Bar Section Council that in Champaign County, the bar association had set up an ombudsman program where a well-respected lawyer in the community would receive comments or complaints regarding judges that did not rise to the level of an ethical violation, where prosecutors or the ARDC would have jurisdiction.

A lawyer could tell the ombudsman that a judge was spitting when he spoke, and this way the lawyer's identity would not have to be disclosed, embarrassing the judge. If there were complaints of a judge sitting on a decision for a lengthy period, the ombudsman could tell the judge that the lawyers and their clients need a timely decision. The system there worked well in Champaign County.

I was determined to bring a system like it to Cook County and was open to the program being available in all of the other counties and circuits as well. I enlisted several active members of the Bench Bar Section Council, and we drafted a proposal suitable for the huge number of lawyers and judges in Cook County. We considered that different panels of intermediaries would be required for the different branches and divisions of the court, where issues in domestic relations may be different from those in criminal or chancery or law cases.

We favored having a diverse panel of actively practicing lawyers of all racial, ethnic, and religious groups, with both genders, and including retired judges as well, so complaining lawyers would feel comfortable as well as the judge being approached. If a former judge might be more easily listened to by the sitting judge, she or he might be more amenable to change the conduct complained of. It might also be possible for the retired judge to understand the reason for the sitting judge's conduct and explain it to the complaining attorney.

When I was on the JEC, I had investigated a judge in a suburban court house who was seeking retention. I learned that many lawyers complained that she did not take the bench until long after the scheduled time. It was felt that she was indifferent to the schedules of the lawyers. What my investigation disclosed was that this judge, hearing criminal cases, was dependent on the availability of a court reporter, the arrival of prisoners coming from the jail adjacent to the courts at 26th and California in

Chicago, many miles away, and the availability of sheriff's deputies.

The judge could have benefited from an intermediary, like me or another experienced retired judge, telling her that she should come out on the bench at the appointed time and explain the problems, stating that the bus of prisoners was late and that she and two other judges were sharing a court reporter. She could offer to make a record for the lawyers who merely wanted a continued date after being tendered discovery by the prosecutor. She could tell the lawyers that she would page them if they wanted to attended other cases in the same building and let them know when the court reporter was available in this room or when their client had arrived on the bus.

Since she did not come out at the proper time, lawyers suspected she was not waiting as well. Transparency would have gone a long way to shift the anger from her to the real source. Without the intermediary program allowing for the lawyers' concerns to be conveyed to her, she was a deer in the headlights set up for a poor evaluation by the bar associations, and she faced the danger of not being retained.

New members of the Section Council expressed the need for the program. Each of the next 20 or more years, as the section council sought the ISBA's approval for a court managed program, refinements were made. One major improvement was the amendment of a Supreme Court rule to protect the intermediary by providing confidentiality for all of the communications similar to those already allowed for the Lawyer Assistance Program.

When I was Vice Chairman of the Bench Bar Section Council pushing the intermediary program, the new Secretary was a downstate judge, Lloyd Karmeier, a bright and affable hard working committee member. He went on to be an appellate judge and then a Supreme Court justice while on the Section Council. The section recommended the rule change and he made it happen. He understood the benefits and sold them to the Supreme Court. The section had the plan of selling the intermediary program to each circuit and have them enact rules suitable to their local situation, just as a group of us from Cook County tried to prevail on the Chief Judge in Cook County to support and implement our program.

Several members of the council, including former Associate Judge James N. Karahalios, Willis Tripler, Appellate Justice Michael B. Hyman, and myself, as past chairs of the section, met with Chief Judge Timothy C. Evans. While he always was cordial and appreciative of our efforts, he never moved an inch to help. After time passed, we all concluded that he was not a supporter of the program. We would have to have the bar association itself set up the program without cooperation from the Circuit Court in Cook County.

Betrayal and Let Down

The experience with Evans was particularly hurtful to me because of our personal relationship, going back to 1969, when he became a lawyer. He began to work in the law department of the city in the tort division. Tim also joined the 4th Ward organization of Claude Holman based upon his introduction to Holman by Glenn Johnson, who had been instrumental in getting Evans a scholarship to attend law school at John Marshall Law School.

Tim Evans had gone to public high school at Hirsh High School on the south side. After he married, he moved to Hyde Park with his bride, Thelma, a practicing pulmonary physician. They had twin daughters, Cathy and Cindy, slightly older than my daughter. They lived in the 5000 South Cornell apartment building, still occupied by my parents, about a block away from our apartment building. Sometimes neither Tim nor Thelma would get home before the girl's nanny had to leave. They regularly asked my mother to care for the girls, and my mother was all too happy to care for them until Thelma got home. My mother would usually give the girls snacks or dinner. Elizabeth would play with the twins on many occasions. Years later, the twins attended Elizabeth's wedding in New York and were treated like members of our family. I have been getting fathers' day cards from the girls for many years.

Tim became a precinct captain in the 4th Ward Regular Democratic Organization and shared the precinct near 48th and Lake Park with a very efficient and affable man, Johnnie Hill. I would sit with and visit with Tim on many occasions at ward meetings and saw how well he related to everyone. Later, having been named the ward organization's president by Alderman Holman in his capacity as ward committeeman, upon the death of Claude Holman, it was my responsibility, with the consensus-approval of the precinct captains, to recommend a successor as committeeman to the chair of the county organization, Mayor Richard J. Daley.

Many members of the organization contacted me and asked me to call a meeting and to express my support for them. It was clear to all that I was not going to be a candidate, being a White man in a predominately Black ward. I considered all of the candidates who expressed an interest and also considered a few others who had not contacted me. I decided that I wanted a man like Claude Holman, who would be intelligent, educated, independent of any special influences, and unbiased and someone I felt I knew.

I came to the conclusion that Tim Evans might be the one to fit my criteria. I consulted Nick Melas, who was the highest-ranking public office holder in the organization. He had been the city sealer before. That position became the Commissioner of Consumer Weights and Measures, later occupied by Jane Byrne. With Claude Holman's and Mayor Daley's help, he had been elected a trustee of the Metropolitan Sanitary District and ultimately became the President, running one of the largest governments in Cook County in a transparent, honest, efficient manner, using his skills and the education acquired at the University of Chicago. He had acquired a master's degree and was deserving of the offices he occupied. Importantly, Nick was the chairman of the ward's executive committee, having been put in that position by Alderman Holman. I believed that Alderman Holman expected and knew we would confer and reach a consensus.

Nick asked me why I thought Tim should be our candidate. We discussed his qualities and shortfalls, and after a thorough discussion, Nick agreed with my choice. We had also discussed the other possible candidates and their strengths and deficiencies. One logical candidate was the Ward Superintendent that Alderman Holman had put in and who supervised about 20 of the workers in the organization. He was supported by the secretaries and staff of the ward office, since they had worked with him on a daily basis. Nick and I felt he was influenced by a man who may be too close to unsavory people.

My next step was to speak to Tim and tell him of our discussion and get his reaction. Tim was not only grateful, but was excited and very desirous of getting the nod. We then arranged for Nick and I to meet with the mayor to get his feedback. Tim was known to the mayor, since the mayor, at the request of Alderman Holman, had made Tim the deputy head of investigations for the city, moving Tim from the law department to that role.

The mayor asked most of the same questions about Tim that Nick had asked me. The mayor was interested in Tim's family, education, work habits, honesty, and ability to communicate and get things done. I tried to be honest and yet wanted to give an unreserved endorsement for Tim. At the end of our meeting, the mayor said, if the precinct captains approved, he would recommend that Tim be approved by the Central Committee of the party.

My involvement in selecting the political successor of my mentor Claude Holman put me inside the room where the decision was made by the king maker, Mayor Daley. I had a firsthand chance to see how he interacted and took in facts. He asked appropriate, direct, meaningful questions that showed me his concern for ethics, character, work effort, and efficiency. He regarded family as a cornerstone of life. I was impressed and saw how at ease he was with his position of power. He invited honesty and created the environment for truth. I was relieved to hear his quiet voice, see the twinkle in his eyes, and see the smile on his face. His handshake was warm.

During the process, I did not know what might be the hardest step in the process. It turned out that getting a majority of the precinct captains on board was the challenge. Each of the other candidates had several friends and the ward superintendent had a block of votes. I allowed open discussion but did not allow a vote since I was not sure of the outcome. While there were no negative comments made about any candidate, I heard murmurs that Tim was not prompt in responding to calls and did not follow up on tasks without many reminders. I adjourned the meeting until a week later, when all of the members of the organization would reconvene. In the meantime, Nick and I persuaded enough precinct captains to understand that certain of the candidates had insufficient strength and that they should be convinced to support Tim. With enough pledges, we convinced McVoy, the ward superintendent, that Mayor Daley favored Tim.

We explained that McVoy's future was with Tim. His position might not be secure with the mayor believing he thwarted his will. McVoy folded. The vote at the second meeting was by acclamation. I never understood why Tim had not truly understood his rise to the position of committeeman was in large part due to my efforts. Once Tim was committeeman, he could call the shots and determine who would be the party candidate for Alderman. He picked himself to run for Alderman and was elected. He served several terms and later under Mayor Harold Washington, the first Black mayor, he became the floor leader and chairman of the most important committee of the city council, Finance. Tim participated in the County Central Committee deliberations on policy and candidate selection. Tim was installed when the party still had tremendous patronage and power. Tim shared some of that power.

When Tim fell out of favor with the voters in the 4th Ward, he lost the next election for alderman to Toni Preckwinkle, who later went on to be President of the Cook County Board of Commissioners. After Tim lost the race for Alderman, he then ran for circuit judge from a subcircuit district centered around the 4th Ward. After his election as a Circuit Judge, he was made a supervising judge and then a presiding judge of the Domestic Relations Division and then the Presiding Judge of the Law Division, when the Presiding Judge of that division moved on to become Chief Judge.

Deja Vu, All Over Again

With the positioning set for Tim Evans by both Chief Judge Harry Comerford and Commerford's successor Chief Judge Donald O'Connell, Tim ascended to the office of Chief Judge. Among those helping Tim, besides the retired chief, Comerford, and retiring Chief Donald O'Connell, were Acting Interim Chief Judge, Henry Budzinski, the Probate Division Presiding Judge, who had run city-wide with me in 1984, and Judge Moshe Jacobius, the Presiding Judge of the Divorce Division.

Moshe was born in Israel and immigrated to the US and settled in the Chicago area, living in the northern suburbs. After service in the office of the Attorney General, he was elected from a subcircuit as a judge of the Circuit Court. Unlike a sabra, one born in Israel who is hard on the outside and soft on the inside, Moshe was soft on the outside and hard on the inside. His inner strength gave him strength to act on his convictions. He had a strong ally in his corner, a strong religious figure whose charitable activities were later under investigation by the state Attorney General. With pressure from a wealthy benefactor, none of the questioned actions in his charitable endeavors saw the light of day, although his wings were clipped for a while—but only a while. His backing did give Moshe a lot of confidence.

Moshe Jacobius did a lot of hard bargaining and lobbying for Tim and would have been at risk if someone else had won—even with his religious supporter. There was a tight contest for the position the first time Tim ran. Shortly before the voting, another very prominent judge in the law division announced his support for Tim, and that tipped the scale. That judge, Bill Maddox, was rewarded by Tim and made the new Presiding Judge of the Law Division. Moshe was rewarded as the new Presiding Judge of the Chancery Division. Tim was consolidating his position and power with those moves. Moshe became the key to

Tim's success in becoming the chief judge as I had been for him to become the committeeman years before. Tim smiled and enjoyed the results. He enjoyed the hard work, cunning, and risk taken by others to ease him into power as chief judge, as he had to become committeeman years before.

When I tried to get out of traffic court as a judge, after being there longer than any other honest judge at the time—8 months, I spoke to Tim, as my friend, and he said he would speak to Chief Judge Harry Comerford on my behalf, but nothing happened until I was transferred out after 11 months. Tim had earlier said he would help me become an associate judge, but I learned later that he did nothing. When I ran for Circuit Judge, he did not push for me during the slating process. Tim never said he spoke to anyone or said anything on my behalf. He only said he would do what he could when I asked him to speak to Comerford or members of the Democratic County Central Committee.

The failure to support the intermediary program was a major disappointment for me, but only one of many disappointments I suffered due to Tim. Tim approaches me whenever he sees me with a smile and a handshake and a hug and he tells whoever is present that "Mike is his great friend." We talk about family and each move on. When I left the bench, I received glowing remarks from many lawyers and judges and with their permission used those remarks in materials I sent with my resume when asked by lawyers considering using my services for arbitrations and mediations. Tim said he did not want to show any favoritism to me or use his office inappropriately. I said all I was asking for was a letter wishing me well after serving the community during my 26 years of service as a judge. Well, he did finally say no and that came out so easily for him.

Maureen and I were disappointed, but not shocked, when Tim moved out and left his wife Thelma when she was ill. He had been dating another woman. He even took that woman to a ceremony in Washington, D.C., where he received an award from then Chief Justice of the US Supreme Court, William Rehnquist, and did so in the presence of his daughters. He became the longest serving chief judge in Cook County, the largest unified court system in the country. He received the award on behalf of the court system.

Until Tim is retired from the bench, Thelma is ineligible to receive any amount of his pension that she is entitled to receive under their divorce decree. They are both close to eighty already. Tim was born June 1, 1943 and is about 14 months younger than me. Thelma is close in age. When Thelma was very ill for a while, Tim let me know he visited her to see what she needed. She lives at the former family home in Kenwood in the 4th Ward. Tim and the girls no longer live in the 4th Ward. The girls see and care for her regularly.

Tim stayed in his judicial office as long as he did because he enjoyed the role, the power, or the perks. He had the advantage of not needing to work on his own or for anyone else. He also had the knowledge and perhaps satisfaction that Thelma would not get a penny of his pension as long as he was working as a judge. She could collect a portion of his pension only upon his death or retirement so long as she was still living. If Thelma died and he remarried, a second wife might get those spousal pension benefits. His daughters might get the money he paid into the system if he and Thelma died before he collected as pension the amount of money that he had paid into the pension system during his years on the bench. They would not be able to receive more than he had paid into the system that had not already been paid to him or his spouse as pension benefits.

On many occasions, I have regretted the vigorous support I gave to a man who showed little gratitude. I never asked for anything inappropriate, unethical, illegal, or embarrassing. I was shown no favor or benefit whatsoever. What I have regretted was not getting truthful and open answers when I asked if he could or would do something on many issues and topics. He only said no once to my request for a congratulatory letter after my retirement. Sometimes I believed he was listening to persons who controlled his conduct with him being only a puppet. I may never know. He acquired a reputation of inaction and delay, never saying no to anyone for any reason. I heard many complaints about him being non-responsive to calls. When some people called me to complain, I could only tell the truth, that I had the same experience.

A Little Here and a Little There, But Not Everywhere

The Intermediary Program Blossoms in Parts of the State, but not in Cook County

In the meanwhile, to advance the intermediary program in as many counties as possible, I had contacted the chief judges in Lake and Winnebago counties on behalf of the Bench Bar Section Council and found their support and witnessed immediate implementation. Justice Lloyd Karmeier arranged for programs to be started in several of the counties feeding into his appellate district in southern Illinois. Yet, there were many areas of the state not implementing any intermediary program. We went to state agencies affiliated with the courts, but they felt it was beyond their purview or felt they did not have the resources to support the activities required. Justice Hyman and I made many presentations to no avail.

We then turned our attention to the leadership of the ISBA to implement a state wide program helping in the various counties and circuits. We faced resistance with the fear of expense. We argued that the volunteer members of the section council would be the vanguard of labor and there should be little or no expense. The leadership declined saying that when the Bar Association started judicial polls and evaluations, they thought it would be inexpensive and it turned out to be a substantial part of the budget.

Although the ISBA was still on record of favoring an intermediary program through the courts, they did not want to be the sponsor. Our arguments that this activity would make practice easier and kinder for its member lawyers and make the system function better for the public fell on deaf ears. While we believed we would wait a few more years with different leadership at the ISBA, I found I was no longer on the section council, after serving all but two years since 1975 when Judge Wachowski and Justice Johnson had me put on as an assistant editor of the newsletter under Dennis Dohm. The project was for me an effort I had invested in for over 40 years without success. Perhaps I should accept defeat. I am ever hopeful though, that other lawyers will carry on the effort and some day in the future there might be an intermediary program in all of the Illinois courts. If just a few judges around the state benefit from the programs that we encouraged, I should be happy for whatever insights they gained.

19 THE WIDE VIEW

A Perspective of History

I had ascended to the bench at age 31 in 1974 in the wake of a national scandal involving President Richard Nixon, who abused his power trying to coverup his and his agents' involvement in a burglary of the Democratic national party headquarters at the Watergate Apartments in Washington, DC. History suggests that his coverup was worse than the crime of burglary. I believe I had a lift in my favor since I was young, fresh, and clean, whereas others selected with me were not so young. Some had a lot of experience in the profession. My connections and lack of experience had to be of prime relevance. As I was sworn in as a judge, I heard Nixon saying, "I am not a crook!" I felt I was going to hit a home run now, by helping make the judicial system work fairly and justly.

    I was thrust into the midst of the other major scandal in my own back yard—Operation Greylord, the code name used by federal investigators looking into our local courts to ferret out corruption and to hold wrongdoers accountable. Upon becoming a judge, I rubbed shoulders with those who went on to fix not only parking cases and minor moving violations, but also drunk driving cases, enabling those criminally charged people to go on again and again to kill or maim others. As I was sworn into office, I received my marching orders to report to Supervising Judge Richard LeFevour at traffic court located at 321 North LaSalle Street in Chicago, where I had started my legal career in 1966. I was like a lamb going to the slaughter, feeling only happiness and delight.

Some of those corrupt judges I rubbed shoulders with moved from traffic court to criminal branch courts where drugs or guns were involved. Some went to domestic relations where children's custody was sold to the highest bidder. In at least one case, a murderer was able to buy his way out of a conviction. Fortunately, years later, an honest judge ordered a retrial, holding that jeopardy had never attached since the judge was bribed. To generate statistics that were plausible, innocent defendants were often found guilty; because of poverty, the defendants had a public defender or they had hired lawyers who did not pay the bribe. We had a system that stole people's children, fortune, liberty, and dignity.

Would the solution to insure justice be the selection of judges by a blue-ribbon panel? Who decides who is good enough to be on the selection panel, and what insures they will pick people who will be ethical as well as bright?

We saw that some of those convicted were in respectable positions before going on the bench, such as Richard LeFevour. Some were bright such as Allen Rosin. The last job, the IQ, or the school attended do not guarantee the best, the brightest, or the most ethical. I saw women and men who were down to earth and did not have the best credentials do great work. Monica Reynolds is a great example. When the Chicago Tribune did its survey of the judges in the Domestic Relations Division, she was one of the six best judges in the division. She worked hard to support her family. When her husband or son stumbled, she was there supporting her family and always showed knowledge of the law, decency, and compassion. She related to all people. Even after she retired, she gave to the community by serving as an arbitrator for only the honorarium in the mandatory arbitration program. She was typical of so many more unsung heroes.

She was conscientious in awarding the best parent custody because she knew that she had that child's future in her hands.

When I attended her funeral and that of my good friend Peter Fitzpatrick, I learned that these two Irish Catholic families were united, with a child of one marrying a child of the other. To find my friends were now family was heartwarming. The world is smaller than I could imagine and there are enough good souls to make life worth the effort, in spite of suffering the transgressions by others bent on profit at the expense of morals, law, decency, and humanity.

My Mentor Goes Home, But Creates My Path Forward

Before I became a judge, I attended the funeral of Claude Holman, who had put a list of things he had to do in a notebook he carried with him. He was in an open coffin in a fine suit, wearing his black rimmed conservative glasses. I felt uncomfortable looking at him, knowing he could not see me. It did not seem right on so many levels. One of the things he had not yet accomplished was to help make me a judge. He was with me in my heart as I was sworn in and everyday thereafter. He had accomplished much in his life. One of those things he accomplished was to help make me a better man. He saw the positive in mankind. He saw what united us and not what divided us. He had produced a television program called "Unsung Heroes" on Chicago's channel 26, broadcasting out of the Board of Trade Building.

He featured people who did good deeds for other people without much fanfare. He asked me to moderate the program. I can't say I became a TV star, since I don't believe too many people watched the program other than my parents, my wife, her parents, and maybe a few others, but the people I interviewed proved the goodness in the hearts of many. I felt inspired to achieve and help others. While the program only lasted a few weeks, it was important to me. Claude Holman, when introduced with all of his important titles, jokingly said as he took the microphone that they missed his title as notary public. He had many hats: lawyer, newspaper editor, television producer, alderman, committeeman, and health committee chairman, but the most significant to me were teacher, mentor, role model, protector, advocate, sponsor, and friend. He never bragged about defeating his challengers each time he was elected alderman, and he respected his opposition, whether it was Cohen, Timuel Black, or others. He never lost an election. He beat very formidable, qualified, and decent people.

Alderman Holman not only invited me to write for his *News Clarion* newspaper, he asked me to take Maureen to see a play, *The Great White Hope*, and give a review of the play for the paper. I discovered the play was about a prize fight pitting a Black challenger against the White champion who was the hope of the Whites. It was a review that challenged me to see things not just as a White man but as though I were a Black man too. I tried to be objective, but reflect both possible biases. He was happy with my work, which pleased me. I tried to apply what I learned in my speech class at Little Rock University about knowing your audience. I spoke to my readership and accomplished my mission, just as when I spoke at ward meetings and larger well attended events, such as the annual fund raiser for the organization. I spoke truthfully from the heart, but was always aware of my perspective and approach, and, of course, my audience. I tried to put gusto into my words to liven the delivery. When I finished, I always received applause. I never knew if the applause were due to appreciation of what I said or relief that I was sitting down at last. I applied the same skills to my advocacy in court.

Maureen and I invited Alderman Holman to our apartment for dinner one evening. Maureen made many dishes that took a lot of time and effort; and they were delicious. It was amazing that while he seemed to enjoy all of the food, he had seconds of white rice that had taken almost no time to make. He said it was the perfect consistency and he truly enjoyed it. After we finished, I took the dishes into the kitchen to clear the table and when I settled back down into my seat, I heard Maureen agreeing to something. Alderman Holman explained to me that as

Health Committee Chairman of the City Council, he had passed an ordinance to create a health center to be located in the north end of the ward. There would be an advisory board to help guide the progress and programing. He had asked Maureen to serve on the board. Maureen had agreed to serve, understanding that the job had no perks and no pay.

I remember accompanying Maureen to the first board meeting and seeing we were the only White people in the room. We did recognize a few people. As the meeting progressed, someone made the comment that we do not want any strangers running our health center. I knew the speaker was referring to Maureen. Maureen, not recognizing that she was the object of the man's disparaging remark, spoke up and agreed that we do have to be sure that no outsiders try to take over. One person I knew who was also put on the board by Alderman Holman was Mrs. Elise Bonner. She knew the man's remark was directed to Maureen and she wasn't going to let him get away with it. She looked at the man and then at Maureen and said, "I know both of you and neither of you are outsiders or strangers. Together we will work to make sure our entire community maintains control."

That ended any chance of rancor or animus. After Alderman Holman died, the city named the facility the Claude W. B. Holman Health Center as a fitting and lasting tribute to his public service in the health area. When the building was completed and we toured the facility, we saw a modern complex that helped people with their health needs when they didn't have the resources to go to private facilities.

At the time, Maureen was a teacher in the Chicago Public Schools. She served in a few schools. One year she was at the Hamline School in Canaryville, around 47th and Ashland, where she found a lot of poverty. She taught the children hygiene, discussing brushing their teeth each day following meals. One girl said she didn't always have time, since she and her sister shared a tooth brush and other children in her family waited to use the washroom. Maureen went out and bought enough tooth brushes for each child in her class and saw the smiles of gratitude. We suspect that the girl who acknowledged she was sharing was not the only one not having her own tooth brush. Maureen had another assignment of very short duration at the Stagg School in Woodlawn, where she was assigned to work in a television-like studio to teach remotely, as many teachers would do 50 years later due to COVID-19. After only a week, she was replaced by a teacher whose brother was the state senator for the area. Clearly, the clout of the other teacher forced Maureen to go elsewhere.

I came to realize that the election of John F. Kennedy in 1960 and Lyndon Baines Johnson in 1964 made the national Democratic party one of the greatest civil rights organizations by passing the Civil Rights Act, creating Medicare, and promoting other progressive programs for our great society. I was living out a dream to be part of the side that was helping the poor, the oppressed, and minorities, unlike those ignoring underprivileged people and focusing their support on the rich, the powerful, and the privileged. I knew within the same Democratic Party were also the bigots, segregationists, and regressive politicians in Congress, mainly from the south, but from the north as well. We had a lot of work to do not just in the south but in our own back yard.

The Perk That Lasts Until Death

One of the residual powers I still enjoy after having been a judge is having the authority and power to officiate at wedding ceremonies and sign marriage licenses, allowing me to be with people at their happiest moment. I usually asked the couples how they met and what attracted them to each other. When there were differences, I probed how their families accepted their decision and the life mate they choose. They told me their respective ages. I learned if they had previously been married and if there were any children born or on the way.

I found that when people called and wanted to be married in the next few days, the weddings usually did not proceed. Of course, there were exceptions. I found sometimes there were great differences in age and the parties were raised with different religious beliefs. I told them of the challenges, having sat in divorce court, and challenged them to discuss how they would raise any children they might have, how they would celebrate holidays, and which rituals were important to each of them. Some of the people I questioned found some of their families' religious practices and customs were more important to them than they thought. I asked if their future spouse wanted to do things differently, would it bother them. When it did, I suggested the couple have an open and candid discussion alone with no other family present. If they could not work out their differences, they were asking for trouble.

When Illinois law allowed civil unions between persons of the same gender and later allowed the definition to be marriage and not merely a civil union, I was enlisted. I came to the conclusion that our state and our society had recognized that everyone should be able to be with the person they love. Every woman and man could love anyone. I did have to alter my ceremonies and in particular alter the titles such as bride and groom and husband and wife to partner for life. I would ask if they cared which person I addressed first. When referring to a man and women, I would say the woman's name first. When I asked for consent to be married to get the response of "I do," I would always ask the man first and get his commitment before asking the woman. Now, with either two men or two women, I wanted their impute. My guess was not always accurate so it was good for me to ask.

I found I was sometimes performing a wedding in a huge beautiful venue with hundreds of people in attendance, but sometimes it was just me and the couple in their apartment or a park. Occasionally, there was a photographer with the couple. There were a few weddings, of the hundreds I did after leaving the bench, that stand out. There was a couple who were in the entertainment business as singers and dancers. They had a major production created for the entry and recessional at their wedding ceremony. The groomsmen and bridesmaids sang and danced. I felt like I was in the middle of a Broadway performance. It was phenomenal.

Another wedding took place at Orchestra Hall, where the couple were affiliated. The first violinist of the Chicago Symphony together with a flutist, oboe player, and base player were three feet from me playing as the bridal party entered and left the hall and during interludes. I had a front row seat to beautiful music and got paid to hear it. It was indeed a treat. The view that day out the window was spectacular as well, seeing the boats in Lake Michigan with a clear expanse in both directions north and south. I was surrounded by elegance.

I was hired to officiate at all of the major venues. I was at museums, libraries, cultural centers, ornate lobbies of office buildings, parks, arboretums, conservatories, dinner ships at Navy Pier, yacht clubs, the White Sox stadium, mansions, roof tops, sky decks, country clubs, art galleries, restaurants, and chapels. Sometimes I was joined by a minister, priest, imam, or rabbi to give a blessing based on a strong family connection. Some priests dressed in street dress so as not to give the impression of my ceremony being sanctioned by the Church. One priest did say he was ready to retire, so he could risk wearing his religious habit. A rabbi referred me to several couples for weddings, since he was converting the non-Jewish partner and wanted to be present before the conversion was complete so they could live together or have children with the benefit of an official marriage license.

I found on many occasions there were people in attendance who I knew and I was always surprised at the connections. When people came from out of town, I realized how small the world is that we occupy. For several weddings, family were on the other side of the world and could share the joy by being on some device to hear or see everything. People in Europe, Africa, and Asia attended my ceremonies. Sometimes, we had a translator convey my words in the family's language. I even had ceremonies where everyone was present, but we had a fluent bilingual guest repeat my words in the language some attendees found more understandable. My nephew Craig, who lived in Ecuador for several years, translated my ceremony into Spanish so that translators could merely read my words in Spanish as I uttered them in English. I had to be careful not to ad lib too much during those ceremonies.

There were a few wedding ceremonies where I had to be sure the bride wanted to proceed. I came to one wedding and, as I always do, asked for the bride or groom to get the license and my fee. At one restaurant venue, I asked and someone pointed to a young man who was in torn jeans and an undershirt. I told him I would not take his time, since I saw he had to change clothes before the wedding. He said he was dressed. He also said he forgot the license. I knew from my psychology classes that he was demonstrating his will not to be married. The bride's father stepped up and was outraged. The groom's mother said she had the license and brought him a shirt and a pair of slacks. The bride was in a beautiful traditional wedding gown. He was cleaned up a bit, but I always wondered how long this marriage lasted. Before leaving, I wished the bride's father well and hoped for the best. He thanked me, but I saw the sadness in his eyes, thinking of his baby moving in with an immature child.

The previous wedding was the only one that was questionable as to commitment from the onset, but I saw other unusual marriages. One involved a traditional Indian wedding, where instead of the groom coming in on an elephant, he arrived on horseback. That wedding was unusual and elegant. I noticed that time in the Indian world is about two and a half hours later than our clock time. A young Indian couple told me how embarrassing it was for them to see the family ignore the value of my time. I noted that some Syrian families were on the same clock as the Indians.

Hispanics also came late, but usually did so only out of necessity because one or more household members were at work and they arrived at the earliest they could get there. Often, when I discussed timeliness with the bride and groom because of another wedding or an event in my family, they would say we will start whenever you say we should. My anxiety level would rise if I saw the couple and their bridal party were not ready and time was passing. I would tell them it was not fair to the people who would be waiting for me.

When I said I had to leave by a certain time, the speed of things usually picked up. On the other hand, some couples wanted to start on time. I counseled them to allow for a five or ten-minute delay, since some people might arrive on time, but by the time they actually entered and found their seats, time would pass. It would be disruptive if many people were entering in the first few minutes, and to bar their entry would be taken as an affront. I advised couples that if I provided a twenty-minute ceremony after waiting five to ten minutes for stragglers, the banquet hall usually needed about twenty to thirty minutes to turn over the seats, so that schedule would work best to avoid over-heated food.

I found that many couples asked me for marital advice, thinking that since I officiated at wedding ceremonies, I was expert in all things related to marriage. Perhaps others knew I had sat in the divorce division. I was always surprised when couples would call me for a ceremony and said that I had married their parents or others in the family, like a sibling. Some said they were in the bridal party for a wedding I did and felt they had auditioned me for the role. I tried to ask how people heard of my name. It was always interesting to me. Some said they had found my website. It was heartening to know the money spent on Google, GoDaddy, and Siteocity was paying off.

I tried to leave my business card with the wedding coordinator at the banquet hall, hotel, or other facility where I officiated. When I was out socially at a place that might cater to weddings, I told them I presided at weddings, and if a couple came and asked for someone, they could suggest my name. Many calls at busy places came with recommendations from those lovely people.

Every once in a while, I would get a card in the mail telling me that a couple had reached a landmark anniversary or they had children. I realized that I might forget many of them, but they would remember the person who married them. Sometimes at weddings, a man or a woman would come over to me and start visiting. I thought they were just friendly, since I usually did not know anyone. I soon realized they knew me from a wedding they had attended, and it might have been their own.

I was surprised one day when I received a telephone call from the wedding coordinator at Chevy Chase Country Club in Wheeling, Illinois, where I had performed many weddings in their two ballrooms and on their terrace. I thought they might be giving me a heads up regarding a referral they had just made. The previous week I had performed a wedding where the plans for the site on their property changed several times due to the changing weather. The couple wanted an outside wedding. I told them what I told all couples about the lack of predictability of weather in the Chicago area. They said they would hope for the best. I asked for their backup plan as I always do, and they said it would be in the ballroom where the reception was already scheduled.

Sure enough, after the employees at Chevy Chase put chairs out on the terrace, the sun disappeared, clouds appeared, thunder sounded, and the rain began. The employees pulled in the chairs. I told the couple that if we waited for the storm to clear, some of the seats might still be wet and ruin the fine clothing of their guests. We waited a few minutes and to the relief of all, the couple yielded to mother nature and we had the ceremony with the guests in their seats at their assigned tables. Some of the guests who heard me speaking with the couple thanked me for urging the move inside.

The call from the wedding coordinator had nothing to do with the previous week's wedding or another future wedding. I was told that two siblings contacted her regarding a memorial service for their mother and asked for a recommendation. Instead of suggesting a clergyman who officiated at another wedding, she and her associates thought I would be ideal. I reminded them that that was not in my comfort zone, but since the date and time requested fit my schedule, I agreed.

I then set on a plan to have a presentable service. I had to get several perspectives about the deceased so that whatever I said would be appropriate and, more important, not inappropriate. I asked if they would suggest persons to be called upon to speak, including the brother and sister. I now had a sense of the ceremony. I would intersperse remembrances by friends and family with things I would say. In order to have appropriate words, I turned to a couple of rabbis I knew who suggested some prayers that no one would find objectionable and might give comfort. I also was guided to prose and poems by noted authors. After I finished putting the service together, I concluded it would be about 30-40 minutes, as they requested, would be soothing and perhaps uplifting, and give some meaning to the women's life. The service went well and at the conclusion I saw tears of remembrance in the eyes of several people. I received many words of appreciation and praise. I found I was being addressed as father or minister and not judge for this Christian assembly. None would suspect that what gave them comfort were the words from the Bible and the words suggested by two rabbis. One of those rabbis was James Gordon, who was also a lawyer and good friend. To date, that is the only memorial service I have been asked to perform.

The episode with the rain at Chevy Chase reminded me of another wedding a few years before, where the reception was to be in a restaurant in Chicago. The ceremony was to be in a park where the couple met, across the street from the restaurant. When I arrived, I saw that rain was on the horizon. I suggested if there were any chance of having the ceremony out in the park, we should start everyone out there immediately and start a few minutes early. All agreed. As we started, newly gathering people saw us and joined the crowd. We then heard the thunder and I gave an abbreviated version of the ceremony ending it quickly as the rain started. I pronounced them husband and wife and ran for my car before getting soaked as they and their family ran for the restaurant and yelled thanks and congratulations.

The last two weddings I will relate here were less than a year after I left the bench. One was scheduled to take place on an afternoon at Buckingham Fountain in Grant Park in Chicago, where the temperature was over ninety degrees. I suggested starting as soon as possible, since I saw some elderly people who looked uncomfortable. I asked for the marriage license that was found in the couple's limousine. I asked for my fee. The bride said to ask the groom who said to asked her parents, who said to ask his parents. It became clear to me that no one intended to pay. I told the couple that unless I was paid, I was leaving and there would be no ceremony. Within minutes, the limousine driver paid me in cash. I never learned what his connection was to the couple, but since I was paid with legal tender, I gave them a beautiful ceremony before we all wilted.

As a result of that hot and steamy wedding and the ones that were rained out due to inclement weather, I always recommended an indoor wedding and asked for a fallback location in the event of bad weather to those insisting on an outdoor location.

The last wedding of note was at the Drake Hotel in Chicago. It is one of the most elegant of places. The ceremony was in their grand ballroom to accommodate about 300 guests. I remember this event for two reasons. One, the processional and recessional each took a long, long time due to the length of the walkway. The grandparents arrived at their seats at the front looking like they had just finished a marathon. When they were seated, and as the bridal party was walking in, I congratulated them as grandparents and also for having made the long walk to their seats. The other reason I remember this wedding was that the father of the bride told me when I went to him for my payment that he would have to send it to me in the future, since he was short of funds. Clearly, he had enough for the hotel and the other expenses, but thought he could have me do it on the cheap.

I had seen a good friend, Barry Greenburg, as people were taking their seats. He and I had shared a cubicle in the General Counsel's Division of the Chicago law department when we both prosecuted liquor and license cases. I told him of the conversation. He said he would speak to the father of the bride, since he knew him. Barry's words motivated the father to come over to me with cash—not even a check. I don't know what I would have done if Barry weren't there to intervene.

When I got home, I shared the story and conveyed the message that in our family we celebrate in a way we can afford. We don't have fun and celebrations on credit or stiffing others. Our word is our bond. Just as Popa Harry, my father-in-law, and Grandpa Ben, my father, committed only to what they could afford. Every event in life is a lesson. Most of the lessons were mine. Here, I shared the experience as a lesson for my daughter and son. I was never again going to be rated poorly in reliability or dependability and I did not expect my children to be seen poorly either.

During the height of the COVID-19 epidemic, when most of the state and federal courts were physically closed and operated by Zoom video and other means, marriage ceremonies were also allowed by video. I performed a few in this manner, requiring the parties to get me the marriage license in advance and to be located in the county where the license was issued. Our system has evolved where not only can a distant guest witness the ceremony from a distant place, but the presiding official may be remote as well. The technology has made everything plausible and possible.

Extended Perks and the Value of a Good Name

My immediate family enjoyed some of the perks I found bestowed on me, and they also suffered the burdens. One day in the summer of 1984, when I was on the campaign trail in my quest to be elected a circuit judge, Maureen and I discovered that we wanted to go to a dedication for a friend at a cemetery. We also were going to a huge picnic for the Lyons Township

Democratic Party, hosted by the Clerk of the Circuit Court. I knew there would be a petting zoo for the children and thought my children might enjoy petting the animals. I also was scheduled to do a wedding—not for a fee, since I was a sitting judge. In consideration of my services, the couple was starting off their marriage by giving to a charity. One good deed deserves another.

The question Maureen and I had was what should I wear so I did not look out of place in any of these venues. At the wedding I would put my judicial robe over my shirt and tie and slacks. At the picnic, I would take off my tie and jacket. At the cemetery, I would wear the tie and jacket. We had it all arranged and made a lot of jokes about the day's events, being careful not to show too much happiness at the cemetery.

For several years, when I was a precinct captain in the 4th Ward Democratic Organization, I received an invitation each fall, as did all workers in the various ward and township organizations in Cook County, to attend the Ringling Bros. Barnum and Bailey Circus at the International Amphitheater, hosted by the 11th Ward Regular Democratic Organization and its leader, Mayor Richard J. Daley. He made everyone feel like they were all members of a huge family. Everyone came with their children and all enjoyed seeing everyone else, including all the leaders and elected officials in the party as well as all of the volunteers.

At first Maureen and I had no children, but then Elizabeth came on the scene and enjoyed the extravaganza. Mayor Daley died a few years before Jeff was born, so Jeff did not get to go to the circus with everyone in the crowd feeling a connection. I did take Jeff years later to a smaller circus that put up a tent at a shopping center at Golf Mill in Niles. For me, it was not the same, but for Jeff, it was exciting since he was just a few years old. I think he enjoyed the hotdogs, popcorn, peanuts, and other snacks as much as the animals and performers. As I have learned, a parent is happy if his kids are happy and cannot be happy if even one of his kids is unhappy.

Thinking back at another wedding I performed makes me think of my name. I had a last-minute conversation with the wedding couple and they gave me instructions to enter the banquet hall through a certain door and take three steps in and then pause for a moment until I heard some music and then to proceed to the front, where the ceremony would be. I did as I was told. I walked in and took three steps and then paused to hear a loud speaker with a voice blasting the words, "and now introducing our surprise guest, MICHAEL JORDAN. With the roar of the crowd, I heard the theme music for the Chicago Bulls being played. As I proceeded to the front, the guests were all on their feet with applause and cheers. It was quite a warm up for the entry of the bride a few minutes later. When the groom reached me, he whispered to me that they did not want me to know for fear I might not consent. My name clearly had value.

It was one evening sometime in 1983 when I entered Congregation Beth Sholom Synagogue in Northbrook for a board meeting that I heard the first Michael Jordan "joke." I saw the executive director, Harvey Gold, who had grown up with Maureen. Harvey said, "Hi, you really played a great game last night." I did not know what he meant. I asked what is that all about? He asked me how I didn't know about the college basketball star Michael Jordan. I said I never heard of him.

Well, beginning that day and almost every day thereafter, I began hearing every sort of joke as Michael Jordan became more and more well known, until he became a Chicago Bulls top scorer and a worldwide celebrity. His name became the most known on the face of this planet. Many of the attempts at humor were repeated many, many, many times. "I thought you would be taller." "I thought you would be darker." "Can you get me some tickets?" I never knew exactly what to say. If I was asked directly if I ever heard that remark or joke before, I would say honestly, "Yes!"

For many years we would get crank calls with people calling our home telephone and asking to speak to "Michael." When I perceived the caller was an eight or nine-year old boy, I would tell him that he reached the wrong number, but I would give his message if I spoke to Michael. When I could tell the caller was an older teen or an adult, I would just hang up. If Elizabeth or Jeff answered, having always been told to be polite, they would merely say he was not available. When the basketball player had a son and named him Jeffrey and he began to play basketball in high school, my son Jeffrey got a few calls as well.

On one occasion when Maureen went to the Jewel Osco drug store to pick up a prescription for me when I had the flu, she was asked if I lived on Essex. She knew of my address in South Shore on Essex Avenue when I was growing up and asked how they would have my old address from a time when there were no computers. The clerk and Maureen finally realized the prescription the clerk had in mind was for "him." At the time, before moving to his mansion in Highland Park, Illinois, he lived on a street in Northbrook named Essex, just a few blocks from the drug store. The clerk found the prescription for the correct Michael Jordan and we knew we better watch out in the future that I was not about to get any performance enhancing drugs or steroids. (We did not know what his prescription was and had no reason to believe it was anything improper.)

I found over time that the name my parents bestowed upon me had magic. When I ran for judge in 1984, the two candidates who filed for the same vacancy in the Democratic primary withdrew and won against other candidates slated with me. I had asked to run for the vacancy of Theodore Swain, who was retiring from the bench. He was a friend from the 4th Ward who I assisted in the precinct. I knew how bright and ethical he was and wanted to fill his vacancy. I think my name scared off the others who originally filed for the Swain vacancy. In the general election, I led the ticket, getting the most votes and trouncing my opponent, another associate judge who was a Republican.

I knew my opponent. When I saw Gerald Rohrer was also running for the Theodore Swain vacancy, I called him and agreed that whoever won would take the other couple out for dinner. Since I won the election, I lost the bet and took the Rohrers out to dinner. I did not mind paying at all, but I realized that while normally Maureen and I would request the no smoking section of the restaurant, Gerry, a chain smoker, got to the restaurant earlier and got seats in the smoking section. He and his wife Pauline had a drink while they were smoking. Maybe that was Gerry's revenge.

I assume the Rohrers must have been toasting my election before we got there. When Maureen and I got home, we each went into the shower to wash off the smoke, sent our clothes to the cleaners, and took anti-histamines. I have allergies to tobacco and Maureen avoids tobacco as well. Years later, when smoking was barred in all restaurants, we would have had a more enjoyable evening. Gerry died early and I assume it was due to his eating, drinking, and smoking habits.

After I left the bench and began my arbitration and mediation practice and was also performing wedding ceremonies, I cannot count the number of times people said to me that they wanted to be able to say they spent the day or evening with Michael Jordan. I tolerated any bad jokes that came my way if they came from people paying for my time. Just recently, I received a new securities case and I asked the case coordinator if I was selected by the staff for this case or if the parties selected me, since I did not know any of the lawyers involved. He said both sides ranked me #1 of the many names tendered to them. I said I assume they like my name. He countered, saying my selection must be based more on my qualifications, since the lawyers and brokerage houses do a lot of screening and checking around. They may like your name, he said, but he believed the selection was made on my experience and background and references that they must have checked before ranking me. I thanked him for his supportive words, but said we will never know.

The next day, when my car radio tuned to the local news station for CBS—780 AM—but I found no reception, I turned to another station and heard the conservative radio host Dennis Prager on 970 AM Radio, interviewing an astrophysicist. The man being interviewed was a recent author and his book dealt with the Nobel Laureates. The author believed that no matter how accomplished each of the laureates was in science, they felt they were imposters recognized for achievements they had no right to accept. When they appeared in Stockholm and signed the receipt for the million-dollar honorarium and the medal and certificate, they saw the names of people who received the science awards in years past and saw names like Enrico Fermi, Albert Einstein, and Sir Isaac Newton, they felt ashamed and undeserving to be in such company.

Each laureate was told that men like Albert Einstein felt inadequate seeing a name like Sir Isaac Newton before them and were told that Newton felt inadequate, saying he was no Jesus Christ. It showed almost everyone puts someone else in history on a high pedestal and can never see the value of their own accomplishments. Hearing that made me think that maybe some of those people picked me for my reputation, even if they were attracted because of my name.

I know my name has some drawbacks as well. When my sister and brother-in-law visited me from Miami and were staying at a hotel in Skokie, they asked me to call when I finished a case I was working on downtown so that we could meet for dinner. I called my sister immediately upon finishing the case to give her fair warning. I was told no one was in the room, but the clerk would take a message for her. I gave my name and expected a call from her. When I got north, I called her again and she asked if I had just finished. I told her I called about an hour earlier and left a message with the clerk. He never gave her my message, believing it was a prank call when I gave my name as Michael Jordan. In the future, I never gave a message without saying it was Judge Michael Jordan. Some close friends and family would ask me if I wasn't a little pretentious. I told them that I found that with calls to lawyers I knew as friends, I needed to say judge or I was screened out as a nuisance call.

I am known in many different ways by many different people. Family that knew me since I was a child call me Michael. Classmates and friends who met me after first or second grade call me Mike. A few classmates from high school who were in my Spanish class may call me Miguel. Those I went to Hebrew School during grade school may say Moshe. Those in religious services in the adult years would look at me when Mendel Sholom ben Benjamin was called up to receive an honor at services. Others call me judge, sir, arbitrator, hearing officer, or chair. Of course, at home I was also Da Da, then Daddy, and now Dad.

Before becoming a judge, I was counsel or the attorney for the city. Whatever the title used, I could usually tell if the person addressing me was friendly or showed animus, disappointment, fear, respect, gratitude, envy, distain, or anger. My actions and position were the triggers. I remember in high school, each fraternity had to offer one member to be an umpire for baseball or a referee for football. I was the designated neutral during many games. I tried to be a fair arbitrator and not a partisan during those few moments. As a result, I sometimes received derisive calls from my own "friends." Then my title might be more of a piece of anatomy spoken either in English or Yiddish. Likewise, in college when I asked for quiet and asked more times than certain fraternity brothers wished to hear since I had an early class the next day and they had a later class, I heard some words I did not think my close friends would use and especially directed against me.

Brotherly Love and Concern

In my view, my sister has been living in other cities for too many years—Little Rock at first, Miami, then Chicago for a short period, and now Denver. I think about her and worry about her although I know that when she is with one of her sons, they look out for her and protect her, or do their best.

One evening when she lived in Coral Gables, a suburb of Miami, I received a call that distressed me to no end. Gayle was in Coral Gables when a police officer signaled for her to pull her car over for a traffic stop. She had her then 12-year-old son Craig in the back seat and wondered if she had exceeded the speed limit. The officer came to the car, abruptly opened her door with his gun drawn and pulled her out of the car, pushing her down onto the street, causing her to suffer bruises and scrapes.

The angry and out-of-control police officer was, unexplainably, yelling, "Stop resisting me," as he continued his violence. At the time there were no cell phone cameras or cameras on police cars or officers. My young nephew was traumatized. The angry policeman arrested Gayle for resisting arrest. It was all nonsense. He had no basis to stop her in the first place and certainly no reason or right to be physically abusive and violent.

All charges were dropped by the prosecutors, but she had been brutalized. I was already a judge when she told me what had happened. I had great power as a judge, but absolutely no power to help my own sister. I thought back and hoped none of the police clients I had represented a year or so before had done anything like what this officer had done to my sister. I can't focus on my sister's experience without feelings of anger, inadequacy, and sadness. No matter how much power, prestige, or income one has, all it takes is one thug in a uniform to destroy your feeling of safety and tranquility. The most recent, more publicized, incidents of outrageous conduct by police officers around the country show how our psychological screening has failed in the hiring of well-grounded police officers. My sister does not speak about this traumatic incident, and never wanting to raise bad memories, I don't ask, but I wonder if she still thinks of that day. I also wonder what scars that left on my nephew. How many other traumatized people are there who suffered the injustice of other police officers? I can only hope that my actions help and do not hurt others.

Now as I move into my 80s and I take renewed efforts to make sure my estate is in order so my family will not be burdened by unnecessary complications, I also reflect upon my life and the choices I made when there were several paths to take. I examine the persons, places, and events that gave me joy and those that gave me discomfort, stress, and worry. I think back only with joy when I married and when we brought home our children after their births. When our first child was born and I was present, I came to believe that a birth of a healthy child to a healthy mother is truly a miracle and there has to be a power greater than humankind. Sometimes, the greatest stress is due to the uncertainties in the lives of those closest to us, whether it be happiness or sadness or health or illness. The more friends we care about, the more happiness and sadness we might face. When I reflect that there may be a power greater than me, some of the burden on me is lighter and my anxiety dissipates.

In my professional life, I had always felt supported and nurtured by those around me, including my supervisors before I became a judge. Once I became a judge, however, I learned of the resentment, hate, and disgust others had for me, and I could not avoid the traps, hurdles, and publicly embarrassing consequences. Only years later did I learn from some of those involved in publicly humiliating me or using me to further their own corrupt goals that I understood why and how bad things had happened to me. Why was I kept in traffic court longer than all of the other judges except those later indicted for corruption? Why did other judges ignore me and walk away when I appeared? I felt isolated and lonely.

I knew I was much younger than those around me, but I felt it was more than age that separated me and them. I learned later that they were crooked and I was not trying to monetize the job. Early in my career on the bench when bad things happened, I was sad and lonely but did not really get in touch with my feelings. I thought the exhaustion I felt when I came home was due to the huge court calls assigned to me. In traffic court, I regularly received the courtroom having the largest number of cases. I would frequently see over 125 cases listed on each call for the room I was assigned for the ninety-minute period before the next call. With four court calls having about 125 cases, I could easily see about 500 people, an impossible task. How much could I hear in the seconds allowed for each case. Fortunately, it was possible with the regularity of having some people who did not appear. It was not possible to provide the appropriate time for each person. I came home drained and needed to lie down for just a few minutes before I could move on with an even keel for the evening.

I felt the stresses not just from corruption around me in the days before the Operation Greylord prosecutions began, but when the substance of my cases could be quite troubling, such as the welfare of children in custody cases. I felt tremendous stress when Judge Gentile was murdered by one of my litigants and then I was put in the court room with the blood stains and other evidence of the events clearly evident to remind me of my own mortality. Later yet, when a morbidly obese man died in my courtroom after disrupting the proceedings by demanding that his case be heard before all others and the sheriff's deputies struggled with him to remove him from the courtroom, I was greatly troubled then as I am today when I think of his tragic loss.

I had learned that the court system and the State of Illinois have an employee assistance program allowing for a confidential referral for counseling. I learned that situational counseling is not only appropriate, but is essential. It got me through several tight pressure-point situations. I knew when my mother died under hospice care and the representative said that members of the family were entitled to counseling, I would take advantage of it and deal with any issues that might have been simmering under the surface. Each of the challenging episodes I mentioned, triggering stress, motivated me to seek and obtain the temporary counseling I needed to reduce the effects, gave me greater insight, and allowed me to move forward and better serve the public. I was particularly able to use a lot of what I learned in helping others, especially in mediations and in groups I facilitated for the Mankind Project.

I have learned that not every act directed at me is due to inadequacies on my part, although when that is the case, I can better recognize and modify my own conduct. I can also appreciate when the events are due to improper motivation by someone else and have nothing to do with me. I have to be aware and take responsibility for my own conduct, but not that of others.

As one goes through life, there are opportunities to learn or to repeat the same bad habits over and over again. I hope from 1974 until now, I have matured and learned a few things I did not know then. I am far from perfect. I have not yet learned all I need to learn, but I am better. Those closest to me, like my wife and children, would acknowledge that I am not perfect—far from it—but I am much more improved than 30 or 40 years ago.

Before COVID-19, I was less reactive and more proactive in facilitating groups of friends to get together for lunches. Now I have organized many Zoom video social meetings for family or for high school classmates. It is not that hard to do, and I enjoy the camaraderie. I invite friends to join with me. As a kid growing up, I often avoided getting together with friends where I thought it might involve playing ball since I was so very bad. In gym, of course, I did play baseball and usually struck out—although there was one occasion where I connected with a ball and hit the ball out between the center field and right field players, scoring a player while I got a double. I might have only gotten a single but the outfielders played me shallow and the ball not only went perfectly between them but went beyond them. I had never experienced that thrill before. It had always been shame and disappointment when I played ball as a kid. I try to have my memories focus on that double.

I did play football with friends in the alley where I could block and throw and catch short passes. When I went to a bowling alley with Larry Lichtenstein and Lawrence Weprin, I got more than my share of gutter balls and rarely got a strike or a spare. With bowling, unlike a team sport, my lack of success did not impact anyone else. When the scores were totaled, my score was much lower than theirs. We also played miniature golf or went to a driving range and I could play as well as I could, but not as well as they played, but it did not interfere with any team score or the fun they had. I was great company and others would always have the benefit of knowing that even on their worst day, they wouldn't be the worst one playing. Tennis and golf were another story. I did not do well, and in tennis I could not keep up a volley. I played once with several different guys on different days, but no one wanted to have a repeat match.

For swimming, since I was always a great swimmer, I was included and we would play in the water and have a great time. I remember going to Rainbow Beach at 78th Street and the Lake with Lawrence a few times and with Mike Friduss, Lee Epstein, and Steve Felsenberg, who were all in Schmegglers fraternity, a year behind me in school but close in age to me. I already mentioned another Schmegglers, Mike Leroy, who played golf with me in high school once at the end of our freshman year, learning that it took me about seven or eight strokes for every one of his. Yes, that one time was the last time. Mike told me recently when I reminded him of that day that he doesn't play golf and had no recollection of us playing golf in high school. I think I really spoiled his experience to the extent he never played again with me or anyone else.

As I have grown older and my contemporaries have aged as well, I have been fortunate to still be able to exercise and walk for miles as long as there are many washrooms along the way. Many of my friends who were quite athletic as kids have various orthopedic problems or balance problems, inhibiting their ability to do now anything like what they could years before. I walk with some at a slower pace for the company. Fortunately, one acquaintance in high school has become one of my best friends in the last ten years. Mike Grossman and I can maintain the same pace and duration. As I noted, I just need a washroom every so often. Mike is wise enough to take advantage of the rest stops as well.

Mike and I seem to have endless topics to discuss, whether international or national politics, family, or mutual friends. If Maureen or I are faced with a medical issue, Mike is my first resource. He has recently retired from his medical practice and I trust his knowledge, his concern for us, and his awareness of resources. He is one of the kindest persons I could have found a friendship with. I had told Maureen that I really enjoyed Mike's company at meetings for our 50th reunion. Maureen suggested, wisely, as always, to call Mike to find common interests and get together. I was smart enough to follow my wife's advice and rekindle a friendship. We had many of the same friends in high school and we were in the same home room division in addition to being together in band and gym. I know there were many other classes together as well. Mike's freshman year college roommate at Miami of Ohio was my friend from the baby buggy period, Billy London. Mike was in groups with Al Lipton, who had become my best friend in college.

While my brother-in-law Jerry was my best man and my brother-in-law Sy was one of those standing up for me at my wedding, several fraternity brothers, including Al Lipton, also stood up for me. I included my roommate of five semesters, Phil Ravid, another roommate, Mike Vold, and Nick Harris, who was a year behind us in school after I had been asked to stand up at his wedding with his lovely wife Aileen Kite. Nick and I lost touch, since he moved several times. We did reconnect and I found he and Aline had moved to California where he had set up a successful medical research and supply company, which he recently sold at a great profit, insuring retirement.

No one knows what the future brings regarding anyone's longevity, so the advice of Judge Abraham Lincoln Marovitz to make a new friend every day is a great goal. It is better to have too many friends than not enough. Maybe now I understand why my grandfather, Hyman Kritzer, spoke to me in his nineties and said it would soon be time for him to die, since his friends had all died. I told him that he still had family like me. He said it wasn't the same. Whenever my friend Al Lipton tells me we have a history, I realize we can talk about people we each went to grade school with whom we shared as classmates in high school and those we both met in high school and college when we were together. We went to the same places, had the same teachers and professors, dated some of the same girls, suffered the same brutal winters, and commiserated as we learned of friends, classmates, fraternity brothers who were ill or dying. Al could not always deal well with death so he cut those conversations short.

Now regarding death, I came to realize the benefits of having some religious ritual to rely upon in times of loss, especially the close personal loss of a parent. While we did not follow all of the rituals, we did allow visitors to give us comfort and take care of us. Each of our parents, as they died, brought great loss and evoked many feelings of sadness, regret, anger, and finally acceptance. Maureen's father's early death was sudden and unexpected. He had visited our house just the day before to see Maureen and Elizabeth when I was at work. Maureen was shocked and felt great loss from the man who had given her unconditional love.

20 WHO CARES ABOUT ONE PERSON'S LIFE?

Why Tell My Story?

The events I experienced show that the good and the bad people we live with do affect us. We must work together in a cooperative way.

I thought that due to my contact with a few figures in local history, I might have a story that would evoke interest in those not exactly looking for a murder mystery or spy novel. It would be recollections of my own life that had touched tens of thousands of other people I had not known until our interactions. I looked back with gratitude to those people I met who were so very generous and kind to me and with hurt to those I met who were so bitter and destructive to me and my career. I realized that whatever limitations, quirks, neurosis, or self-centeredness close family or friends had, I received a gift from everyone. If nothing else, I learned how to rise above the limiting message some gave me and to believe I could dream the impossible dream and advance on my own achievements and connections I had forged.

I hope that I have been a positive force in the lives of others, particularly my two children, giving them the message that they are capable of reaching their dreams but urging them to accept that if the dream is an impossible dream, to revise and plan and develop another dream that can be reached. May all of my extended family feel a connection to me and believe I cared about them all the best way I could.

As I learned in the memorial service that I conducted at Chevy Chase Country Club in Wheeling, the dates of our birth and death are not as important as the dash in between that symbolizes how we lived and what we did and what benefits society received from our time spend on this earth. When I was actively involved in the Mankind Project with the Warrior program, I was urged to create a mission for my life. I was to consider something positive that overcame my negative tendencies. A mission was not always achieved but it was the goal for all of my words, actions, and thoughts. My mission was to resolve conflict with love and acceptance. I had to avoid creating conflict. I had to set aside my judgmental nature and act out of a place of love, accepting people as they are rather than rejecting them and their ideas and actions unless they reflected my own.

After an interaction, I ask myself if my action in some way fulfilled my mission. Often, I disappointed myself but pledged to myself to do better, always wanting the mission to be fulfilled. The mission is never completed but is a continuing challenge. In a Jewish way, it is a constant fight between the evil inclination and the good inclination—*Yetzer Hare* and *Yetzer Tov*. We all have within us the potential to do great evil and the potential to do great good. We must all live life to its fullest with the proper intentions and a mission fitting for us designed to do the most good that is possible, and the least bad. We were taught to be aware of our feelings, not just physical, and intellectual, but emotional and spiritual as well. Every person needs a mentor and someone to mentor. It is like having a buddy for swimming when I was in summer camp. Safety required a buddy. Life requires a mentor to help guide us and someone to mentor which is key to maintaining our own sense of direction for life.

I do express my unlimited gratitude to every one of those people who I hope will be rewarded in time if they haven't been so far. Thank you for reading this flow of words that reflect my thoughts on the one hand, but may also give a glimpse into my soul on a more spiritual level. You have not intruded. You have been invited and welcomed to see I was not perfect. I was a work in progress. Until my last breath, my work continues. From the date of my birth, April 7, 1942, until a date not yet known to me, when death will come for me, I have to make the dash between those dates meaningful and positive. It is never too late to give substance and meaning and greater value to my life.

I will hopefully still have many more productive years ahead of me, where I can make the dash between my birthdate and my death date more meaningful and productive in helping others. Every day is one I can use for good. I hope to continue my work, since little heavy physical lifting is required. The skills of arbitrating, mediating, writing, lecturing, and generally engaging people will keep my mind active and alert. My diligence in exercise will allow me to function physically and invigorate my energies. I don't know how to slow down in one way without slowing down in every other way. As long as people continue to call upon me for help, I plan to serve. If the COVID-19 virus is subdued, perhaps greater in-person socializations will again be possible, but variants emerge and more booster shots may need to be developed.

Maureen and I have had our first two Moderna COVID-19 vaccinations and had our third, fourth, and fifth as boosters. We will get other booster shots as directed. We have worn masks when with others and observed social distancing while others have given up some precautions. We are doing what we can to survive and thrive. We try to protect our bodies that house our souls and do what we can to be involved in the world around us. We will continue to follow the science going forward.

I have gone through the editing process for the words I have written. How nice life would be if we had an auto correct as we go through life or the ability to redo our choices, actions, and words like the rewrite of a script for a play or movie or a second take where things did not go as planned or they did, but once we saw them unfold, we knew they should have been said or done differently. We could be a more perfect people and less harmful to each other if we had the power of the retake. We don't have that power, so all we can do is think more before we act and act cautiously. I can't do the impossible, so I have gone through the editing process to find clarity and certainty for the reader of my story. I have done my best, although I cannot guarantee perfection! Until the last breath, one has a chance for acknowledgment of wrongs and some opportunity to take a different course and do right or better. Once our writing is put out into the world, the words are permanently recorded. I have told my story. Others can then retell my story.

Made in the USA
Monee, IL
16 December 2022